"This is a gem of a book. Masterfully conceived and executed, *Turning Points in American Church History* is smart, lively, and highly instructive. With expert command of the scholarly literature and the voice and heart of a teacher, Elesha Coffman brilliantly distills nearly five centuries of Christian history into thirteen vibrant episodes. Christians and non-Christians, scholars and novices, college and seminary students, church groups and armchair readers will all find the book illuminating, accessible, and engaging. A rare feat."

—**Kristin Kobes Du Mez**, Calvin University; *New York Times* bestselling author of *Jesus and John Wayne*

"More than a dozen academic surveys of American church history grace the field, and each displays distinctive strengths. Yet Coffman's volume offers the strongest overall combination of focus, clarity, research, conciseness, and wit (yes, wit). I would assign this work before any of the others to virtually any seminary, university, or Christian formation class. It is a truly brilliant contribution."

—**Grant Wacker**, Duke Divinity School (emeritus)

"Colonialism, race, religious freedom. Coffman reminds us how much of American history is bound up with the history of Christianity. After reading this accessible work, Christian readers in America will better understand their own story, and those outside the faith and outside the nation may get a better idea of what all the fuss is about when it comes to American Christianity."

—**Malcolm Foley**, Baylor University

"If you are looking for a captivating introduction to the story of American Christianity, you would do well to start here. This sweeping, swiftly paced book brims with insights and is guaranteed to leave readers with much to ponder and debate. Coffman not only brings church history to life but also underscores its undeniable, ongoing centrality to United States history writ large."

—**Heath W. Carter**, Princeton Theological Seminary

"Elesha Coffman's smart, carefully constructed, and richly informative book shows us the power of a really good question, a gift more valuable than a library full of answers. She has issued the best invitation possible, asking us to think, consider, and then keep on asking good questions about what she aptly calls the 'lumpy and angular' story of American Christianity in all its diversity and depth."

—**Margaret Bendroth**, author of *Good and Mad: Mainline Protestant Churchwomen, 1920–1980*

"Believe it or not, church history is essential for understanding the origins of the United States and the development of our national culture. Elesha Coffman selects a few well-chosen events from the past five hundred years, each one yielding vivid insights and revealing just how often the church lies at the center of American society. This surprisingly comprehensive series of historical highlights demonstrates the numerous yet profound and often unseen connections between religion, race, gender, and politics. A reliable guide and handy resource, *Turning Points in American Church History* is not to be missed."

—**Gerardo Martí**, Davidson College; author of *American Blindspot*

TURNING POINTS

in AMERICAN CHURCH HISTORY

How Pivotal Events Shaped a Nation and a Faith

Elesha J. Coffman

Foreword by Mark A. Noll

Baker Academic
a division of Baker Publishing Group
Grand Rapids, Michigan

Published by Baker Academic
a division of Baker Publishing Group
Grand Rapids, Michigan
www.BakerAcademic.com

Printed in the United States of America

Library of Congress Cataloging-in-Publication Data
Names: Coffman, Elesha J., author.
Title: Turning points in American church history : how pivotal events shaped a nation and a faith / Elesha J. Coffman.
Description: Grand Rapids, Michigan : Baker Academic, a division of Baker Publishing Group, 2024. | Includes bibliographical references and index.
Identifiers: LCCN 2023022908 | ISBN 9780801097492 (paperback) | ISBN 9781540967503 (casebound) | ISBN 9781493445394 (ebook) | ISBN 9781493445400 (pdf)
Subjects: LCSH: United States—Church history.
Classification: LCC BR515 .C63 2024 | DDC 277.307—dc23/eng/20230710
LC record available at https://lccn.loc.gov/2023022908

24 25 26 27 28 29 30   7 6 5 4 3 2 1

To my mentors and my students

Contents

Foreword

Mark A. Noll

Readers of this book are going to get triple their money's worth. They will be encouraged to *think* about the question of "turning points": What, after all, makes some developments, individuals, or happenings in Christian history more important than others? They will find out a great deal about important events that over the past five centuries explain the whys and wherefores of *American church history*. In the process, they will also learn a lot of simple *American history*. Each of these contributions deserves brief elaboration, here in reverse order.

Although the book is devoted to church history, it also makes a real contribution by teaching a great deal about the American past in general. We begin, for example, with a chapter explaining why Protestant Christianity rather than Catholic Christianity long dominated in what became the United States. To understand that significant reality, however, we really need to grasp the importance of a naval battle between Spain and England that took place far from American shores and decades before the first permanent European settlement in the "new world."

Similarly, the chapter late in the book on the 1963 Birmingham church bombing shows why race relations have been, are, and will continue to be so important for all American churches. But to understand that obvious fact, we need to have at least some understanding of the not-so-obvious facts of African American history in the years after World War II. When this book is read for personal benefit, as a text assigned for a college or seminary class, or for adult education in church, those who take it seriously will come away with a clearer grasp of the American contexts in which the Christian faith has developed in this part of the world.

As Elesha Coffman spells out clearly in her introduction, the "turning points" approach is not designed for a comprehensive treatment. Instead, it is designed to provide sufficient details on selected events so that readers understand those events in greater depth and, more importantly, why those particular events can be considered significant. The strength of longer, more complete textbooks is that they provide more information; the weakness is that quantity of information can easily overwhelm quality of insight. By limiting itself to only thirteen events, this book explains each one more fully and, in so doing, makes room for the personal—the human—factors that can be mentioned only in passing in comprehensive treatments.

When Coffman examines the appointment of John Carroll as the first supervisor of Roman Catholic missions in the new United States, she explains how relatively insignificant the Catholic population was in those days as well as why factors surrounding that appointment anticipate what will be much higher Catholic numbers and much more obvious Catholic importance in later history. In addition, by taking time to set out this story as a "turning point," Coffman can show readers why Carroll's personal history made him an ideal individual for this crucial initial appointment.

In the same way, the chapter on the Scopes Trial of 1925 explains why the issues involving science and faith, evolution and the Bible, are important. But it also reveals some of what drove William Jennings Bryan and Clarence Darrow to take part in that trial and how their personal stories help us gain a better understanding of their well-publicized confrontation. From each of the chapters, readers should come away with a better grasp of the big picture while also benefiting from the kind of human detail that puts flesh on the dry bones of mere historical recitation.

From my own experience, however, the greatest value of the "turning points" approach is its ability to transform readers from passive consumers into active participants. In the introduction, Coffman sets out the process that led her to choose the thirteen events featured in the book. As she does so, she shows that the process involved judgment at every step, explains why she asked others for their opinions, and sets out the need to think carefully about alternatives. Ideally, each person who comes to this book will join in that process by asking their own questions: Are the reasons for designating this particular event as a turning point sufficient? What do others reading the book find most compelling about the way an individual turning point is described? Can you think of other events that might have been even more important than the events given their own chapter here?

For myself, I have greatly enjoyed thinking about what thirteen events I would have selected for this book and why I would have made those selections. As it happens, I think that Coffman has made excellent choices, particularly because of how she explains why she found each one important. But . . . but . . . doesn't the American Revolution deserve a place, since it led to a Constitution that separates church and state for the nation, with the states soon following close behind? Or what about the founding of the Woman's Christian Temperance Union in 1874, which led to its leader, Frances Willard, becoming one of the most significant women in American public life? Or didn't the Hart-Celler Immigration and Nationality Act of 1965 spark the great expansion of ethnic churches that have become so important for contemporary Christian life?

If this book fulfills its author's purposes, readers will discover more than just what she thinks was important. They will also be using what they know about American history and their own church experiences to ask similar questions about the events chosen as the book's turning points. If that happens, those who are learning about history will themselves become historians.

As a final word, the inclusion of a hymn and a prayer with each chapter, as well as the excerpts from primary sources, offers the crucial reminder that the history of Christian churches is always a history of worship, devotion, and personal engagement. And for those who want to find out more, the suggestions for further reading at the end of each chapter provide excellent guides pointing out ways to go.

Acknowledgments

Bringing this book to print took an unusually long time, owing to a job change and a global pandemic. I am grateful to my editor at Baker Academic, Bob Hosack, for sticking with the project through years of delay. Mark Noll provided the idea and structure for the book as well as valuable insights throughout its composition. A semester of research leave at Baylor University enabled me to finish the manuscript at long last. I give thanks to my department chairs, the College of Arts and Sciences, and the Baylor Library staff for essential institutional support.

I fear that I cannot even remember all the fellow historians who made suggestions on chapters that span centuries of historical time and nearly ten years of my own life. All of these colleagues lent their expertise by reviewing at least one chapter: David Bains, Brandon Bayne, Seth Dowland, Robert Elder, Elizabeth Flowers, Jennifer Graber, Ronald Johnson, Adam Laats, Thomas Rzeznik, and Angela Tarango. Grant Wacker read every word. Members of faculty writing groups in Dubuque, Waco, and online read drafts and fielded queries: Christopher James, Jacob Kohlhaas, Martin Lohrmann, Amanda Osheim, Troy Troftgruben; Ricardo Álvarez-Pimentel, Daniel Barish, Marilia Corrêa, Julie deGraffenried, Marcelo Boccato Kuyumjian, Lauren Poor, Andrea Turpin, Daniel Watkins; Kate Carté, Mary Kupiec Cayton, Nicole Kirk, Jenny Wiley Legath, Rachel Lindsey, Tisa Wenger, and Rachel Wheeler. A conversation with Paul Harvey yielded the outline for chapter 5. Church history students at the University of Dubuque Theological Seminary helped to build early chapter bibliographies. Jennifer Collins and May Young at Taylor University graciously offered the use of an office on a summer break. Lily Coffman and Skylar Ray assisted with image research.

The strengths of the book reflect the contributions of all these people and many more who joined spirited discussions on social media. The errors are my own.

Introduction

Not many people feel a burning need to know about American church history. Students of American history might recognize a need to know about wars and presidents and economic policies, but church history seems like a niche topic, one obscure little shelf in the bookstore. Students of church history might thrill to the triumphs of the early church, the otherworldliness of the medieval period, or the battles of the Reformation, yet be skeptical that anything truly kingdom-altering ever happened in the United States. Seminary students might wonder why they have to take church history at all, when courses on the Bible, preaching, and ministry seem so much more relevant. Lay readers might feel the same way, believing that what makes Christianity compelling is what God is doing in the world today, not what church people did in the past. According to Esther 6:1, King Xerxes figured that reading history books would put him to sleep! Not exactly a ringing endorsement.

But people do need to know about American church history. American Christians, especially, need to know about it, but so does anyone who interacts with them.

For one thing, Christianity has been the dominant religion in the territory that became the United States since the period of European colonization. The people who lived in this place could embrace Christianity, wrestle with it, reinterpret it, reject it, build institutions to spread its influence or try to curb those institutions, but they could not ignore it. Narratives of American history that minimize the impact of Christianity, then, are incomplete at best, misleading at worst. Which is not to say that the United States is or ever has been a "Christian nation." Rather, Christianity is an indelible part of the nation's story, no less than geography or the Constitution or the legacy of enslavement. A history of the United States with Christianity cut out would be like a map of the United States minus the Mississippi River basin—it would have a gaping hole in the middle.

1

For those of us who are American Christians, church history helps to explain how our faith took the shape that we inhabit. Although varieties of American Christianity (Protestant, Catholic, and Orthodox; homegrown and immigrant; conservative and progressive) have their own distinctive shapes, they are lumpy and angular in some context-specific ways. In other words, American Christianity is distinctively American because it has an American history. That is, in many ways, the argument of this book.[1] Missiologist Andrew Walls describes this phenomenon as the outworking of the principles of incarnation and translation, noting that everywhere the gospel traveled, it was embodied and spoken anew.[2] American Christianity is not the only enculturated form that exists; American Christianity is distinctively American just as Nigerian Christianity is distinctively Nigerian, Korean Christianity is distinctively Korean, and so on. Distinctively American influences include racial and denominational diversity existing in tension with white, Protestant political dominance, as well as geographic expansiveness and an economic system that favors entrepreneurship. American Christianity cannot be reduced to these features, but neither can it be understood without considering them.

It might be tempting to see embodiment and language as distractions, the dirt that must be cleared away to reveal nuggets of Christian truth. But these are also the factors that enable historical study. Embodiment and language created the artifacts available to historians. It is difficult, if not impossible, for a historian to see God's tracks in the historical record, but we can examine the actions of the people who embodied the faith and attend to their words. For Christian historians, these people are our ancestors, sometimes our antagonists, and our great cloud of witnesses (Heb. 12:1).

All of this lumpy history matters to Christians because we do not receive an impervious faith straight from ancient texts or from the realm of the supernatural. (My graduate adviser, Grant Wacker, called that the "sacred meteor" theory of religious transmission.) For good or for ill, we receive faith from the people who came before us. We need to know who they were and be able to recognize the imprint of their hands on the "faith that was once for all entrusted to the saints" (Jude 1:3 NRSV). We might want to place our own hands in the same grooves they stamped, or we might hold the tradition at a new angle, embracing it differently before passing it on. Christianity has been both durable and malleable over the years. These qualities could be viewed as weaknesses

---

1. An academic argument is not like Monty Python's "Argument Clinic" sketch, verbal jousting for the sake of being contrary. An academic argument is more like a scholar saying, "I have looked at this material, and here's what I think is the best way to understand it."

2. Andrew F. Walls, *The Missionary Movement in Christian History: Studies in the Transmission of Faith* (Maryknoll, NY: Orbis Books, 1996).

or as exactly the strength required to persist, across wildly different contexts, for two thousand years.

Readers of this book who are not Americans or not Christians might feel, at times, like they have stumbled into someone else's family reunion. The names might be strange, the narratives perplexing. Yet these readers also can benefit. At the very least, a reader who encounters new names and terms in this book will recognize them when they show up again in other history books or in news coverage. Christians outside the United States can gain perspective on their American cousins, and on themselves, by learning how a shared faith adapted to a foreign context. And even Americans who never cross the threshold of a church will be, when conversant with history, better able to navigate a landscape full of steeples. In the first college class I ever taught, "World Religions in America" at Duke University, a student said that the towering Gothic chapel on campus intimidated her, and she hoped that learning more about religion would help her live in its shadow. I had not anticipated that answer to my question about why students had enrolled in the class, but it was a good one.

Why "Turning Points"?

In 1997, one of my mentors, Mark Noll, published a book titled *Turning Points: Decisive Moments in the History of Christianity*. He devised the format as a way of covering a lot of material while avoiding the tendency of survey texts to feel like they are eighty-five miles long and an inch deep. In his book's introduction, he identified three advantages of focusing on turning points:

- It provides an opportunity to select, to extract from the immense quantity of resources available for studying the history of Christianity a few striking incidents and so to bring some order into a massively complicated subject.
- It provides an opportunity to highlight, to linger over specific moments so as to display the humanity, the complexity, and the uncertainties that constitute the actual history of the church, but that are often obscured in trying to recount the sweep of centuries.
- It provides an opportunity to interpret, to state more specifically why certain events, actions, or incidents may have marked an important fork in the road or signaled a new stage in the outworking of Christian history.[3]

3. Mark A. Noll, David Komline, and Han-Luen Kantzer Komline, *Turning Points: Decisive Moments in the History of Christianity*, 4th ed. (Grand Rapids: Baker Academic, 2022), xvi.

Noll used his book for teaching, and I have used it as well. So have countless other people in academic and church settings, keeping the book in print through four editions. The book you are now reading arose from my own need for a primer on American church history that could be squeezed into the closing weeks of a seminary history course and then used by my students in their congregations.

There are, of course, shortcomings of the turning-points approach. The significance of some of the events chosen for this book could be debated. (In fact, you are encouraged to do so!) Many important events that could have been selected are omitted or mentioned only in passing. Although I endeavored to shine the spotlight on men and women representing a range of times, places, races, ethnicities, and traditions, some coverage areas remain dim. A different author might have given more sustained attention to Roman Catholicism, for example, or to historic peace churches, or to Latino and Asian Americans. Groups whose status as Christian churches has been contested, such as the Church of Jesus Christ of Latter-day Saints (Mormons), Jehovah's Witnesses, and Christian Science, appear only peripherally here. In choosing these thirteen dates, I was especially attuned to events or trends that showed up in both my US history courses and my church history courses, judging them to be moments when those intertwined narratives converged to make a powerful intervention in the American story. I acknowledge the limits of my expertise and imagination, and I hope that the book is broadly useful in spite of them.

Admittedly, some of the events in this book are easier to classify as turning points than others. Perhaps the events associated with violence or deep cultural conflict (such as King Philip's War, churches splitting over slavery, and the Birmingham church bombing) lend themselves most readily to a narrative arc with a sharp rupture between what came before and what proceeded afterward. Many of the events here might be better categorized as launch points: the institutional birth of American Catholicism, the emergence of the Black church tradition, the advent of Pentecostalism. It would have been easier to identify turning points in a narrower, more linear narrative, such as the history of one American denomination; broader coverage necessarily incorporates a plethora of arcs, bouncing and crossing all over the place. Rather than attempting to determine precisely what turned into what else at each point, then, it might be helpful to think of each highlighted event as a hook on which to hang a lot of information. It is impossible to remember every detail from a survey text or course, but if you can recall a few items *and can explain why they mattered*, you have come away with wisdom that you can apply elsewhere.

Following Noll's model, each chapter in this book begins with a hymn and ends with a prayer. The hymns and prayers can be analyzed as primary sources, similar to the sidebars and block quotes embedded in the text.[4] They can also be read devotionally, as a way of entering into the lived religion of the historical figures surveyed. Noll opened sessions of his church history class with recordings of hymns, with which he would hum along. I have occasionally included communal singing in my own history classes. It is always worth remembering that Christian traditions are more than their formal theology or their denominational organization charts; they bring people together and connect them to God, or else they die out. If you are interested in the sounds of the featured hymns, nearly all of them can be found online at Hymnary.org.

Where I Started

As I mentioned, Mark Noll was one of my mentors. I took his graduate-level church history class at Wheaton while I was editing *Christian History* magazine, which had offices up the road from the college. I was working on a magazine issue about Dante Alighieri and the *Divine Comedy* at the time, so I wrote a paper on financial misdeeds in the *Inferno* that I could reuse as an article. Noll wrote in the margin of the paper, "You might want to study this subject more seriously," meaning at the doctoral level. So I did, getting my PhD in the Graduate Program in Religion at Duke.

Ironically, I had known very little about Christian history when I became editor of *Christian History* just two years after graduating from Wheaton with a degree in English literature. I grew up attending a variety of Protestant churches in central Indiana, but I never heard about Christian thinkers of the past, or where denominations came from, or how it happened that my county, home to two Christian colleges and scores of congregations, was also the site of the state's last known lynching, in 1930. Not being a history major as an undergraduate, I did not encounter this information in college either. Only through my work at the magazine, the handful of graduate classes I took at Wheaton, and then my doctoral studies did I begin to get a sense of how significantly cultural context shaped Christian life and how much variety there was within the Christian tradition across time and space. I learned that not all Christians read the same Bible—not the same translation, of course, but not even the same number of books! (Because of decisions made by various church authorities centuries ago, the Protestant Bible has sixty-six books, the Roman Catholic has seventy-three, and the longest Bible, used in the Ethiopian Orthodox Church,

---

4. Primary sources are texts, images, or other artifacts that provide a firsthand account of the past. Secondary sources, by contrast, offer after-the-fact analysis and interpretation. They are often, but not always, written by scholars.

has eighty-one.) Christians in some times and places proudly served in the military, while others were devout pacifists. Depending on when and where they lived, as well as which church they belonged to, Christian women were exhorted to remain single and celibate or to marry and bear many children, to preach and make disciples or to be silent. "There's a wideness in God's mercy," proclaims a nineteenth-century English hymn, and there's a wideness in the Christian tradition too.

Like any author, I have opinions about the topics I write on. My opinions inform my perspective, as does my demographic identity. I can write only as the person I am: a white, English-speaking, American, Protestant woman, born in what is often called "the year of the evangelicals." But perspective differs from partisanship. I think that it is useful, for a project like this one, that I have lived in every region of the United States, in small towns and larger cities, and have attended a variety of churches, including Mennonite, Wesleyan, Baptist, Presbyterian, Episcopal, and nondenominational. It is not my goal in this book to steer anyone toward or away from any expression of faith. No author can be entirely objective, but I have tried hard to be fair. I was taught that it is a historian's duty to paint a picture that the historical actors would recognize, even if they would not want to buy it and hang it on their wall.

How a Book Like This One Gets Written

Although I hold a PhD in American religious history and have been teaching and writing about the subject for more than fifteen years, by academic standards I am an expert on only a few topics.[5] My wheelhouse is twentieth-century mainline Protestantism, which barely makes a showing in this book. For each of the chapters that follow, then, I started either by having a conversation with an expert on that topic or by pulling a lot of books from library shelves and reading articles in academic journals. In every case, I looked for stories with broad but manageable scope, studded with memorable personalities. Once I had a narrative framework, I began writing.

The process of writing inevitably took me down evidentiary rabbit trails. To be honest, that is probably my favorite part of being a historian. More than once I had so many tabs open on my computer that my browser crashed—journal articles, scholarly blogs, library websites, Wikipedia pages (yes, even professionals consult them, judiciously), historic magazines and newspapers, digitized

5. My two previous books are *The Christian Century and the Rise of the Protestant Mainline* (New York: Oxford University Press, 2013) and *Margaret Mead: A Twentieth-Century Faith* (Oxford: Oxford University Press, 2021).

out-of-print books. My desk got just as messy. Occasionally, I crowdsourced a question. About a dozen scholars on social media helped me choose the hymn for chapter 11, "The Old Rugged Cross," informed by their research on fundamentalist revivals. The hymn at the start of chapter 6, "Lucis Creator," was like nothing I had ever seen before, so I asked two choir directors to look at it. They, in turn, reached out to musicologists they had trained with, and emails raced around several Midwestern universities. Even though none of us could track the tune to its source, the chase felt more like play than work.

When I had corralled all of this material into a chapter draft, I shared it with other scholars for feedback. Many of these people are thanked in the acknowledgments. Because this book is primarily intended not for other scholars, however, but for students and general readers, I solicited feedback from nonspecialists too, including college and seminary students, my teenage daughter, and colleagues in different fields. When I edited *Christian History*, most of the magazine's authors were academics, but most of the readers were not. The main occupational categories among readers were pastor, teacher, and, mysteriously, dentist. What I learned to do in that job was to translate what scholars had concluded, based on mountains of archival research and sometimes fierce professional fights, into words that made sense to people who had never been to an archive or a scholarly conference.[6] It's a challenge to write chapters that pass scholarly muster while conveying meaning and significance to people in other walks of life. Readers who want more engagement with primary and secondary sources can follow the footnotes and dig into the "Further Reading" sections. Readers without such inclinations can skip those parts and get to the next chapter a little quicker.

Before wrapping this up with a "Further Reading" list of general works on American church history, I'd like to offer a few words on, well, words. Calling this book *Turning Points in American **Church** History* hints at its center and its boundaries. A book on American *religious* history would include many traditions other than Christianity. A book on American *Christian* history might spend more time on spirituality, or trends in religious thought that wove in and through different churches, or notable individuals. *Church* history includes ideas and individuals, certainly, but in many ways its basic unit of analysis is Christian institutions, such as denominations or benevolent organizations. Functionally, it is convenient to study institutions because they have archives, and they usually last long enough to invite reflection on both continuity and change over time. They are amenable to historical analysis in ways that ideas

---

6. At scholarly conferences, professors and graduate students read papers to one another in badly lit, garishly carpeted hotel ballrooms. Sometimes there is coffee. I actually love academic conferences. Being a person who reads footnotes, perhaps you would too.

and individuals often are not. But writing church history entails a specific kind of humility as well.

The main US-based academic society for scholars who study the history of Christianity is the American Society of Church History. Its academic journal is also called *Church History*. Periodically, the members of that guild have discussed changing the name to something more capacious or peppy, but in 2013 the society's president, Laurie Maffly-Kipp, made a case for retaining the name, despite sharp declines in church affiliation among Americans. Maffly-Kipp, a historian of African American Christianity, said in a presidential address later published as "The Burdens of Church History":

> Because of my mental conversations with [Episcopal Rector] George Bragg, [African Methodist Episcopal Bishop] Richard Allen, and many others who lived prior to the mid-twentieth century, I cannot avoid the nagging feeling that since the church and church history mattered for them, I must take it seriously and understand it. Like it or not, there is a staying power to the notion of church history. Recognizing what it has been can only help us better understand our past, and, perhaps, better understand ourselves as scholars in the process. . . . As the novelist and critic Marilynne Robinson wrote, "History is a little forgiving. We need only be ready to put aside what we think we know, and it will start to speak to us again."[7]

Reflecting my own humility, as well as my Protestantism, I will not refer in this book to "the church" as a visible institution encompassing all Christians. I can say on Sunday that I believe in the "holy catholic church,"[8] but on working days my scholarly tools are best adapted to the study of churches—congregations, denominations, or other groupings labeled in this book as movements or traditions. The exact labels for these various levels of organization and affinity are not terribly important. The connections among and friction between Christians in various institutions, by contrast, are important. They are the evidence historians can see of the operation of a mystical body that we perceive only dimly. I cannot say which is the truest church, much less which

---

7. Laurie Maffly-Kipp, "The Burdens of Church History," *Church History* 82, no. 2 (June 2013): 353–67. Quotation from Marilynne Robinson, *The Death of Adam: Essays on Modern Thought* (New York: Houghton Mifflin, 1998), 149.

8. The phrase "holy catholic church" is rendered differently in different versions of the Apostles' Creed. This creed is a statement of key Christian beliefs dating to the fourth or fifth century, and its original language was Latin. It is often recited during Protestant church services, much less often in Roman Catholic services, and it does not appear in the Eastern Orthodox liturgy. Sometimes the word "Catholic," or "Church," or both are capitalized. Some Protestants say instead "holy Christian church," to distinguish themselves from Roman Catholics; others, understanding the Latin term *catholicam* to mean "universal," are comfortable reciting it.

of the people who have called themselves Christians were truly saved. What I can do is tell their stories, and share their words, and try to hear what they have to teach me.

FURTHER READING

All these books can be purchased new or used online. You are also likely to find them in an academic library.

Albanese, Catherine L. *America: Religions and Religion*. 5th ed. Boston: Wadsworth, 2012.

Allitt, Patrick. *Major Problems in American Religious History*. 2nd ed. New York: Cengage Learning, 2012.

Brekus, Catherine A. *The Religious History of American Women: Reimagining the Past*. Chapel Hill: University of North Carolina Press, 2007.

Brekus, Catherine A., and W. Clark Gilpin, eds. *American Christianities: A History of Dominance and Diversity*. Chapel Hill: University of North Carolina Press, 2011.

Butler, Jon, Grant Wacker, and Randall Balmer. *Religion in American Life: A Short History*. 2nd ed. New York: Oxford University Press, 2011.

Byrd, James P., and James Hudnut-Beumler. *The Story of Religion in America: An Introduction*. Louisville: Westminster John Knox, 2021.

Gaustad, Edwin S., Mark A. Noll, and Heath W. Carter, eds. *A Documentary History of Religion in America*. 4th ed. Grand Rapids: Eerdmans, 2018.

Gaustad, Edwin S., and Leigh Schmidt. *The Religious History of America: The Heart of the American Story from Colonial Times to Today*. Rev. ed. New York: HarperCollins, 2004.

Griffith, R. Marie. *American Religions: A Documentary Reader*. Illustrated ed. New York: Oxford University Press, 2007.

Marsden, George M. *Religion and American Culture: A Brief History*. 3rd ed. Grand Rapids: Eerdmans, 2018.

Noll, Mark A. *A History of Christianity in the United States and Canada*. 2nd ed. Grand Rapids: Eerdmans, 2019.

Williams, Peter W. *America's Religions: From Their Origins to the Twenty-First Century*. 4th ed. Urbana: University of Illinois Press, 2015.

The Old World Order Upended

The Defeat of the Spanish Armada, 1588

Christians from the New Testament to the present have used the language of the psalms and the images of the Old Testament to locate themselves in sacred time and space. For example, Paul's exhortation at the synagogue in Pisidian Antioch, recorded in Acts 13, recounts Israel's history and quotes psalms and prophets to make the point that, "What God promised our ancestors he has fulfilled for us, their children, by raising up Jesus" (Acts 13:32–33 NIV). Psalm singing has a long history in worship, especially among Reformed Christians. The early 2000s chorus that begins with the line "These are the days of Elijah" similarly collapsed the distance between the ancient, holy past and the speaker's present.

Standing in this tradition, England's poetry-writing Queen Elizabeth I (reigned 1558–1603) drew on Exodus and the Song of Deborah, found in Judges 5, to identify herself as a female leader of God's people expressing gratitude for divine deliverance. Her "Song on the Armada Victory, December 1588" was sung as she processed to St. Paul's Cathedral.

> Look and bow down Thine ear, O Lord.
> From Thy bright sphere behold and see
> Thy handmaid and Thy handiwork,
> Amongst Thy priests, offering to Thee
> Zeal for incense, reaching the skies;
> Myself and scepter, sacrifice.

My soul, ascend His holy place.
Ascribe Him strength and sing Him praise,
For He refraineth princes' sprites
And hath done wonders in my days.
He made the winds and waters rise
To scatter all mine enemies—

This Joseph's Lord and Israel's God,
The fiery Pillar and day's Cloud,
That saved his saints from wicked men
And drenched the honor of the proud;
And hath preserved in tender love
The spirit of his turtle dove.[1]

———————▼———————

On July 29, 1588, Lord Admiral Charles Howard and his wily vice admiral, Francis Drake, received word that Spanish ships had been spotted at the mouth of the English Channel. The news came as no surprise. Spain's King Philip II had declared his intention to assemble a massive naval force, the Armada, back in 1581, and while details about the fleet's composition and objectives were murky, the project as a whole was, in one historian's estimation, "the worst-kept secret in Europe." Acting on earlier intelligence, Drake had attacked the still-forming fleet at Cadiz, Spain, in spring 1587, sinking about thirty ships and delaying the force's assault for more than a year. The summer of 1588 had abounded in rumored sightings and speculations regarding where the Armada would head, and when. Finally, as July turned to August, the wait was over.[2]

The English still did not know exactly what the Spanish hoped to accomplish. As it happened, the Armada constituted only half of Philip's plan. The ships, under the command of the Duke of Medina Sidonia, were supposed to gain control of the English Channel and then help transport an army, under the command of the Duke of Parma, from the Netherlands over to southern England—a bit like the D-Day invasion of Normandy in reverse. Neither duke viewed his task with much enthusiasm. Medina Sidonia feared that his fleet, which had sailed from Lisbon, Portugal, way back on May 30, lacked sufficient provisions for the battle. Parma thought it would be better to complete his campaign against the fractious Dutch Protestants before taking on their English abettors. Philip, however, had run out of patience and compelled his commanders to proceed.

1. Leah S. Marcus, Janel Mueller, and Mary Beth Rose, eds., *Elizabeth I: Collected Works* (Chicago: University of Chicago Press, 2000), 411.
2. De Lamar Jensen, "The Spanish Armada: The Worst-Kept Secret in Europe," *Sixteenth Century Journal* 19, no. 4 (Winter 1988): 621–41. Incidentally, because England was late in adopting the Gregorian calendar, some accounts of the clash with the Armada give dates ten days earlier than those given here.

The complexity of this operation hinted at the far-reaching consequences of the overall conflict. Spain was, at the time, the preeminent power in Europe. Philip ruled not just Spain but also lands that are now Portugal, the Netherlands, Belgium, Luxembourg, and much of Italy. During his short marriage to "Bloody Mary" Tudor (1554–58), he even counted England and Ireland among his territories. Lucrative colonies that had been established by Spain and Portugal, and thus fell under Philip's sway, ringed the coasts of South America, Africa, and India. Colonies also dotted the Pacific, which was nicknamed the "Spanish Lake" in recognition of the nation that ruled its vast waters.

Additionally, Philip saw himself as the champion of Catholic Christendom, divinely appointed to bring rebellious lands back into the Roman pope's fold. Philip inherited this responsibility, as well as many of his lands, from his father, Holy Roman Emperor Charles V, who had been the nemesis of Martin Luther and the other first-generation Protestant reformers. (Charles's attentions had been divided between European and global conflicts too. While he was meeting with Luther at the Diet of Worms in 1521, conquistador Hernán Cortés was planning to break the Aztec Empire by besieging its capital, Tenochtitlan.) Philip's orders to naval commander Medina Sidonia, rendered in a nineteenth-century translation, specified that his fleet sailed "to serve God, and to return to his church a great many of contrite souls, that are oppressed by the hereticks, enemies to our holy catholick faith, which have them subjects to their sects, and unhappiness." In keeping with this mission, the ships' sails bore red crosses—the Crusader emblem—and all on board were to confess and take Communion. Both the political and the religious future of huge swathes of territory, including what would centuries later become the United States, hung in the balance.[3]

Philip's multifaceted power earned him an array of enemies. Some Europeans who supported his religious aims were leery of his political and economic might. Muslim Moors still resented the Reconquista that had pushed them off the Iberian Peninsula a century earlier, while Ottoman Turks challenged Spain for dominance in the Mediterranean and central Europe. Philip's chief antagonist, though, was England. Its Protestant queen, Elizabeth I, persecuted Catholics at home while supporting the Dutch rebels and sending privateers, such as the notorious Drake, to plunder Spanish ships carrying treasure from the colonies. Elizabeth had to be stopped. For added incentive, Pope Sixtus V offered Philip one million gold ducats if he could prove that his forces landed on the English

3. William Oldys and John Malham, *The Harleian Miscellany: Or, A Collection of Scarce, Curious, and Entertaining Pamphlets and Tracts, as Well in Manuscript as in Print, Found in the Late Earl of Oxford's Library; Interspersed with Historical, Political, and Critical Notes*, vol. 2 (London: Robert Dutton, 1809), 42–43.

Wikimedia Commons / Royal Museums Greenwich

This anonymous sixteenth-century English painting depicts the types of ships involved in the Battle of Gravelines.

shore. Money, power, and the ascendance of "true" religion were incredibly potent motives on all sides.

Battle commenced on July 31, 1588, with about one hundred thirty ships in the Spanish fleet and two hundred in the English. The fleets were more evenly matched than these numbers might indicate, but they had different capabilities and fighting styles. Though there were moments of high drama, for the most part the battle for the English Channel was a slow-moving series of skirmishes, retreats, and accidents. Both sides shot off large quantities of ammunition without much damage to show for it. By August 6, the English had chased the Spanish to Calais, France, where Medina Sidonia hoped to resupply and join forces with Parma. While the fleet waited in the harbor for Parma to get his troops and transport barges together, Admiral Howard launched a nighttime attack of fireships—eight unmanned boats, set ablaze, guns loaded, were towed toward the Spanish and then unleashed on the tide. No Spanish ships caught fire, but several were damaged in the scramble to escape. The next day, England took advantage of the disarray and a favorable wind to press its attack. After fierce fighting at the Battle of Gravelines (named for a nearby port in the Spanish

Netherlands), the hobbled Armada opted to head home—not by the direct route, back through the English Channel, but by sailing all the way around the British Isles, counterclockwise.

Spain had lost a few ships and scores of men by this point, but it was the Armada's retreat that made the campaign a disaster. A strong wind set the fleet on its circuitous course, and storms continued to batter the poorly supplied ships as they fled. Dozens of ships wrecked off the coasts of Scotland and western Ireland, which jutted farther into the Atlantic than the Spanish maps had indicated. Many sailors who survived the wrecks were slaughtered onshore by English garrisons wary of invasion. The remnants of the Armada that straggled home stood at maybe half the strength of the force that set out. England's ships fared much better, but that nation lost perhaps as many as half of its sailors by the end of the year too, mostly killed by disease.

Although many problems contributed to the Armada's failure—low supplies, bad communication, unwieldy ships, unreliable guns—one has stood out in nearly every account of the defeat: the wind. The English and Dutch struck celebratory medals with the inscription "God blew, and they were scattered," a reference to Job 4:9. Philip reportedly attributed the result of the contest to the elements, telling his unsuccessful veterans, "I sent my fleet against men, not against the wind and waves."[4] Participants on all sides took for granted that God had directed the outcome for his own purposes.

Discerning a divine hand behind events was very common in the sixteenth century, among Protestants and Catholics alike, but the move served different purposes on either side of the English Channel. By displacing blame to (super)natural forces, Philip preserved the belief that his navy could have won the battle and could very well win the next one. Elizabeth, meanwhile, could plausibly claim that God favored Protestants and would aid them in the future. This claim was the most important legacy of the defeat of the Armada. With a rising power, England, in the Protestant camp, the dream of a reunified Catholic Christendom faded, and imperial control of the New World became an open, and very hotly contested, question.

Age of Conquest

The nation eventually known as Spain enjoyed a long head start on colonizing the New World, one that a single naval defeat, however spectacular, could hardly erase. (Like most European countries on a twenty-first-century

---

4. Colin Martin and Geoffrey Parker, *The Spanish Armada* (London: Hamish Hamilton, 1988), 255.

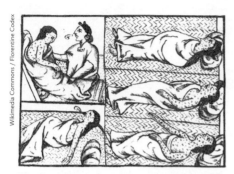

The Florentine Codex, a sixteenth-century compendium of knowledge about New Spain, noted the devastating effects of smallpox on the Indigenous population. Nahuatl text accompanying this image describes slow deaths from starvation, as people became too weak to care for one another.

map, Spain was in the fifteenth century a collection of kingdoms with varying degrees of independence.) In 1492, monarchs Ferdinand and Isabella famously sent Christopher Columbus to sail the ocean blue, seeking a new trade route to Asia. Instead, of course, he landed in the New World—specifically, an island in what is now the Bahamas—where he found friendly Indigenous people (whom he mistakenly called "Indians"), natural beauty, and gold. His letter to the court at Madrid, published in Latin for wide distribution, extolled the riches to be gained and the souls to be won through the establishment of Spanish colonies.

Broadly speaking, Spanish colonies in the New World followed Columbus's plan to develop seaports, agricultural plantations, and mining, optimally of gold but also of silver and other metals. All of these ventures required considerable labor, which initially was provided by Indigenous workers who were enticed by European goods, compelled by tribute requirements, or enslaved. Within a few decades of colonization, however, a combination of violence and exposure to European diseases nearly wiped out the Indigenous people. Bartolomé de las Casas, a Spaniard who arrived as part of the colonial venture but became its fiercest critic, claimed that by 1542 the Native population of Hispaniola (the island now shared by Haiti and the Dominican Republic) had plummeted from three million to barely two hundred. His count was plausible; the "Great Dying" that followed European arrival in the Americas is estimated to have killed 90 percent of the Indigenous population within a century of first contact. A Caribbean slave trade, followed by the Atlantic slave trade, arose to supply fresh bodies for the fields and the mines.[5]

Spanish colonizers also pursued Columbus's call to convert the Natives to Catholic Christianity, though never with the same fervor that the conquistadors displayed in their pursuit of treasure. Las Casas's career in the New World illustrates the complicated role of religion in the Spanish enterprise. He immigrated to Hispaniola in 1502 to become an *encomendero*, an estate holder entrusted by pope and king to oversee Indigenous people while appropriating their land and

5. Bartolomé de las Casas, *A Short Account of the Destruction of the Indies* (1542). The Spanish original, *Brevísima relación de la destrucción de las Indias*, was translated anonymously in 1689.

Excerpt from the Letter of Christopher Columbus to Luis de Sant Angel, 1493

The famed explorer understood his mission as a blend of commerce, Christianity, and conquest.

Hispaniola is a marvel. Its hills and mountains, fine plains and open country, are rich and fertile for planting and for pasturage, and for building towns and villages. The seaports there are incredibly fine, as also the magnificent rivers, most of which bear gold. The trees, fruits and grasses differ widely from those in Juana. There are many spices and vast mines of gold and other metals in this island. They have no iron, nor steel, nor weapons, nor are they fit for them, because although they are well-made men of commanding stature, they appear extraordinarily timid. . . .

At every point where I landed, and succeeded in talking to them, I gave them some of everything I had—cloth and many other things—without receiving anything in return, but they are a hopelessly timid people. . . . [I] gave a thousand good and pretty things that I had to win their love, and to induce them to become Christians, and to love and serve their Highnesses and the whole Castilian nation, and help to get for us things they have in abundance, which are necessary to us. They have no religion, nor idolatry, except that they all believe power and goodness to be in heaven. They firmly believed that I, with my ships and men, came from heaven, and with this idea I have been received everywhere, since they lost fear of me. . . .

Our Redeemer has given victory to our most illustrious King and Queen, and to their kingdoms rendered famous by this glorious event, at which all Christendom should rejoice, celebrating it with great festivities and solemn Thanksgivings to the Holy Trinity, with fervent prayers for the high distinction that will accrue to them from turning so many peoples to our holy faith; and also from the temporal benefits that not only Spain but all Christian nations will obtain.

"The Letter of Columbus to Luis de Sant Angel Announcing His Discovery,"
UShistory.org, http://www.ushistory.org/documents/columbus.htm.

extracting their labor. Even after he was ordained a priest in 1507, he continued to defend the estate holders' treatment of the Indigenous Taíno people. Then some newly arrived Dominican friars began to preach against the abuses, with one demanding of the *encomenderos*, "Tell me by what right of justice do you hold these Indians in such a cruel and horrible servitude?" Las Casas objected to this criticism and convinced the king of Spain to recall the Dominicans from Hispaniola.[6]

Then Las Casas had a change of heart. Through hearing passionate sermons, studying the Bible, and witnessing additional atrocities as a chaplain during the conquest of Cuba, Las Casas came to agree that the Spanish treatment of the Indigenous people was wrong. He joined the Dominican order and spent the rest of his life documenting colonial horrors and advocating better treatment for the Native population. He also engaged in, and wrote about, peaceful evangelization. His work influenced Pope Paul III to issue, in 1537, the bull *Sublimis Dei*, which declared the Native people to be fully human, worthy of salvation rather than enslavement. Though a powerful statement, the pope's words were routinely ignored in the colonies and reversed by later popes.

Spain was not the only nation to jump early into colonial ventures. Portugal actually set out first, exploring the western coast of Africa beginning in 1419 and reaching India by 1498. Columbus would have sailed on behalf of Portugal rather than Spain if the former's king had been able to fund him. After Columbus returned from his first voyage, to avoid hostilities between the two countries, Spain and Portugal signed the 1494 Treaty of Tordesillas to divide the globe into two spheres of influence. Foundational to the globe-carving project was the Doctrine of Discovery, articulated by Pope Alexander VI, stipulating that any land not already ruled by a Christian prince could be "discovered" and colonized. In the Americas, the treaty line gave modern-day Brazil to the Portuguese and everything else to the Spanish, which is why Portuguese remains the official language of Brazil, while Spanish predominates nearly everywhere else south of the Rio Grande. The Doctrine of Discovery had more far-reaching consequences, serving as a basis for American "manifest destiny" ideology and imperialism.

France tried to establish a presence in the New World in the sixteenth century, but it faced fierce opposition abroad as well as an especially bloody series of religious conflicts at home. Its first colonizers belonged to the embattled Protestant minority, called Huguenots, who sought safe haven in present-day Brazil and, later, Florida. The Portuguese destroyed the first settlement in 1560, and the Spanish ended the second in 1565. A decade after the 1598 Edict of Nantes ended the French Wars of Religion, French colonization began again in Quebec, far from the Spanish and Portuguese strongholds in the Caribbean and South America. This time, the French colonizers' religion was Catholicism. Even though Huguenots had been granted toleration in France, they were not allowed to settle in France's North American territories.

6. George Sanderlin, ed. and trans., *Witness: Writings of Bartolomé de Las Casas* (Maryknoll, NY: Orbis Books, 1993), 67.

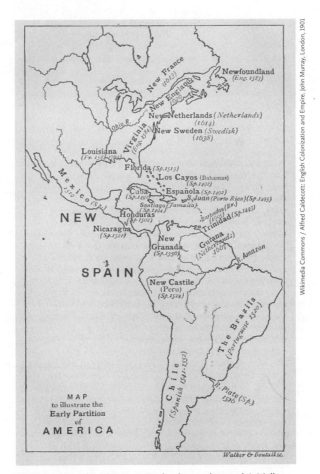

As depicted on this 1901 map, England was a late and, initially, fairly minor player in the European quest for colonial territory in the Americas.

The Dutch began colonial ventures at the close of the sixteenth century. Though technically still part of the Spanish Empire, several northern Dutch provinces adopted Protestant (Reformed) Christianity in the 1560s and declared their independence from Philip's rule in 1581. (These were the rebels that the Duke of Parma was fighting when he was called away to join the Armada.) Lacking a strong home base, the Dutch mounted a commercial rather than imperial colonial operation via the Dutch East and West India Companies. Initially, the Dutch specialized in the Asian spice trade. As an extension of their Eighty Years' War (1568–1648) for independence from Spain, the Dutch also disrupted Spanish and Portuguese trade wherever they could.

Although it would eventually surpass all of these global empires, England got off to a late, slow start. Prior to its defeat of the Spanish Armada, all that England had managed in the New World were minor attacks on Spanish treasure ships—essentially, piracy—and Walter Raleigh's mysteriously failed colony, Roanoke, off the coast of what is now North Carolina. England's first permanent settlement in the Americas—Jamestown, Virginia—fared little better. The 104 English men and boys who founded Jamestown in 1607 included many gentlemen but few of the laborers or tradesmen who could make the place habitable. There were no women among the initial colonists either. The group did include one disgraced Church of England preacher, Robert Hunt. Hunt acquitted himself fairly well as the group's chaplain before, like most of the settlers, he died within months of his arrival. The "Starving Time" of 1609–10 claimed all but sixty of the five hundred colonists who had either survived from 1607 or come on a later supply ship.

Clearly, Elizabeth's naval victory over Spain did not lead inexorably to the ascendance of English-speaking, Protestant America. But the defeat of the Armada made such a development *imaginable*, a necessary prelude to its actualization. The event altered visions of the future across Europe. Here is an assessment made by Pulitzer Prize–winning historian Garrett Mattingly:

> For the spectators of both parties, the outcome, reinforced, as everyone believed, by an extraordinary tempest, was indeed decisive. The Protestants of France and the Netherlands, Germany and Scandinavia saw with relief that God was, in truth, as they had always supposed, on their side. The Catholics of France and Italy and Germany saw with almost equal relief that Spain was not, after all, God's chosen champion. From that time forward, though Spain's preponderance was to last for more than another generation, the peak of her prestige had passed.[7]

Elizabeth's and Philip's successors, James I of England and Philip III of Spain, formally ended hostilities with a peace treaty in 1604. The document declared that God, looking with pity on the calamities of his people, "has powerfully extinguished the raging flame by a firm confederacy of the most potent princes of the Christian world."[8] As "confederates," the rulers of England and Spain agreed to treat one another primarily as trade rivals rather than mortal enemies. Neither could eliminate the other's religion or territorial claims. As a result, the Western Christian world would remain divided between Protestants and

7. Garrett Mattingly, *The Armada* (Boston: Houghton Mifflin, 1959), 400–401.
8. *A General Collection of Treatys, Manifestos, Contracts of Marriage, Renunciations, and Other Publick Papers, from the Year 1495, to the Year 1712*, vol. 2, 2nd ed. (London, 1732), 131. (The English here is modernized; the original quotation is available at http://books.google.com/books?id=U8nYFSTQhXcC&pg=PA131&output=html.)

Catholics, who, even in times of relative peace in Europe, reestablished their rivalries everywhere else they traveled.

Competing Empires

Narratives of American history often begin with New England, but this approach obscures most of colonial history and gives rise to the erroneous impression that ethnic diversity and religious diversity are recent developments. Colonial America was a far more complicated place, where Indigenous groups asserted territorial sovereignty before European powers invoked God's aid for very different projects. Nothing remotely resembling the United States in culture or geography emerged until the late eighteenth century.

Because massive death and displacement of Indigenous people followed swiftly after European contact, it is difficult to sketch how the lands that would become the United States were populated beforehand. The territory was definitely not blank, "virgin" wilderness but rather was full of living cultures and artifacts of earlier civilizations. Population density was much lower north of the Rio Grande than south of it, and most population centers were on the east or west coast. Levels of organization varied from small, kinship-based groups that mostly stayed in one settled area to confederations of tribes ranging across hundreds of miles. Early Spanish and French maps noted the locations of settlements with drawings of dwellings or people while designating territories as they understood them—for example, "tierra de los Pampopas," "tierra de los Carrizos," and "tierra de los Cujanes" on a 1728 Spanish map of the Gulf Coast. Significantly, Anglo-American maps were more likely to render Native American territories as empty spaces, projecting the attitude that Robert Frost expressed centuries later in his 1961 inaugural poem: "The land was ours before we were the land's."[9] Nonetheless, according to historian Juliana Barr, "Taking in all of North America in 1789, more than three-quarters of the continent remained under Indian rule as well as half of the so-called sovereign territory of the United States."[10]

European territorial claims draped over this patchwork of preexisting sovereignties with varying degrees of permeability. By the end of the sixteenth century, the Viceroyalty of New Spain stretched from what is now northern California east to Florida and south to Panama, encompassing Mexico, Central

9. The poem, "The Gift Outright," was written in the 1930s but not published until 1942. Frost recited it at the inauguration of President John F. Kennedy.

10. Juliana Barr, "Geographies of Power: Mapping Indian Borders in the 'Borderlands' of the Early Southwest," *William and Mary Quarterly* 68, no. 1 (January 2011): 44. While usage has varied, "Indian" is no longer the preferred academic term for Native Americans.

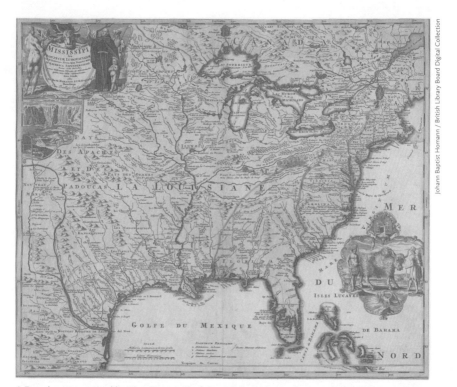

A French map acquired by King George III of Great Britain shows the names and settlements of Indigenous groups. Europeans knew that the land was not merely empty space awaiting discovery.

America, and the Caribbean, as well as the Philippines and Mariana Islands across the Pacific. (Spain's territories in South America were administered separately.) Though vast, Spain's holdings within the borders of today's United States yielded little profit. Conquistadors who had explored the North American interior found no riches to plunder, only mountains, deserts, plains, and deadly swamps. As far as the king of Spain was concerned, the point of maintaining a presence in these forbidding regions was mainly to keep other European explorers well away from the wealth of Mexico.

Because New Spain's northern reaches offered scant economic value, missionaries exercised a comparatively greater influence there than they did in what is now Mexico or Central America. In and around Florida, after the Huguenot settlers had been dispatched, Franciscan friars established a series of *doctrinas*, or mission centers, and *visitas*, or outposts, where Native Americans were taught Catholic religion and Spanish culture. At its height, in 1675, this effort involved forty friars ministering to twenty thousand Native people in thirty-six churches. In subsequent decades, Native American resistance and pressure from English settlers reduced the Franciscan presence to just two missions near St. Augustine.[11]

Accounts of life at Spanish missions varied widely. In some portrayals, friars braved numerous hardships to live peacefully among the Native people, respecting their cultures as much as possible while bringing them the blessings of the sacraments and of European agricultural techniques. In other portrayals, harsh priests demolished symbols of Indigenous culture, banned games, enforced monogamy, and whipped anyone who defied their authority. All these things happened at different times and places. The personalities and approaches of the missionaries varied, as did Indigenous responses.

How the narrative of the Spanish missions took shape depended on the writer's audience and intention. The English were especially fond of playing up Spanish atrocities, fostering a "Black Legend" to discredit Spanish colonialism while legitimating their own. Ironically, the information fueling the Black Legend often originated among the Spanish themselves. Bartolomé de las Casas's pleas for better treatment of the Native people were used by Spain's enemies to argue that the country should be stripped of all its colonies. There is, unfortunately, very little surviving record of these events from an Indigenous perspective.

One well-documented example of missionizing and resistance comes from New Mexico, the remotest, poorest corner of New Spain. Life was hard there for missionaries, colonists, and the Pueblo people, and the resulting tensions were great. In 1680, the Pueblos' anger over their mistreatment—including the arrest and beating of forty-seven medicine men—boiled over into the Pueblo Revolt, led by one of the medicine men, Popé. He spread word that if the Pueblos killed or drove off the Spanish, their ancestral gods would return to bring peace, health, and prosperity. This promise held great appeal because the Pueblos' situation was dire (drought and high taxes had pushed them to starvation) and because, while many Pueblos partook of Catholic sacraments and participated in Catholic worship, they continued to follow their traditional religion as well. Such religious blending was very common among evangelized Native populations and enslaved Africans throughout the Americas. Of course, the Europeans blended Christianity with other elements of their ancestral cultures too, but they rarely noticed this tendency in themselves.

During the Pueblo Revolt, warriors from multiple towns seized the Spaniards' horses, to prevent them from fleeing, and destroyed their settlements. Perhaps one-fifth of the one thousand colonists died, or perhaps more. The

Pueblos directed special fury toward churches, religious symbols, and priests, although they preserved some religious symbols and repurposed them as signs of their own power. Within the span of a few weeks, the whole colonial project in New Mexico was dismantled—by far the most effective Indigenous uprising against Europeans in American history. But the rains and harvests did not return. Popé lost his leadership position the next year, and in 1692 the Spanish reclaimed the territory without a fight.

The more famous missions in California were built much later, between 1769 and 1833. In an effort to win souls, and to make the Native people more productive and compliant taxpayers to the Spanish crown, Franciscans under the leadership of Fray Junípero Serra traveled north along the coast, establishing a string of missions one-day's journey apart. Native people from dozens of tribes who came to the missions (sometimes seeking food or work and sometimes because they were forced to come) labored in construction, agriculture, and domestic tasks, attended daily Mass, and followed the priests' moral instruction—or else. Serra initially estimated that the process of making the Native people into Christian, Spanish subjects would take ten years, at the end of which mission lands would be distributed among an Indigenous population left in the care of parish priests. The Native people never did regain their land. Instead, they remained under mission authority until the first native Mexican governor of Alta California issued a "Proclamation of Emancipation" in 1826, granting them the right to become Mexican citizens.

From the start, French colonization of the New World differed from the Spanish enterprise. As French explorers worked their way up the St. Lawrence River, around the Great Lakes, and down the Mississippi River, they encountered no great cities to seize, no gold to mine, and little land that could easily be turned into plantations. Instead, the region offered furs. The best way to get furs was to trade with Indigenous people who knew the land and its animals. Because French traders needed Native people as partners, they tended to have better relations with them than did other Europeans. It also helped intercultural relations greatly that the French settlements were generally sparse, which meant fewer conflicts over resources and fewer outbreaks of disease.

In terms of religion, the Jesuit missionaries who worked in French territories adopted a more culturally sensitive approach than did most of the Spanish Franciscans. They took pains to learn Native languages and translate spiritual concepts into local idioms. Still, conversion proceeded slowly and proved fragile when disease and European weapons ravaged Indigenous populations, or when the presence of foreigners exacerbated tribal rivalries while also introducing environmentally harmful competition for furs. Several missionaries were killed,

The Huron Carol

Canada's oldest Christmas song was written by Jesuit missionary Jean de Brébeuf in about 1642. It combined a text in the Huron language with a French folk melody. Three verses are presented here in English translation.

'Twas in the moon of winter-time
When all the birds had fled,
That mighty Gitchi Manitou
Sent angel choirs instead;
Before their light the stars grew dim,
And wandering hunters heard the hymn:
"Jesus, your King is born, Jesus is born,
In excelsis gloria."

Within a lodge of broken bark
The tender Babe was found,
A ragged robe of rabbit skin
Enwrapp'd His beauty round;
But as the hunter braves drew nigh,
The angel song rang loud and high:
"Jesus, your King is born, Jesus is born,
In excelsis gloria."

O children of the forest free,
O sons of Manitou,
The Holy Child of earth and heaven
Is born today for you.
Come kneel before the radiant Boy
Who brings you beauty, peace and joy.
"Jesus your King is born, Jesus is born,
In excelsis gloria."

Translated into English by Jesse Edgar Middleton in 1926. This version is available at https://www.hymnsandcarolsofchristmas.com/Hymns_and_Carols/huron_carol.htm.

among them Father Jean de Brébeuf (author of "The Huron Carol"), and many Native Christians perished as well.

As was the case with Spain, France's main Western-Hemisphere colonial strength lay outside the borders of what is now the United States. French adventurers and missionaries, most famously Louis Joliet and Father Jacques Marquette, were the first Europeans to explore the Mississippi River in the seventeenth century, but these journeys were followed up by trade alliances rather than missions or settlements. In all of New France, there were just a few thousand white colonists by 1663, and only around fifteen thousand by 1700. Though defended well by their Native allies, French territories became ripe targets for the British and, later, the Americans as they pushed west from the Atlantic Coast.

Aside from England, whose colonies are the focus of the next few chapters, the other European country to gain a foothold in North America was the Netherlands. In 1609, the English sailor Henry Hudson, backed by the Dutch East India Company, sought the ever-elusive Northwest Passage to Asia by traveling up the river that now bears his name. He got only as far as present-day Albany, New York, which marked the extent of the Dutch colony as well. New Netherlands attracted a few more settlers than did New France but not nearly enough to flourish or to resist the encroachment of the English. Its chief legacy was the establishment of New Amsterdam, the cosmopolitan trading hub rechristened as New York City in 1665, the year after Britain took control of the territory.

Mapping History

From the earliest days of exploration, Europeans put their stamp on America by naming, or renaming, its settlements and natural features. A look at these names helps us remember the colonial past and better understand the religious dimensions of the various European endeavors. Although the world they attempted to erase still peeks through in place names from Massachusetts to Malibu, a fuller recovery requires looking past modern maps, using tools such as the Native Land Project (https://native-land.ca).

All of the American colonial holdings took their names from their European parents: Nueva España, Nouvelle-France, Nieuw-Nederland, New England. These names signaled both ruptures and continuities with the Old World. This relationship echoed, sometimes implicitly and sometimes quite explicitly, Christian hopes for the renewal promised in the Bible. As Columbus claimed to a member of the Spanish court in 1500, "God made me the messenger of the new heaven and the new earth of which he spoke in the Apocalypse of St. John after having spoken of it through the mouth of Isaiah; and he showed me the spot where to find it."[12]

---

12. G. B. Spotorno, *Memorials of Columbus* (London: Treuttel & Wurz, 1823), 224.

The names Columbus gave to the islands he visited on his first voyage sacralized the landscape while also claiming it for his patrons. First came references to the Savior (San Salvador) and his holy mother (Santa Maria de la Concepción). Next came homages to the monarchs who backed him (Fernandina, Isabella) and their country (Española). The ship *Santa Maria* ran aground on Española on Christmas morning, so Columbus named the settlement there La Navidad.

Many Spanish missions and settlements were named for saints. Naming a place after a saint was understood to invite that saint's protection, and it also identified a feast day to celebrate, enacting a new cultural heritage. The California missions invoked a number of figures tied to the spirit of the missionary project: San Luis Rey de Francia and San Juan Capistrano to recall the courage of crusaders, Santa Barbara and Santa Ines in memory of brave martyrs, San Diego and San Francisco in honor of two famed preachers. The Spanish also named places for angels (San Miguel, San Gabriel) and holy symbols, such as Santa Fe (faith) and Santa Cruz (cross).

French colonial place names in the United States were more of a mixed bag. Some invoked saints (such as St. Louis and Sault Ste. Marie, or "Rapids of St. Mary"), some explorers (such as the towns, lake, and river named for Samuel de Champlain), some Old World cities (such as Montpelier, Vermont, named after a city in southern France), and some merely described natural features (such as Detroit, in reference to the strait of the river on which it stood). Surviving Dutch names mostly recall early settlers (Stuyvesant, Bronx), royalty (Nassau), or places in the Netherlands (Harlem).

English colonists most often named new places after the ones they left, starting with Plymouth. They also inscribed their spiritual hopes on the map of the new land. As Puritan divine Cotton Mather wrote in his spiritual history of America, "Geography must now find work for a Christianography in regions far enough beyond the bounds wherein the Church of God had, through all former ages, been circumscribed."[13] Hence Salem (short for Jerusalem), Concord (meaning harmony or agreement), Providence, Philadelphia (with reference to Rom. 12:10 and Rev. 3:7–13), and the hundreds of other American sites bearing biblical names, from Antioch to Zion.

To be sure, not all of the biblically named places in America were founded by the English or during the Colonial era. Later immigrants from all sorts of countries continued the tradition of writing their dreams on the map, settling in New Bern, New Braunfels, and New Prague; New Canaan, New Lebanon, and New Palestine. It was as if God's promise in Revelation 21:5—"Behold, I

---

13. Cotton Mather, *Magnalia Christi Americana; or, The Ecclesiastical History of New England*, ed. and abr. Raymond J. Cunningham (New York: Frederick Ungar, 1970), 16. The original was published in London in 1702.

am making all things new"—applied especially to them, and especially here, in
what they perceived to be a young and hopeful land.

Jean Ribault, a Huguenot, led the first Protestant colony in what is now the United
States, the doomed settlement at Fort Caroline, Florida. In 1565, the Spanish
governor of the territory killed him and every other man who would not abjure
his "heretical" faith (save a handful who escaped). Reportedly, Ribault died praying, or perhaps singing, Psalm 132. He would have known it by heart, because
Huguenots, in keeping with the practice instituted by John Calvin, sang only the
Psalter in worship. But Ribault made a substitution in the first line, applying it not
to David but to himself, and by extension applying other verses to the land on
which he stood and the enemies who opposed him. The version here is excerpted
from the Geneva Bible, the Bible of English Protestants in the sixteenth century.

> Lord, remember me with all my affliction,
> Who sware unto the Lord, and vowed unto the mighty God of Jacob, saying,
> I will not enter into the tabernacle of mine house, nor come upon my pal-
> let or bed,
> Nor suffer mine eyes to sleep, nor mine eyelids to slumber,
> Until I find out a place for the Lord, an habitation for the mighty God of
> Jacob. . . .
> For the Lord hath chosen Zion, and loved to dwell in it, saying,
> This is my rest forever: here I will dwell, for I have a delight therein.
> I will surely bless her vittles, and will satisfy her poor with bread,
> And will clothe her Priests with salvation, and her Saints shall shout for joy.
> There will I make the horn of David to bud: for I have ordained a light for
> mine Anointed.
> His enemies will I clothe with shame, but on him his crown shall flourish.[14]

FURTHER READING

Anderson, Emma. *The Betrayal of Faith: The Tragic Journey of a Colonial Native Convert.*
Cambridge, MA: Harvard University Press, 2007.

Bayne, Brandon. *Missions Begin with Blood: Suffering and Salvation in the Borderlands of
New Spain.* New York: Fordham University Press, 2021.

Eccles, W. J. *The Canadian Frontier, 1534–1760.* Albuquerque: University of New Mexico
Press, 1983.

---

14. The text of the Geneva Bible is available online at https://textusreceptusbibles.com/Geneva
/19/1. Spellings have been modified for readability.

Elliott, John H. *Empires of the Atlantic World: Britain and Spain in America, 1492–1830*. New Haven: Yale University Press, 2007.

Glaser, Lynn. *America on Paper: The First Hundred Years*. Philadelphia: Associated Antiquaries, 1989.

Hackel, Steven W. *Children of Coyote, Missionaries of Saint Francis: Indian-Spanish Relations in Colonial California, 1769–1850*. Chapel Hill: University of North Carolina Press, 2017.

Jacobs, Jaap. *The Colony of New Netherland: A Dutch Settlement in Seventeenth-Century America*. Ithaca, NY: Cornell University Press, 2009.

Knaut, Andrew L. *The Pueblo Revolt of 1680: Conquest and Resistance in Seventeenth-Century New Mexico*. Norman: University of Oklahoma Press, 1988.

Maltby, William S. *The Black Legend in England: The Development of Anti-Spanish Sentiment, 1558–1660*. Durham, NC: Duke University Press, 1971.

O'Brien, Jean M. *Firsting and Lasting: Writing Indians Out of Existence in New England*. Minneapolis: University of Minnesota Press, 2010.

Phillips, William D., Jr., and Carla Rahn Phillips. *The Worlds of Christopher Columbus*. Cambridge: Cambridge University Press, 1992.

Rodriguez-Salgado, M. J., and Simon Adams, eds. *England, Spain, and the Gran Armada, 1585–1604: Essays from the Anglo-Spanish Conferences, London and Madrid, 1988*. Savage, MD: Barnes & Noble Books, 1991.

Scully, Robert E. "'In the Confident Hope of a Miracle': The Spanish Armada and Religious Mentalities in the Late Sixteenth Century." *Catholic Historical Review* 89, no. 4 (October 2003): 643–70.

Stewart, George R. *Names on the Land: A Historical Account of Place-Naming in the United States*. Boston: Houghton Mifflin, 1958.

Taylor, Alan. *American Colonies: The Settling of North America*. New York: Penguin, 2001.

2

The Limits of Religious Freedom

Roger Williams Banished from Massachusetts, 1635

As Reformed Christians, the Puritans continued the Calvinist practice of singing only psalms in worship. They were not, however, content to keep singing the translations of those psalms found in the hymnbooks they brought with them from Europe. They wanted to sing their own versions, translated more faithfully (if less poetically) from the Hebrew by their own ministers.

Within years of arriving in the colonies, the few dozen Puritan "divines," as ministers were called, in New England divvied up the psalms among themselves and produced new versifications. These appeared in 1640 as the *Bay Psalm Book*, the first book published in British North America. Psalm 1 emphasized many key Puritan concepts, including God's providence and the need to distinguish the wicked from the godly.

> O Blessed man, that in th'advice
> of wicked doeth not walk:
> nor stand in sinners way, nor sit
> in chayre of scornfull folk.
>
> But in the law of Iehovah,
> is his longing delight:
> and in his law doth meditate,
> by day and eke by night.

And he shall be like to a tree
    planted by water-rivers:
that in his season yields his fruit,
    and his leafe never withers.

And all he doth, shall prosper well,
    the wicked are not so:
but they are like unto the chaffe,
    which winde drives to and fro.

Therefore shall not ungodly men,
    rise to stand in the doome,
nor shall the sinners with the just,
    in their assemblie come.

For of the righteous men, the Lord
    acknowledgeth the way:
but the way of ungodly men,
    shall utterly decay.[1]

On October 8, 1635, Roger Williams appeared before the General Court of Massachusetts for the fourth time in two years. He had not killed anyone or stolen anything. He had not blasphemed or broken the Sabbath. He had, however, proclaimed "diverse new and dangerous opinions," despite repeated admonitions to hold his tongue. In a fledgling colony that understood itself to be building a model Christian civilization at the edge of a howling wilderness, that offense was beyond bad enough.

The heads of the Massachusetts Bay Colony wanted to like Williams. A charming man in the prime of life, Cambridge-educated, ordained, he met the colony's stringent criteria for true faith. He took his religion, especially his Bible, very seriously. He was sufficiently disgusted with the Church of England to leave it behind, even though that meant crossing an ocean with his young wife. Crucially, Williams could also articulate his conversion, recalling the moment in his childhood when "the Father of Lights and Mercies touched my Soul with a love to himself."[2] He should have been exactly the sort of man to lead a New England congregation and take a prominent place in its society.

1. The text of an existing copy of the Bay Psalm Book is available online at https://tile.loc.gov /storage-services/service/rbc/rbc0001/2008/2008amimp02405/2008amimp02405.pdf.

2. Roger Williams, *George Fox Digg'd Out of His Burrowes*, in *Publications of the Narragansett Club*, ed. J. Lewis Diman, 1st ser., vol. 5 (Providence, 1872). The quotation is from a section titled "To the People Called Quakers." The original was written in 1673 and published in Boston in 1676.

Granted, on the spectrum of belief represented in Massachusetts in the 1630s, Williams stood at one end. The colony was settled by Puritans, English Protestants who objected to the *via media*, or "middle way," between Catholicism and Protestantism that Queen Elizabeth I had steered in an effort to bring peace to her religiously torn realm. Puritans got their name from their drive to purify the church of its "popish" remnants. They also held themselves to a high standard of personal purity, and they longed to construct a purer society. In these projects, the Puritans took their cues from John Calvin (1509–64), whose city, Geneva, had been called by the Scottish founder of Presbyterianism, John Knox, "the most perfect school of Christ that ever was in earth since the days of the apostles."[3]

There were, however, two kinds of Puritans. Separating Puritans ("Separatists") believed that the Church of England was so corrupt that true Christians had to separate themselves from it totally. A group of Separatists left England for religiously tolerant Holland in 1608 and then, in 1620, sailed to the New World on the *Mayflower*. Prevented by waves and weather from reaching their intended destination, Virginia, they instead founded Plymouth Colony on Cape Cod. American history recalls them (not very accurately) as the Pilgrims who celebrated the first Thanksgiving in 1621.

Nonseparating Puritans favored reforming the Church of England from within. This effort hit a wall, though, after King Charles I succeeded his father, James I, in 1625. Charles minimized Puritan influence on the government when he disbanded Parliament, and his chosen head of the church, Archbishop William Laud, reintroduced Catholic practices and severely punished anyone who worshiped differently. Without entirely abandoning the hope of reforming England and its church, Puritans began emigrating in large numbers in the 1630s, settling in the Massachusetts Bay Colony.

When Roger Williams arrived in 1631, Puritans had just founded Boston, and the tiny town invited him to be its minister. After spending some time in the church, though, he determined, "I durst not officiate to an unseparated people, as, upon examination and conference, I found them to be."[4] In other words, the Boston Puritans were not pure enough. Williams next tried the larger Puritan town of Salem, but when the church in Boston advised the church in Salem not to offer Williams a position, he moved farther south to Plymouth Colony, to minister among the Separatists.

By the end of 1633, Williams had worn out his welcome in Plymouth too. Plymouth governor William Bradford noted that Williams "fell into some strange

3. John Knox to Anne Locke, December 9, 1556, in *The Works of John Knox*, ed. David Laing, 6 vols. (Edinburgh, 1855), 4:240.

4. Roger Williams to John Cotton, in *The Complete Writings of Roger Williams*, ed. Reuben A. Guild et al., 7 vols. (New York: Russell & Russell, 1963), 6:356.

A Model of Christian Charity

Puritan lay leader John Winthrop delivered the sermon containing these excerpts to the emigrants aboard the *Arbella* in 1630. It is best known for the phrase "city on a hill," a celebration of American exceptionalism, but it is also noteworthy for its dire warnings about what would happen if the colonists failed to love one another.

> Thus stands the cause between God and us. We are entered into covenant with Him for this work. We have taken out a commission. The Lord hath given us leave to draw our own articles. We have professed to enterprise these and those accounts, upon these and those ends. We have hereupon besought Him of favor and blessing. Now if the Lord shall please to hear us, and bring us in peace to the place we desire, then hath He ratified this covenant and sealed our commission, and will expect a strict performance of the articles contained in it; but if we shall neglect the observation of these articles which are the ends we have propounded, and, dissembling with our God, shall fall to embrace this present world and prosecute our carnal intentions, seeking great things for ourselves and our posterity, the Lord will surely break out in wrath against us, and be revenged of such a people, and make us know the price of the breach of such a covenant.
>
> Now the only way to avoid this shipwreck, and to provide for our posterity, is to follow the counsel of Micah, to do justly, to love mercy, to walk humbly with our God. For this end, we must be knit together, in this work, ▶

opinions, and from opinion to practice, which caused some controversy between the church and him."[5] Some of Williams's opinions related to his rigid separatism, such as his condemnation of colonists who worshiped in nonseparated churches on their visits back to England. Other opinions related to English treatment of Native Americans. The English king had no right to give the Native people's land to the settlers, Williams argued, and thus the royal patents authorizing the Puritan colonies were invalid.

As if these judgments were not upsetting enough, Williams also repeatedly questioned magistrates' authority, both in Plymouth and after his return to Salem. The disagreement was complicated. Contrary to caricatures of Puritan Massachusetts as a theocracy, meaning a place ruled by God through the

5. Quoted in Joseph Barlow Felt, *The Ecclesiastical History of New England*, vol. 1 (Boston: Congregational Library Association, 1855), 187.

as one man. We must entertain each other in brotherly affection. We must be willing to abridge ourselves of our superfluities, for the supply of others' necessities. We must uphold a familiar commerce together in all meekness, gentleness, patience and liberality. We must delight in each other; make others' conditions our own; rejoice together, mourn together, labor and suffer together, always having before our eyes our commission and community in the work, as members of the same body. So shall we keep the unity of the spirit in the bond of peace. The Lord will be our God, and delight to dwell among us, as His own people, and will command a blessing upon us in all our ways, so that we shall see much more of His wisdom, power, goodness and truth, than formerly we have been acquainted with. We shall find that the God of Israel is among us, when ten of us shall be able to resist a thousand of our enemies; when He shall make us a praise and glory that men shall say of succeeding plantations, "may the Lord make it like that of New England." For we must consider that we shall be as a city upon a hill. The eyes of all people are upon us. So that if we shall deal falsely with our God in this work we have undertaken, and so cause Him to withdraw His present help from us, we shall be made a story and a by-word through the world. We shall open the mouths of enemies to speak evil of the ways of God, and all professors for God's sake. We shall shame the faces of many of God's worthy servants, and cause their prayers to be turned into curses upon us till we be consumed out of the good land whither we are going.

John Winthrop, "A Model of Christian Charity," The Winthrop Society, https://www.winthropsociety.com/_files/ugd/9a2d3b _4d9f243ce4b34c0fad7f4f41df29d992.pdf.

unquestionable judgments of religious leaders, magistrates (the governor's assistants) were civil officers, elected by the freemen of the colony. Clergy were not allowed to run for this office. This system did not, however, sever church and state. Ministers advised the governor and his assistants and figured prominently at the General Court. Freemen, the only people who could vote, originally had to be church members, as did the magistrates. Moreover, Puritans understood their colony to be based not just on a charter from the king but also on a covenant with God, as described in "A Model of Christian Charity," a sermon by Massachusetts Bay governor John Winthrop. For a people endeavoring to build a holy commonwealth, godliness mattered as much outside the church as within it.

Williams fundamentally disagreed with the Puritan blending of religious and civil authority. Such blending, he believed, defiled the church, which should be pure, unworldly, and wholly unlike the Catholic Christendom from which

The Trial of Anne Hutchinson

The year after Williams's departure, Anne Hutchinson was also banished from Massachusetts. The reasons were somewhat similar—she, too, proclaimed opinions that challenged the magistrates—but also complicated by her gender and by her declaration, at the end of her testimony, that God spoke to her directly. Here is the beginning of the transcript of her 1637 trial.

MR. WINTHROP, GOVERNOR: Mrs. Hutchinson, you are called here as one of those that have troubled the peace of the commonwealth and the churches here; you are known to be a woman that hath had a great share in the promoting and divulging of those opinions that are causes of this trouble, and . . . you have spoken divers things as we have been informed very prejudicial to the honour of the churches and ministers thereof, and you have maintained a meeting and an assembly in your house that hath been condemned by the general assembly as a thing not tolerable nor comely in the sight of God nor fitting for your sex, and notwithstanding that was cried down you have continued the same, therefore we have thought good to send for you to understand how things are, that if you be in an erroneous way we may reduce you that so you may become a profitable member here among us, otherwise if you be obstinate in your course that then the court may take such course that you may trouble us no further, therefore I would intreat you to express whether you do not hold and assent in practice to those opinions and factions that have been ▶

Protestants had broken. Such blending also violated individual conscience. For Williams, faith counted only if it was freely chosen. The colonists had left a country where all residents, regardless of piety, were required to belong to the established, national church and faced punishment if they did not worship in the state-sanctioned manner. Why on earth would the colonists want to replicate the oppressive arrangement they had fled?

Williams's position on oaths highlighted both aspects of his concern. To be freemen, males age sixteen and older had to swear loyalty to the colony and its leaders. The oath ended, conventionally, "So help me God." Williams did not believe that *free* men owed obedience to a government that dictated their adherence not only to the "second table" of the Ten Commandments (murder, theft, adultery) but also to the "first table," the explicitly religious commandments handled in court already, that is to say, whether you do not justify Mr. Wheelwright's sermon and the petition.

MRS. HUTCHINSON: I am called here to answer before you but I hear no things laid to my charge.

GOV.: I have told you some already and more I can tell you.

MRS. H.: Name one, Sir.

GOV.: Have I not named some already?

MRS. H.: What have I said or done?

GOV.: Why for your doings, this you did harbour and countenance those that are parties in this faction that you have heard of.

MRS. H.: That's matter of conscience, Sir.

GOV.: Your conscience you must keep or it must be kept for you.

Thomas Hutchinson, *The History of the Province of Massachusetts-Bay* (Boston, 1767), 482–83.

Harper's Magazine, 102 (Dec. 1900–May 1901)

A 1901 magazine illustration portrays men's consternation as Anne Hutchinson taught a mixed crowd in her home.

about worship. "Forced worship stinks in God's nostrils," he later wrote. But Williams also feared that asking an unregenerate man to say "So help me God" meant worshiping with him, and it was wrong to worship with the unregenerate. So Williams hated the oath because he loved liberty and because he sought separation from the ungodly.[6]

All these issues came to a head at Williams's October 1635 trial. There, the General Court had to figure out what to do with a man who argued:

First, that we have not our land by patent from the King, but that the natives are the true owners of it, and that we ought to repent of such receiving of it by patent.

6. Roger Williams to John Mason, June 22, 1670. This letter and others can be found in John Russell Bartlett, ed., *Letters of Roger Williams, 1632–1682* (Providence: Narragansett Club, 1874).

Secondly, that it is not lawful to call a wicked person to swear, to pray, as being actions of God's worship.

Thirdly, that it is not lawful to hear any of the ministers of the parish assemblies in England.

Fourthly, that the civil magistrate's power extends only to the bodies and goods and, outward state of men, etc.[7]

The stance for which Williams became famous, the last on the list above, was actually the least important at the time. And there was more to the story.

As opposition to his ideas mounted, Williams had urged the church he led in 1635, the church at Salem, to separate itself from the rest of the Massachusetts Bay Colony. This was a bridge too far. The church withdrew its support for Williams, as did John Cotton, a powerful Puritan divine who had spoken in his defense at his previous trials. The court banished Williams, giving him six weeks to leave the colony.

Walls of Separation

John Haynes, the stern governor who presided over Williams's banishment, intended to ship the troublemaker back to England and thus remove his influence from the colonies. John Winthrop, the more circumspect former and future governor, privately suggested to Williams another course: start a new settlement on Narragansett Bay, land that was not included in the king's patent. During his six free weeks after trial, granted in part because Williams's wife was due to deliver their second child, Williams gathered resources and friends for the new settlement. When emissaries of the court came to seize him for his voyage back across the Atlantic, he was gone.

With the help of Narragansett tribe members who deeded him land and provided food, Williams founded Providence, Rhode Island. (Unlike other Englishmen, Williams had developed good relationships with the Native people, learning their language and customs while treating them with respect.) He declared it a haven for anyone willing to abide by its civil rules, allowing "Liberty of Conscience" for religious matters. The aim of this system, for Williams, was not to minimize the influence of faith but to preserve it. As he wrote in an open letter to John Cotton, the Bible proved that the Jews in the Old Testament and the earliest Christians in the New Testament kept themselves separate from the world, but "when they have opened a gap in

7. Roger Williams, *Mr. Cotton's Letter Examined and Answered*, ed. Reuben Aldridge Guild, 1st ser., vol. 1 (Providence: Narragansett Club, 1866), 40–41. The original was published in London in 1644.

A monument in Providence, Rhode Island, shows Narragansett people welcoming Roger Williams in 1636.

the hedge or wall of separation between the garden of the church and the wilderness of the world, God hath ever broke down the wall itself, removed the candlestick, etc., and made His garden a wilderness, as at this day."[8] The references to Genesis 2–3, Isaiah 5:5–6, and Revelation 2:5 stressed what was at stake in rightly dividing church and world, sacred and profane. Violate the boundary, Williams warned, and you will not see paradise in this world or the next.

Questions about how Christians could be in the world but not of it (John 17:13–19) had swirled for centuries before Williams weighed in. Puritan framing of the issue echoed an early fifth-century conflict between the Donatists, a North African church faction, and Augustine, the leading theologian of the day. During Roman persecutions a century earlier, some Christians had handed over their Scriptures to avoid punishment. Donatists believed that these traitors should never be restored to fellowship, because only faithful believers belonged in the church. The main body of the Western church, however, found this punishment too severe and this definition of the church too restrictive.

8. Williams, *Mr. Cotton's Letter*, 108.

Augustine countered the Donatists with an appeal to the parable of the wheat and tares, found in Matthew 13:24–30. (John Cotton, Cotton Mather, and other Puritan divines cited the same parable when they faced opposition within their churches.) Imagining a field mixed with good plants and weeds, representing the children of God and the children of the evil one, Jesus advises the disciples to let both grow up until the harvest, when God's angels can sort them out. Using this parable, Augustine argued for an *invisible* church, whose true membership was known only to God, rather than a *visible* church, with membership limited to people who were deemed sufficiently godly.

While Augustine's interpretation of Matthew 13:24–30 might seem to support a hands-off approach to the church, he combined it with a highly intervention-ist reading of Luke 14:16–24. In that parable, several people decline a servant's invitation to his master's banquet. The master becomes angry and tells the servant to "compel them to come in." Augustine took this verse to mean that the government—the Christianized Roman Empire, in his day—could force people to attend church, suppressing any heretics or schismatics (such as the Donatists) who got in the way.

This debate flared again in the sixteenth century. The so-called magisterial Reformers, among them Martin Luther and John Calvin, upheld Augustin-ian views of the invisible church and of the coercive role of the government. Magistrates in Geneva and in the Massachusetts Bay Colony derived their authority from this way of thinking. So did the monarch and the archbishop in England.

In contrast, radical Reformers believed the commingling of saints and sin-ners, and of civil and religious authority, to be a deadly error. Many radical Reformers came to be called Anabaptists because they rejected infant baptism (which was administered to babies, who could neither repent nor choose faith) in favor of believer's baptism (which was administered only to people mature enough to do both). Insisting on believer's baptism, they argued, would produce a visible church of true Christians who obeyed the New Testament directive to "repent and be baptized."

Because infant baptism also conferred citizenship in the sixteenth century, rejecting it was widely seen as subversive as well as theologically incorrect. Anabaptists were slaughtered by Catholics and Protestants alike, especially after tragedy befell the Anabaptist city of Münster in 1535. As an army summoned by its deposed Catholic bishop took up positions outside the city, within its walls a radical (and, one suspects, unhinged) preacher, John of Leiden, declared himself the successor to King David, took multiple wives, and exercised dictatorial rule over the starving, panicked population. Eventually, the bishop's forces retook the city and put its leaders to death. Mainstream Anabaptists' resolute pacifism could not overcome the taint of association with this disaster, which Puritans invoked to discredit their own Anabaptist critics.

Puritans attempted to combine both views of the church. As Calvinists, they believed that God elected some people for salvation through his sovereign choice alone, and only he knew whom he had chosen. God sowed the wheat. But they also believed that their covenant with God depended on mutual love and communal labor, with all persons pulling together, in Winthrop's words, "as members of the same body." Letting the tares thrive until judgment day simply was not an option.

The New England colonists tied themselves in knots trying to pursue both the unity promised by an invisible church and the purity found in a visible one. The project seemed possible among the first generation of immigrants because practically all of them were committed Puritans who qualified as "visible saints"—people who displayed every sign of numbering among the elect. But what about their children, all of whom were baptized as infants but only some of whom later made a profession of faith? Could they be communing members of the church? Voting members of society? And what about *their* children?

In 1662, some New England churches addressed this dilemma with the Half-Way Covenant. Ministers who supported this policy, foremost among them Solomon Stoddard, allowed those who had been baptized but never professed personal faith to take Communion, reasoning that they might belong to the invisible church despite lacking a hallmark of visible sainthood. The Half-Way Covenant also allowed these baptized but "unconverted" churchgoers to bring their children (the grandchildren of the visible saints) to be baptized. The policy extended the outreach and authority of the church from its core members to a wider segment of society. It promoted unity at the expense of purity.

Roger Williams, on the other hand, decoupled the pursuit of social unity from the pursuit of church purity. Regarding unity, he endeavored to keep governance in his new settlement minimal, resolving disputes by mutual consent whenever possible and allowing everyone the freedom to worship, or not worship, as they pleased. Fewer rules, he hoped, meant fewer fights. Things did not quite work according to plan, however, and eventually Williams had to form a government and even go to England to secure a royal charter. "Roger Williams spent much of his time criticizing civil magistrates and trying to circumscribe their activities," wrote biographer Edwin Gaustad. "The rest of his time he spent assisting such magistrates or becoming one himself."[9]

---

9. Edwin S. Gaustad, *Liberty of Conscience: Roger Williams in America* (Grand Rapids: Eerdmans, 1991), 122.

Regarding purity, Williams moved in the direction of more rules, searching for a church that followed the model of the New Testament in every particular. Any deviation from this divine pattern, he believed, rendered a church invalid. Initially, his quest for the true church led him to cofound the first Baptist church in North America with about twenty fellow believers. In 1638, one member of this group rebaptized him, and then he rebaptized the others. The church maintained strict separation from other churches and from civil affairs, which should have pleased Williams. The following year, though, he left that church too, and he never joined another. He confessed in a 1652 pamphlet, *The Hireling Ministry None of Christs*:

> In the poor small span of my life, I desired to have been a diligent and constant observer, and have been myself many ways engaged, in city, in country, in court, in schools, in universities, in churches, in Old and New England; and yet cannot, in the holy presence of God, bring in the result of a satisfying discovery, that either the begetting ministry of the apostles or messengers to the churches, or the feeding and nourishing ministry of pastors and teachers, according to the first institution of the Lord Jesus, are yet restored and extant.[10]

Better to belong to no church, Williams decided, than to belong to one that fell short of the New Testament ideal. He considered this choice lonely but necessary. His critics saw it as the logical result of his egotistical fanaticism. Cotton Mather, John Cotton's grandson and author of a well-known history of New England called *Magnalia Christi Americana*, subtitled his chapter on Williams "The Spirit of Rigid Separation in One Remarkable Zealot."

A Lively Experiment

The phrase "a wall of separation between church and state" is usually associated with Thomas Jefferson, who used it in an 1802 letter to the Danbury, Connecticut, Baptist Association. Freedom of religion is usually associated with the Bill of Rights, ratified in 1791. Roger Williams forged both concepts much earlier, which is why his banishment and subsequent founding of a new colony signaled a turning point in American church history—indeed, in all of Western history.

The Pilgrims and other Puritans did, as the storybooks say, come to America for religious liberty, but not in the sense understood today. In England, the Puritans suffered penalties for not supporting a church they found theologically lax, unreformed in its worship, and willing to employ ministers who scarcely knew

---

10. Roger Williams, *The Hireling Ministry None of Christ's*, quoted in James D. Knowles, *Memoir of Roger Williams, the Founder of the State of Rhode-Island* (Boston: Lincoln, Edmands, 1834), 172.

the gospel and seldom preached it. In New England, the Puritans could tighten up all these areas without opposition from king or archbishop. Effectively, they sought the freedom to be very strict.

Williams and the other founders of Rhode Island pioneered the modern idea of religious liberty, and they convinced the crown to give them permission to try it out. The royal charter for the colony, issued by King Charles II in 1663, called it "a lively experiment," a test of the claim that religious freedom would engender truer piety and a more stable society than either the established Church of England or the covenanted New England Way. In revolutionary language, the document declared that "no person within the said colony, at any time hereafter shall be any wise molested, punished, disquieted, or called in question, for any differences in opinion in matters of religion, [provided that they] do not actually disturb the civil peace."[11] The Dutch had flirted with such ideas, but no European government had yet embraced them.

Few observers believed that this experiment would work. The king hedged his bet, noting that the "remote distance" of the colony meant that the "unity and uniformity" of England would be little troubled no matter what happened on the other side of the ocean. In New England, the residents of nearby colonies watched eagerly for "Rogue's Island" to fail. The Reverend John Woodbridge Jr., of Killingworth, Connecticut, called it "the Asylum for all that are disturbed for Heresy, a hive of hornets, and the sink into which all the rest of the Colonies empty their heretics."[12] News of land squabbles, occasional mob violence, and complaints about Williams's leadership fueled this criticism.

Actually, one kind of "heretic" was unwelcome even in Rhode Island: Quakers, who called themselves the Religious Society of Friends. The founder of the Quakers, Englishman George Fox (1624–91), tried many churches before determining that none met his spiritual needs. Then one day he heard a voice telling him, "There is one, even Christ Jesus, that can speak to thy condition."[13] Fox became convinced that church buildings, ordained ministers, and religious rituals only got in the way of communication with God, who was revealed instead by an "inner light" possessed equally by all people. The Quakers' sometimes ecstatic, unstructured worship earned them their nickname.

Like the Anabaptists before them, the pacifist Quakers aroused enmity everywhere they went. The notion of the inner light led Quakers to renounce injuring or enslaving anyone else, but it also led them to renounce deferring

11. Rhode Island Royal Charter of 1663. A transcript of the document is available at https://docs.sos.ri.gov/documents/civicsandeducation/teacherresources/RI-Charter-annotated.pdf.

12. Quoted in Bruce C. Daniels, *New England Nation: The Country the Puritans Built* (New York: Palgrave Macmillan, 2012), 74.

13. *Quaker Faith and Practice*, 5th ed., 19.02, https://qfp.quaker.org.uk/passage/19-02/.

THE FIRST FEDERAL CONGRESS · 1789

WITHOUT FREEDOM OF THOUGHT
THERE CAN BE NO SUCH THING AS WISDOM
& NO SUCH THING AS PUBLICK LIBERTY
WITHOUT FREEDOM OF SPEECH
BENJAMIN FRANKLIN 1722

This mural in Great Experiment Hall at the US Capitol highlights two key freedoms—religion and the press—enshrined in the First Amendment to the Constitution.

to anyone else, be it their social "betters," clergy, or civil authorities. Fox often got in trouble for not tipping his hat to gentlemen, for instance. In response to such violations of social hierarchy, England charged Fox and his followers with blasphemy. Massachusetts imprisoned Quakers, whipped them, and sent them back on the ships they had arrived in. Four Quakers were killed by hanging on Boston Common between 1659 and 1661 before King Charles II ordered a stop to the executions.

The Quakers' rejection of organized religion and emphasis on a private spiritual sensibility might have appealed to Williams, but members of the group claimed more freedom than he was willing to allow. Their quakings might be works of Satan, he argued in a 1672 debate. Quaker women were said to run naked through the streets. (They really did, on occasion, as did a few men, ostensibly in imitation of Isaiah.) There was just no telling what the Quakers might do on the strength of their private convictions, Williams declared. Their seeming humility thinly cloaked a spiritual pride that was sure to cause mayhem.[14]

14. See Williams, *George Fox Digg'd Out of His Burrowes.*

Even for Roger Williams, then, religious freedom had its limits. If people were to live together in peace, a balance must be struck between individual expression and social order, lest liberty descend into chaos or a new kind of tyranny. Williams knew that he did not want his colony to look like John Winthrop's city on a hill or like European Christendom. It was less clear what it would look like instead.

Establishment and Free Exercise

Religious freedom in America has been a balancing act ever since Williams began his lively experiment. The First Amendment to the US Constitution, adopted in 1791, contains two religion clauses: "Congress shall make no law respecting an establishment of religion, or prohibiting the free exercise thereof." Bookshelves groan with analyses of what these phrases meant to the founders of the nation and what they might mean now that the country is far more diverse, and the federal government far more active, than the founders could have imagined. The following paragraphs briefly touch on the questions raised by this single sentence:

Congress shall make no law: This language applies only to the federal government. At the time the First Amendment was adopted, the states took varying positions on religion, with New England states tending to preserve elements of the Puritan (later, Congregationalist) vision, Southern states extending privileges to the Anglican/Episcopal Church, and Middle states allowing the broadest freedoms—while still, in many cases, enjoining a baseline belief in the Christian God. Can states or cities make laws about religion? Is taxing an institution the same as making a law about it?

Respecting an establishment of religion: "Establishment" has meant many things to many people over the years, including religious tests for office (only people who affirm a religious oath can serve in government); use of tax money to pay clergy or otherwise support religious work; "blue laws" that restrict activities such as operating businesses, selling alcohol, or playing sports on Sunday; and prayers, Scripture readings, or Christian holiday celebrations in public schools or on public property. Which of these things actually constitute "establishment" of religion? Is exempting an institution from a tax or penalty equivalent to supporting the institution, and is that support equivalent to establishment?

Or prohibiting the free exercise thereof: Many interesting cases in First Amendment law have centered on this clause. The private religious activities of America's white, Protestant majority—attending church, owning a Bible, donating money to religious causes—have never been contested. When those private activities spill into the public realm—when church services get very loud, when

Bible verses are inscribed on a courthouse monument, when a prominent citizen gives a lot of money to a politically active religious group—conflicts have arisen. Until recently, though, most of the notable free-exercise cases were brought by religious minorities, people who claimed religious justification for activities such as using peyote in ceremonies, refusing military service, marrying across racial lines when it was illegal to do so, or wearing a veil in a driver's license photo. Are these activities religious? Do they pose a danger to the religious people themselves, their neighbors, or their children? If they do pose a danger, does the right to free exercise of religion outweigh the risks?

In addition to the First Amendment, courts have often looked to the writings of Thomas Jefferson to settle church-state questions. There is no conclusive evidence that Jefferson read Williams, but both men argued that individual conscience must reign supreme in religious matters and that civil government should concern itself with keeping the peace, not fostering faith. They differed on what calamity they hoped to avoid. For Williams, breaching the wall of separation would bring God's wrath, while for Jefferson, the consequences were more earthly: hypocrisy and meanness, false religions, tyranny, and corruption.

Principles governing twentieth-century interpretation of the establishment and free-exercise clauses were known by shorthand references to the cases in which they were articulated. The "Lemon test," derived from *Lemon v. Kurtzman* (1971), asserts that any law pertaining to religion "must have a secular legislative purpose; second, its principal or primary effect must be one that neither advances nor inhibits religion; finally, the statute must not foster an excessive government entanglement with religion." Each "prong" of the test is intended to prevent establishment of religion. In the 1971 case, a Pennsylvania law allowing some public funds to be used by private schools was struck down because, even though the law stipulated that the funds be used only for instruction in nonreligious subjects (a secular purpose), all the beneficiaries of the law were teachers at Catholic schools, thus putting the state in the business of advancing religion.

Regarding free exercise, courts refer to the "Sherbert test," derived from *Sherbert v. Werner* (1963). In that case, Adell Sherbert, a South Carolina textile mill worker who was also a Seventh-day Adventist, was fired from her job because she refused to work on Saturday, the Adventist Sabbath. She was subsequently denied unemployment benefits on the grounds that she had not suffered religious discrimination but had merely quit her job. The Supreme Court sided with Sherbert, offering a multipart test to protect the free exercise of religion.

Under the Sherbert test, if a person holds a *sincere* religious belief that is *substantially burdened* by government action, the government can pursue its action (in this instance, denying unemployment benefits) only if there is a *compelling state interest* involved and if the state is using the *least restrictive means* to achieve

Thomas Jefferson, Virginia Statute for Religious Freedom, Enacted 1786

Whereas, Almighty God hath created the mind free;

That all attempts to influence it by temporal punishments or burthens, or by civil incapacitations tend only to beget habits of hypocrisy and meanness, and therefore are a departure from the plan of the holy author of our religion, who being Lord, both of body and mind yet chose not to propagate it by coercions on either, as was in his Almighty power to do, . . .

That to compel a man to furnish contributions of money for the propagation of opinions, which he disbelieves is sinful and tyrannical; . . .

That our civil rights have no dependence on our religious opinions any more than our opinions in physics or geometry, . . .

That it tends only to corrupt the principles of that very Religion it is meant to encourage, by bribing with a monopoly of worldly honours and emoluments those who will externally profess and conform to it; . . .

That it is time enough for the rightful purposes of civil government, for its officers to interfere when principles break out into overt acts against peace and good order;

And finally, that Truth is great, and will prevail if left to herself, that she is the proper and sufficient antagonist to error, and has nothing to fear from the conflict, unless by human interposition disarmed of her natural weapons free argument and debate, errors ceasing to be dangerous when it is permitted freely to contradict them:

Be it enacted by General Assembly that no man shall be compelled to frequent or support any religious worship, place, or ministry whatsoever, nor shall be enforced, restrained, molested, or burthened in his body or goods, nor shall otherwise suffer on account of his religious opinions or belief, but that all men shall be free to profess, and by argument to maintain, their opinions in matters of Religion, and that the same shall in no wise diminish, enlarge or affect their civil capacities.

"Virginia Statute for Religious Freedom," https://en.wikipedia.org/wiki/Virginia_Statute_for_Religious_Freedom.

that interest. The italics added here highlight the four components of the test as well as its interpretive trip wires. How can a court, or anyone, determine the sincerity of another person's beliefs? What makes a burden "substantial" or a state interest "compelling"? How far must the government go to devise minimally restrictive ways to achieve its goals?

Many aspects of modern American life would be totally bewildering to the colonists and Founding Fathers, but John Winthrop, Roger Williams, and Thomas Jefferson would all recognize the difficulty of balancing crucial but sometimes opposing interests: religion and government, individual freedom and social harmony, private and public, minority and majority, liberty and peace.

As King Charles II predicted, the United States' approach to religious freedom has been a lively experiment, complete with trials and errors, explosions and unexpected discoveries. No one is happy with all of the results. A strong case can be made, though, that America's continuing religious vitality—in contrast to the religious apathy in much of Europe—springs from the tensions Americans have chosen to live with.

The most famous version of this argument was made by Alexis de Tocqueville, a Frenchman who visited the country in 1831 and published his observations as *Democracy in America*. "When I arrived in the United States," he wrote, "it was the country's religious aspect that first captured my attention. The longer I stayed, the more I became aware that this novel situation had important political consequences. In France, I knew, the spirit of religion and the spirit of liberty almost always pulled in opposite directions. In the United States I found them intimately intertwined: together they ruled the same territory."[15]

Overall, de Tocqueville was mightily impressed by American religion. The various churches worshiped differently but worked together to support public morality. Compared with their European counterparts, he found American churches less rigidly formal, and American clergy less apt to become embroiled in political power struggles. The virtues preached in American pulpits mitigated citizens' tendencies toward selfishness and greed. Not quite the city on a hill, the United States nonetheless represented for de Tocqueville strong evidence of the value of Christianity.

> It is reasonable to assume that habit rather than conviction dictates the religious practices of at least some Americans. In the United States, moreover, the sovereign is religious, hence hypocrisy must be common. Nevertheless, Christianity maintains more actual power over souls in America than anywhere else. There is no better illustration of the usefulness and naturalness of religion, since the country where its influence is greatest today is also the country that is freest and most enlightened.[16]

Winthrop might have argued (quite rightly) that de Tocqueville overlooked the social inequalities and lack of Christian charity that marked early nineteenth-

15. Alexis de Tocqueville, *Democracy in America*, trans. Arthur Goldhammer (New York: Library of America, 2004), 340–41.
16. De Tocqueville, *Democracy in America*, 335–36.

century America. Williams would not have been comfortable with religion as a "sovereign" authority. Jefferson would have bridled at hypocrisy and questioned both the usefulness and the naturalness of religion. Undoubtedly, though, the America shaped by all three men is a congenial place to hold such a debate. Religious liberty necessarily entails the freedom to disagree.

▼

In an oft-reprinted poem, Roger Williams recounts the cold journey from Massachusetts in the winter of 1536 while declaring a continuing faith in God's provision.

> God makes a Path, provides a Guide,
>   And feeds in Wildernesse!
>   His glorious Name while breath remaines,
>   O that I may confesse.
>
> Lost many a time, I have had no Guide,
>   No House, but Hollow Tree!
>   In stormy Winter night no Fire,
>   No Food, no Company:
>
> In Him I have found a House, a Bed,
>   A Table, Company:
>   No Cup so bitter, but's made sweet,
>   When God shall Sweet'ning be.[17]

FURTHER READING

Barry, John M. *Roger Williams and the Creation of the American Soul: Church, State, and the Birth of Liberty.* New York: Viking, 2012.

Davis, James Calvin, ed. *On Religious Liberty: Selections from the Works of Roger Williams.* Cambridge, MA: Belknap, 2008.

Gaustad, Edwin S. *Liberty of Conscience: Roger Williams in America.* Grand Rapids: Eerdmans, 1991.

Green, Steven K. *Separating Church and State: A History.* Ithaca, NY: Cornell University Press, 2022.

Gunn, T. Jeremy, and John Witte Jr., eds. *No Establishment of Religion: America's Original Contribution to Religious Liberty.* New York: Oxford University Press, 2012.

Morgan, Edmund S. *The Puritan Dilemma: The Story of John Winthrop.* 3rd ed. New York: Pearson Longman, 2007.

17. Roger Williams, untitled poem, in *The Complete Writings of Roger Williams*, ed. Reuben A. Guild et al., 7 vols. (New York: Russell & Russell, 1963), 1:103–4.

Noll, Mark, Nathan O. Hatch, and George M. Marsden. *The Search for Christian America.* Westchester, IL: Crossway, 1983.

Sehat, David. *The Myth of American Religious Freedom.* New York: Oxford University Press, 2011.

Van Engen, Abram. *City on a Hill: A History of American Exceptionalism.* New Haven: Yale University Press, 2020.

Vowell, Sarah. *The Wordy Shipmates.* New York: Riverhead, 2009.

Wenger, Tisa. *Religious Freedom: The Contested History of an American Ideal.* Chapel Hill: University of North Carolina Press, 2017.

3

A Collision of Cultures

King Philip's War, 1675–76

Samson Occom (1723–94), a member of the Mohegan Nation, converted to Christianity during the First Great Awakening, received ministerial training, and was ordained a Presbyterian minister in 1759. He was the first Native American to publish in English. Among his works are at least six hymn texts, including the poignant "A Son's Farewell," or "I Hear the Gospel's Joyful Sound."

> I hear the gospel's joyful sound,
> An organ I shall be,
> For to sound forth redeeming love
> And sinner's misery.
>
> Honor'd parents fare you well,
> My Jesus doth me call,
> I leave you here with God until
> I meet you once for all.
>
> My due affections I'll forsake,
> My parents and their house,
> And to the wilderness betake
> To pay the Lord my vows.

Then I'll forsake my chiefest mates,
That nature could afford,
And wear the shield into the field,
To wait upon the Lord.[1]

It started with one death. Then, three more. By the time the bloodshed abated roughly eighteen months later, it would be, in proportion to population, the deadliest war in American history.

The first man to die was John Sassamon, a "praying Indian" (the English term for Native Christians) of the Massachusett Nation. Orphaned, possibly during a smallpox epidemic, Sassamon grew up in an English home, learning the colonists' language and religion. He became a valued interpreter, working closely with Puritan missionary John Eliot to translate the Bible and establish the "praying town" of Natick, where Native people could be evangelized and acculturated to English ways. Eliot thought so highly of Sassamon that he arranged for a semester's study at Harvard College in 1653.

In the 1660s, Sassamon continued to mediate between English and Native American representatives, but his loyalty seemed to have shifted. He served as a personal secretary to the Wampanoag sachem (or chief) Metacom, whom the English called King Philip. Sassamon represented the sachem in land negotiations and treaties, including a treaty that averted war between Metacom and the Plymouth Colony in 1671. Falling short of Eliot's hopes, Sassamon never converted Metacom to Christianity. Sassamon might have disappointed Metacom too. By 1673, Sassamon was back on English land, ministering to the praying town of Namasket.

In January 1675, Sassamon brought an unwelcome message to Plymouth governor Josiah Winslow: Metacom was conspiring with other nearby sachems to wage war on the colonists. Winslow ignored the report because, as Puritan divine Increase Mather later wrote, reflecting English prejudice, "It had an Indian original, and one can hardly believe them when they do speak the truth."[2] Not getting the reward or protection for which he had likely hoped, Sassamon left Plymouth. Within a week, he disappeared.

The next month, Sassamon's body was found beneath the ice of a pond near his home. Had he fallen in? Had he killed himself? Or had he been murdered— and if so, by whom? Rumors prompted an investigation, and by June the English believed they knew what had happened: Metacom had learned of Sassamon's

1. Joanna Brooks, "Six Hymns by Samson Occom," *Early American Literature* 38, no. 1 (2003): 77–78.

2. Increase Mather, *A Relation of the Troubles Which Have Happened in New-England* (Boston, 1677), 74.

report of the coming war, so he had dispatched three of his men to kill the traitor. An eyewitness came forward to describe the murder. Equally damning, when one of the accused was ordered to approach Sassamon's body, the corpse bled— a sign taken as supernatural confirmation of guilt. A jury of twelve Englishmen and six Native Americans ordered execution by hanging for all three conspirators.

Mary Rowlandson and her children were captured during King Philip's War. One child died; Mary and the other two survived. Her account of the experience became a colonial bestseller, with historically inaccurate woodcuts. (Mary did not have a gun, for example.)

Perhaps Metacom and his advisers had additional reasons for wishing Sassamon dead. Mather claimed (with characteristically erratic seventeenth-century spelling), "No doubt but one reason why the Indians murthered John Sausaman, was out of hatred against him for his Religion, for he was Christianized, and baptiz'd, and was a Preacher amongst the Indians . . . and was wont to curb those Indians that knew not God on the account of their debaucheryes."[3] Sassamon represented a cultural blending that made people on both sides uncomfortable. He was too tied to his Native background to be trusted by the governor of Plymouth, too English to be trusted by other Native people.

The execution of Metacom's men sparked a stunningly cruel war that ranged across southern New England. Metacom and his allied Native nations destroyed many inland colonial settlements, driving the English back to the coast. The modestly better-supplied English and their Native allies fought back, frequently killing scores of their enemies in retaliation for raids or for the capture of English settlers. Both sides slaughtered women and children as well as warriors. Both sides tortured the living and mutilated the dead. By the time a Wampanoag Christian with the English name John Alderman killed Metacom, in August

3. Increase Mather, *A Brief History of the War with the Indians in New-England* (London, 1676), 2.

1676, hundreds of colonists and their allies had been killed, while thousands of their Native opponents had fallen in battle, starved, died of disease, or been sold into slavery. Many of the so-called praying Indians, who had been herded into camps by the English—ostensibly for their own protection—perished as well.

The flow of blood prompted a flow of ink, as the colonists wrote numerous accounts of the war with a variety of goals in mind. Early accounts, published in London, aimed to thrill readers with gory details while also assuring friends (and investors) in the old country that New England's Christians were winning the war against the infidels. Slightly later accounts, first published in the colonies, extracted moral lessons about God's providence. For example, the official report of the Massachusetts government stated,

> The Righteous God hath heightened our Calamity and given Commission to the Barbarous Heathen to rise up against us, and to become a smart Rod, and severe Scourge to us, in Burning and Depopulating several hopeful Plantations, Murdering many of our People of all sorts, and seeming as it were to cast us off . . . hereby speaking aloud to us to search and try our ways and turn again unto the Lord our God from whom we have departed with a great Backsliding.[4]

Generally unstated, but foundational to all of these accounts, was an attempt by the colonists to distinguish themselves from the "savage" Native population and from the cruel Spanish, whose infamous maltreatment of Indigenous Americans served to justify English colonial expansion. New Englanders *had* to be better than the Native nations and the Spanish or else their colony did not deserve to succeed.

The colonists might have learned from King Philip's War that they were not, in fact, better than anyone else, and they could have moved forward with humility and greater cultural sensitivity. This did not happen. As a result, the war was in many ways less a turning point than an archetype, a model of the misunderstandings and violence that attended white interactions with Indigenous people for the rest of American history. As award-winning historian Jill Lepore wrote, "In a sense, King Philip's War never ended. In other times, in other places, its painful wounds would be reopened, its vicious words spoken again."[5]

And yet, this bleak stretch of the historical record is not without moments of turning to the Lord, both on the part of white Christians and, against all odds, on the part of some Native Americans as well. The rest of this chapter will move

---

4. *Laws and Ordinancies of Warre, Pass'd by the General Court of the Massachusets* (Cambridge, 1675), 32.

5. Jill Lepore, *The Name of War: King Philip's War and the Origins of American Identity* (New York: Vintage, 1998), xiii.

The Conversion Narrative of Ponampam

Missionary John Eliot translated and published the conversion narratives of several Native Americans in 1652 as a way of publicizing his work and convincing the leaders of the Massachusetts Bay Colony to authorize a church for the "praying Indians" at Natick. These narratives, though shaped by conventions of the day and substantially edited, are the closest we can come to hearing the voices of the Native people themselves, including a Massachusett man named Ponampam, who confessed,

Before I prayed to God, I committed all manner of sins; and when I heard in the catechism that God made me, I did not believe it, because I knew that I sprang from my father and mother; and therefore I despised the word, and therefore again I did act all sins, and I did love them. Then God was merciful to me and let me hear that word, that *all shall pray from the rising to the setting sun*"; and then I considered whether I should pray, . . . and what would become of me if I did not pray, and what would become of me if I did pray. But I thought if I did pray, that Sachems would be angry; because they did not say pray to God; and therefore I did not pray; but considering of that word that all should pray, I was troubled, and I found in my heart that I would not pray to God; and yet I feared that others would laugh at me; and therefore I did not pray. . . .

Then I heard that word, that God sent Moses into Egypt, and promised *I will be with thee*. That promise I considered, but I thought that it was in vain I did seek, and I was ashamed I did so; and I prayed, O God, teach me *truly* to pray, not only before men, but before God, and pardon all my sins.

Again I heard that word that Christ taught through every town and village, *repent and believe and be saved*; and a little I believed this word, and I loved it; and then I saw all my sins, and prayed for pardon.

Again I heard that word, *he that casteth off God, him will God cast off*; and I found in my heart that I had done this, and I feared because of this my sin, lest God should cast me off, I having cast off God. Then I was troubled about hell, and what shall I do if I be damned. Then I heard that word; if ye repent and believe, God pardons all sins; then I thought, "O that I had this!" I desired to repent and believe; and I begged of God, "O give me repentance and faith!" freely do it for me. And I saw that God was merciful to do it. But I did not attend to the Lord only at sometimes, and I now confess that I am ashamed of my sins; my heart is broken and melted in me; I am angry at myself; I desire pardon in Christ; I betrust my soul in Christ, that he may do it for me.

Martin Moore, *Memoir of Eliot, Apostle to the North American Indians* (Boston: Goldsmith, Crocker & Brewster, 1842), 88–91.

ahead in time, examining key figures and episodes in the fraught relationship among Anglos, Native Americans, and Christianity. Because chapter 1 addressed Spanish and French Catholic missions, this chapter will focus on Protestants.

Revival and Relocation

Though perhaps half of the Massachusett converts to Christianity survived King Philip's War, mission work among them—which had never enjoyed robust support from the colonists—did not recover. Native Christians rebuilt only four of the destroyed praying towns, and no missionary took John Eliot's place when he died in 1690. Few white men (or women) were willing to live among the Native people and attempt to learn their language and customs. More common was the attitude expressed by Cotton Mather in 1710: "The best thing we can do for our Indians is to Anglicise them."[6] Out of this perception grew boarding schools, such as Moor's Charity School, founded by Congregational minister Eleazer Wheelock in 1755. Wheelock hoped that by removing promising youths from their homes, educating, and Anglicizing them, he could train up Native ministers to return and "civilize" their people.

The revival known as the First Great Awakening (more on this event in the next chapter) jump-started numerous evangelistic endeavors, including ministry to Native Americans. David Brainerd, who was expelled from Yale for siding with the pro-revival "New Lights" against the more staid college administration, spent a short but fruitful career preaching to Housatonic and Delaware Native groups in New York, Pennsylvania, and New Jersey. After Brainerd's death from tuberculosis in 1747, theologian Jonathan Edwards—who also spent part of his career preaching to Native Americans—compiled a biography of Brainerd so inspiring that John Wesley, the founder of Methodism, advised every preacher to read it. David's brother, John, continued this ministry until his death in 1781.

Samson Occom, a Mohegan man, also caught the fervor of the Great Awakening and subsequently received a Christian education at Moor's Charity School. Licensed to preach in 1747, he was not granted full ministerial credentials for another dozen years, owing to white ministers' reluctance to count a Native man as their equal. For the same reason, Occom was never paid at the same level as white ministers. He supplemented support from an overseas mission agency, the Society in Scotland for Propagating Christian Knowledge, by teaching school, raising his own food, and selling handcrafts.

6. Collections of the Massachusetts Historical Society, series 6, vol. 1 (Boston, 1886): 401. Available online at https://www.masshist.org/mhs-collections.

Though hampered by low pay, Occom established better rapport with the Native Americans in his care than did white ministers. After finishing at the charity school, he followed a group of Mohegans who settled at Montauk, on Long Island. He performed the full range of ministerial functions: three worship services on Sunday and one on Wednesday evening, plus burials and visitation of the sick. He also taught day school and night school, with an emphasis on spelling and catechism. On top of this work, according to his 1768 autobiography, he sat as judge in the community, hosted many visitors, and "was fetched often from my Tribe and from others to see into their Affairs Both Religious, Temporal,—Besides my Domestic Concerns." After a white minister who spent some time in Montauk left, Occom reported drily, there was a "remarkable revival of religion."[7]

Rev. Samson Occom is portrayed in standard ministerial dress, but the arrows on the back wall hint at his Mohegan identity.

National Portrait Gallery, Smithsonian Institution

Occom received sufficient renown for his work that Wheelock tapped him for a preaching tour of Britain in 1766–67, organized to raise money for a new Native school. The trip was a success, but when Occom returned to New England, he found that Wheelock had altered plans for the school, moving it from Connecticut to New Hampshire, naming it Dartmouth (after an earl who had made a generous pledge), and positioning it primarily as a college for the sons of white colonists. Occom broke with Wheelock and returned to life among Native people, moving with them from Long Island to western Connecticut, then to an Oneida reservation in central New York. Other Native Christians joined the group there in a settlement called Brothertown.

Relocation was a constant challenge for Native Americans in the eighteenth and nineteenth centuries. As the white population of the country grew, settlers purchased, seized, or swindled Native land, pushing the various tribes to the interior of the continent. The moves were physically challenging, sometimes

7. Samson Occom, *A Short Narrative of My Life*, typescript, Dartmouth College Archives, in Bernd Peyer, *The Elders Wrote: An Anthology of Early Prose by North American Indians, 1768–1931* (Berlin: Reimer, 1982), 12–18.

deadly. In 1782, a group of Christian Munsee led by David Zeisberger, a Moravian (a German pacifist church), were forced from their settlement near modern Pittsburgh to the windswept shores of Lake Erie. When a party of Munsee returned to their former towns to gather supplies for the winter, militiamen stationed at Fort Pitt massacred ninety of them—men, women, and children.

Relocation also took a mental toll. Broadly speaking, Native traditional religions view the land as spiritually significant—and not just the land in general but specific mountains, rivers, and other features on the landscape. While many Native groups had always moved frequently, setting up temporary dwellings in response to changing seasons or conflicts with other tribes, their religions were not infinitely portable. Leaving traditional lands necessitated rethinking tribal identity and the relationship between people and place. Complicating matters greatly, Native Americans who relocated in the years after European contact were often survivors of war, disease, or both. They carried only pieces of their cultures as they went, combining those pieces with the fragments of other tribes, constantly reinventing their lives and livelihoods on unfamiliar ground.

For a while, Native groups on the borders of Anglo America were able to carve out pockets of security by playing rival powers against one another. The French and Indian War (1754–63) was so named because the French and their Native allies, notably Algonquians and Mohawks, worked together to halt the westward movement of the English. Other Natives, such as the Iroquois, sided with England in that conflict. Native peoples also took sides during the American Revolution, seeking an ally that would treat them with respect. England continued to cultivate Native allies after it lost its American colonies, hoping to undermine the new nation and retake its territory. Following the War of 1812, though, England relinquished its claims to the Great Lakes region, leaving Native people no government to deal with but the zealously expansionist United States.

The later history of the Brothertown community exemplifies the American government's approach to Native groups. Because of lingering unrest after the War of 1812, and because white settlers wanted the land, the federal government pressured the Native Christians gathered at Brothertown, New York, to move west. After laborious treaty negotiations, these Native people, who were descended from several Christianized tribes, secured land near Green Bay, Wisconsin, and moved there in the early 1830s. Almost immediately, white Americans coveted that land too and made moves to acquire it under the 1830 Indian Removal Act. To avoid removal, the Brothertown group converted their communal land to individual properties and requested US citizenship. In 1839, by an act of Congress, they became the country's first Native American citizens.

Ironically, when the Brothertown Nation sought federal recognition and financial assistance under new Bureau of Indian Affairs guidelines in the late twentieth century, the Bureau of Indian Affairs determined that the acquisition of citizenship in 1839 had terminated the Brothertown Nation's identity as a tribe. They had no standing to request benefits. A few thousand members of the Brothertown Nation still bear the name, though, and continue to press for recognition. Their tribal symbol features a cross, and their elected officers include "Peacemakers."

Christianization and Civilization

To soothe white Americans' conscience, and to make Natives less likely to forcibly resist their treatment, the federal government in the nineteenth century advocated efforts to educate, evangelize, and civilize Indigenous people. The government did not, however, have much in the way of funds or personnel to devote to this project. Protestant churches, by contrast, had considerable reserves of both. Despite the separation of church and state effected by the Constitution, for decades the government effectively outsourced work with Native Americans to Protestant missionaries.

Collaboration between the federal government and Protestant missionaries was not seamless. In 1830, the state of Georgia, in a campaign to force Cherokees off their land, passed a law ordering whites to leave Cherokee territory. Two white missionaries, Samuel Worcester and Elizur Butler, refused to go and were imprisoned. Worcester's case proceeded to the Supreme Court, which ruled in his favor, but President Andrew Jackson's rapacious administration disregarded the decision and kept pressuring the missionaries, and the Cherokees, to leave. Eventually, Worcester capitulated and moved to Native American Territory (now Oklahoma) to prepare for the Cherokee migration. The Cherokee followed, walking the Trail of Tears in 1838–39. As many as four thousand of the more than sixteen thousand Cherokees who began the journey died before completing it.

More often, missionary and government goals basically aligned, as white Americans sought to turn the Native Americans into darker-skinned versions of themselves. Many of these white Americans genuinely believed their religion and culture to be a superior route to happiness in this life and blessedness in the next. Some aspects of the project were even egalitarian. As an 1849 article in the *Baptist Missionary Magazine* phrased it, "The office of the gospel is to bring the heathen nations to be, in these respects, such as Christian nations are; to put every people under heaven on the highest platform of civilization and religion, of art and science, of learning, prosperity, and usefulness, of happiness

White Visions of Native Assimilation

House Committee on Indian Affairs, January 22, 1818

In the present state of our country, one of two things seems to be necessary: either that those sons of the forest should be moralized or exterminated. Humanity would rejoice at the former, but shrink with horror from the latter. Put into the hands of their children the primer and the hoe, and they will naturally, in time, take hold of the plough; and, as their minds become enlightened and expand, the Bible will be their book, and they will grow up in habits of morality and industry, leave the chase to those whose minds are less cultivated, and become useful members of society.

American State Papers, class 2, *Indian Affairs*, vol. 2, p. 151. This document is available online at https://memory.loc.gov/ammem/amlaw/lwsplink.html.

United Foreign Mission Society, May 5, 1823

Let then, missionary Institutions, established to convey to them the benefits of civilization and the blessings of Christianity, be efficiently supported; and, with cheering hope, you may look forward to the period when the savage shall be converted into the citizen; when the hunter shall be transformed into the mechanic; when the farm, the work shop, the School-House, and the Church shall adorn every Indian village; when fruits of Industry, good order, and sound morals shall bless every Indian dwelling; and when throughout the vast range of country from the Mississippi to the Pacific, the red man and the white man shall everywhere be found, mingling in the same benevolent and friendly feelings, fellow citizens of the same civil and religious community, and fellow-heirs to a glorious inheritance in the kingdom of Immanuel.

Records of the UFMS Board of Managers, quoted in Robert F. Berkhofer Jr., Salvation and the Savage: An Analysis of Protestant Missions and American Indian Response, 1787–1862 (Westport, CT: Greenwood, 1977), 10–11.

and social advancement."[8] However painful the introduction of white culture might be for the Native Americans, Anglos reasoned, being left alone to wander in darkness was surely worse.

To effect such a radical change in the Native population, it was necessary to start young, so schools became the cornerstone of the work. By the end of

---

8. "Influence of Missions on the Temporal Condition of the Heathen," *Baptist Missionary Magazine* 29, no. 4 (April 1849): 102.

the nineteenth century, the federal government oversaw more than 250 schools enrolling more than twenty thousand pupils. The schools varied significantly; there were day schools and residential schools, some with the flavor of a military academy, others emphasizing manual labor. As in the public schools of the era, the Bible suffused the curriculum. Discipline was strict, and dress codes were rigid. In numerous ways, the schools created a rupture between the Native world and the white world. When students arrived by train or were dropped off by their parents, little time was allowed for goodbyes. Students received new, American names and were required to speak English on campus.

As a musician, author, and activist, Zitkala-Ša lived in both Native and Anglo worlds. Her Sioux name meant "Red Bird," but she also used the English name Gertrude Simmons Bonnin.

Zitkala-Ša, a Yankton Dakota Sioux writer educated at White's Manual Labor Institute in Wabash, Indiana, in the 1880s, recalled an especially traumatic introduction to school life. She hid under her bed to escape having her hair cut. In her tribe, only mourners or cowards wore short hair. But when a school matron found her, "I remember being dragged out, though I resisted by kicking and scratching wildly. In spite of myself, I was carried downstairs and tied fast in a chair. I cried aloud, shaking my head all the while until I felt the cold blades of the scissors against my neck, and heard them gnaw off one of my thick braids. Then I lost my spirit."[9] Despite this experience, Zitkala-Ša succeeded in school, became a fine musician, and even took a teaching position at another Native American school. Later, though, she became a Native rights activist, critical of white schools and the Christianity taught there.

It was not publicly known at the time how many Native children died at such schools, but in 2021 mass graves were uncovered at sites in Canada, followed by calls to investigate more sites there and in the United States. Quite often, the plan to (as school founder Captain Richard H. Pratt phrased it) "kill the Indian, and save the man" accomplished only the killing. In 2022, Pope Francis apologized for the trauma inflicted at the Canadian residential schools. "What

9. Zitkala-Ša (Gertrude Simmons Bonnin), "The School Days of an Indian Girl," *Atlantic Monthly* 85 (February 1900): 187.

A Failure to Communicate

Corabelle Fellows taught at a mission school for Dakota and Lakota tribal groups from 1884 to 1888. She recounted a conversation about God with an old man named Gray Hawk, whose grandson she had just treated for a burn on his arm.

"Tell me," I said, "about your Wankan-Tanka. I do not know how big or brave he is nor where his tepee stands."

"*Wankan-Tanka mahpie acta*" ("The Great Spirit has gone up into the heavens"), he said in the tone of one explaining to a very young child.

"Then, if I cannot see him, tell me how he looks."

With that he told me, not by words so much as by facial expression and the worshipful tones of his deep old voice, that Wankan-Tanka, he of the most brave heart, listens to and loves best those who can suffer much pain and exert much courage and strength; that he comes down to the tepee where a brave lies dead and escorts him upon a round of all the happy hunting grounds of heaven, letting him choose and be completely satisfied with the one among them all which he most desires. . . . ▶

our Christian faith tells us is that this was a disastrous error, incompatible with the Gospel of Jesus Christ," he said. "It is painful to think of how the firm soil of values, language and culture that made up the authentic identity of your peoples was eroded, and that you have continued to pay the price of this."[10]

In some places, church-state collaboration in work with Native Americans ranged far beyond education. Sheldon Jackson (1834–1909), a Presbyterian missionary, spent the years after his 1858 graduation from Princeton Seminary planting churches in Wisconsin, Minnesota, Colorado, Wyoming, Montana, Utah Territory, Arizona Territory, and New Mexico Territory. These churches mostly served white miners and settlers, but Jackson encountered many Native Americans on his travels through this vast territory as well. Then a number of events came together to refocus his mission.

In 1867, the United States purchased Alaska from Russia, despite having no particular plans for the place. In 1868, Ulysses S. Grant ran for president with the slogan "Let us have peace," meaning both a peaceful reconstruction of the

10. Christopher White, "In Canada, Pope Francis Tells Indigenous People He Is 'Deeply Sorry' for Abusive Schools," *National Catholic Reporter*, July 25, 2022, https://www.ncronline.org/news/vatican/canada-pope-francis-tells-indigenous-people-he-deeply-sorry-abusive-schools.

[To mourn the fallen brave], men and women tortured themselves, the only way they knew to show the depth and sincerity of their grief. The men thrust sharp sticks through the calves of their legs and went out chanting their lament for the dead in a minor and monotonous tone. They took the path of most hazard of beast and weather, and it became a trail of blood, for they went on and on to the very limit of their endurance. . . .

All this, Gray Hawk explained, was that the Great Spirit might have proof of men's power to suffer. Only through suffering, also, might men prove their love for the dead. Only through suffering might the living hope to please the all-brave, all-enduring Great Spirit. Gray Hawk here became very despondent, and fell into *hannedipi* (a god-seeking dream).

"And now," he said, "the Great Father at Washington has forbidden the Sun Dance!" How could the Great Spirit now know that the Sioux desired to please him?

I was unable to bring any comfort with my story of my Great Spirit who asked only kindliness among all men together to be pleased.

Kunigunde Duncan, *Blue Star: The Story of Corabelle Fellows, Teacher at Dakota Missions, 1884–1888* (1938; repr., St. Paul: Minnesota Historical Society Press, 1990), 114–17.

South and a westward expansion of white settlement that minimized conflict with Native Americans. Grant appointed Ely S. Parker, a Seneca tribe member, as the first Native Commissioner of Indian Affairs and also appointed churchmen as agents among Native populations, judging them to be more trustworthy than political appointees. Finding a role within this new policy, in 1870 the Presbyterian General Assembly declared that it "views with deep concern the unevangelized condition of the aboriginal population of our land" and "authorizes the Board of Missions to put forth its utmost efforts" to evangelize and civilize the Native Americans.[11]

In response to these initiatives, Jackson quickly added Native American missions in the Rocky Mountain West and Pacific Northwest to his work. In the later 1870s, he helped raise funds for mission stations in Alaska. He also traveled to Washington, DC, to lobby for legislation setting up government and infrastructure for the new territory. In 1885, Jackson was appointed General Agent of Education in Alaska—on the payroll of the federal Bureau of Education—while also still serving as a missionary-at-large for the Presbyterian Board of Home

11. *The Biblical Repertory and Princeton Review,* vol. 42 (New York: Charles Scribner & Co., 1870), 432.

Missions. In addition to overseeing churches, mission stations, and schools, Jackson attempted to introduce reindeer farming to Alaska, providing Native Alaskans a new source of food, fur, and transportation.

Reindeer farming did not prosper, and when a number of other Presbyterians took public positions in Alaska (even the governor, John Brady, was a former missionary), critics smelled corruption. Jackson was never accused of a crime, but a 1906 investigation into the Alaska situation complained of "denominational favoritism."[12] Brady resigned as governor following the report, and Jackson ceased work for the Bureau of Education in 1908. Oversight of Alaska, and of Native affairs elsewhere, became more strictly a government concern, driven by politics rather than evangelism.

Native and Christian

Different writers have framed the narrative of Native American interactions with Christianity in starkly divergent terms. The position of "Christian Native American" has been difficult to define or to inhabit. James Treat, a religion scholar and member of the Muscogee (Creek) Nation, wrote in 1996,

> Today, native Christians throughout the United States and Canada are continuing their centuries-long struggle for religious self-determination. Denominational missionaries have settled in native communities preaching a gospel of cultural conformity, condemning native religious history on the basis of ignorance, and dictating artificial criteria for institutional acceptability. Academic anthropologists have toured native communities looking for pure, primitive culture, dismissing native religious adaptability as tragic acculturation, and attempting to reduce human experience to ethnographic data. Government agents have dominated native communities in the service of colonial expansion, enforcing laws that restrict native religious freedom, and manipulating political power through bureaucratic patronage. Radical activists have defended native communities against these and other impositions, calling for the outright rejection of "the white man's religion" and the immediate revival of esoteric indigenous traditions. Native Christians have been called heretical, inauthentic, assimilated, and uncommitted; they have long endured intrusive definitions of personal identity and have quietly pursued their own religious visions, often under the very noses of unsuspecting missionaries, anthropologists, agents, and activists.[13]

12. Norman J. Bender, *Winning the West for Christ: Sheldon Jackson and Presbyterianism on the Rocky Mountain Frontier, 1869–1880* (Albuquerque: University of New Mexico Press, 1996), 191.

13. James Treat, "Introduction: Native Christian Narrative Discourse," in *Native and Christian: Indigenous Voices on Religious Identity in the United States and Canada*, ed. James Treat (New York: Routledge, 1996), 8–9.

Buffeted by these competing agendas, what possibilities exist for Native American Christians? The following examples highlight a few twentieth-century Native American contributions in the areas of church leadership, theology, and religious practice.

Charlie Lee (1926–2003) grew up on a Navajo reservation in New Mexico. When teachers at his residential school noticed his prodigious artistic talent, he was sent to another school in Santa Fe that specialized in the arts. Soon his paintings appeared in prestigious galleries and museums, including the Smithsonian Institution. Yet he was unsatisfied with his life and with the mainline Protestant Christianity to which he had been exposed in school. Then, while visiting a friend in Arizona, he encountered Assemblies of God (AG) missionaries and attended Pentecostal worship.[14] The experience changed his life.

Lee gave up art, except as a sideline, to attend Assemblies-affiliated Central Bible Institute in Missouri. One of his teachers advocated a relatively new perspective on missions and evangelism: the "Indigenous principle," which defined the goal of missionary work as rooting new churches in the cultures of evangelized people, then training up Indigenous leaders to sustain those churches after the missionaries left. Acting on this principle, in 1951 Lee returned to his childhood reservation to preach the gospel in Navajo. After securing land from the tribal council, he built a church and led its transition from being a funded mission to, in 1976, the first self-sustaining Native American church within the AG.

Even after Lee's church received denominational status, though, Native Americans lacked representation on the church's General Council. The Indigenous principle was easier to articulate than to embrace, and Native leaders challenged the AG to practice what it preached. After years of requests from these leaders, the AG created a position for a part-time representative but gave the holder of the position no funding and no specific duties. Eventually, in the mid-1990s, Native Americans and members of other ethnic minorities in the church organized fellowships for evangelism and the training of leaders within their communities. The fellowships still lacked funding or specific responsibilities, but at least they afforded a measure of autonomy.

In the realm of theology, the 1960s and 1970s saw a confluence of rights activism and liberation theology among Native Americans. Liberation theology, which gained traction among Latin American Catholics, African Americans,

---

14. Mainline Protestantism is the center-left, ecumenical form of twentieth-century American Christianity associated with denominations such as the Episcopal Church, the Presbyterian Church (USA), the United Methodist Church, the American Baptist Churches (USA), the Evangelical Lutheran Church in America, the Disciples of Christ, and the United Church of Christ. On Pentecostalism, see chap. 10.

and other groups, posits that Christ's life and teachings proclaim a message of liberation from poverty and injustice. In this interpretation, Christianity ceased to be a "white man's religion" and could become a potent force for social change.

The combination of Native American activism and liberation theology invited critique as well. In 1988, Robert Allen Warrior, an Osage man then on the faculty of Stanford University, published an article titled "Canaanites, Cowboys, and Indians," arguing that his people did not fit the typical liberation narrative. A key story in that narrative is the exodus, in which God delivers his people from slavery in Egypt. Instead of identifying with the Old Testament nation of Israel, though, Warrior identified with the Canaanites—the original occupants of the promised land. "The conquest stories, with all their violence and injustice, must be taken seriously by those who believe in the god of the Old Testament," Warrior wrote.[15] He did not see liberation theology, or any Christian theology, offering much hope for Native Americans.

Another Native American university professor, William Baldridge (Cherokee), agreed with Warrior's reading of the Old Testament but offered a ray of hope from the New Testament. In Matthew 15, Jesus heals the daughter of a Canaanite woman who persists in seeking his help after he initially declines to answer her plea. "The story tells us that if we Canaanites will live out our faith, we can change the very heart of God," Baldridge wrote in a response to Warrior. "And if we can change the heart of God we can hope to change the hearts of his chosen people, even those who identify themselves as Christians."[16]

Regarding religious practice, James Treat's edited volume *Native and Christian* offered numerous examples of integration and innovation, some more successful than others. Rosemary McCombs Maxey, a Muscogee tribe member and a United Church of Christ pastor, described participation by some white members of her denomination in traditional Native American practices, such as the vision quest and the sweat lodge. Maxey appreciated the cross-cultural exchange but wondered whether it was fitting for outsiders to drop in on ceremonies that were designed to foster deep community. She preferred the idea of welcoming a diverse, ecumenical crowd to the Lord's Table, where "our various voices, the voices of all creation, and the voice of the Creator can speak and be heard."[17]

15. Robert Allen Warrior, "Canaanites, Cowboys, and Indians: Deliverance, Conquest, and Liberation Theology Today," *Christianity and Crisis* 49, no. 12 (September 11, 1989): 264.

16. William Baldridge, "Native American Theology: A Biblical Basis," *Christianity and Crisis* 50, no. 8 (May 28, 1990): 182.

17. Rosemary McCombs Maxey, "Who Can Sit at the Lord's Table? The Experience of Indigenous Peoples," in Treat, *Native and Christian*, 48–49.

Alberta Pualani Hopkins, a native Hawaiian and member of the Episcopal Church, had a less welcome experience at the Lord's Table. Back in 1893, a group of American businessmen, including the sons of Protestant missionaries sent to evangelize the islands, overthrew Hawai'i's Christian queen, Lili'uokalani, and made Hawai'i a US protectorate. (For more of this story, see chap. 9.) Amid commemorations of this event in 1993, the Episcopal Church in Hawai'i scheduled a worship service of healing and hope. Organizers planned to use traditional Hawaiian foods, poi and coconut water, as eucharistic elements, as they had done before at a large church event. Days before the service, though, the white bishop announced that the service must feature traditional Western elements, bread and wine. Hopkins wrote, "I don't know if the bishop understood the irony of his decision in the context of a service meant to heal the alienation of an entire people in the place of their birth. I only know that at a moment when I was dealing with the hurt of an act one hundred years ago that made my ancestors instant foreigners in the only place they had to call home, my bishop had made me a foreigner in the church I had considered my spiritual home."[18] Hopkins advocated changes to clergy recruitment and training that would encourage a more ethnically diverse priesthood and more sustained attention to cultural imperialism within the church. Without these changes, she feared that racism would remain a problem ritually acknowledged but never effectively addressed.

Forgotten but Not Gone

To return to the event that began this chapter, what does it mean for historian Jill Lepore to write, "In a sense, King Philip's War never ended"? The conflict has been almost entirely forgotten outside New England, reduced to a paragraph or two in a history textbook. The last named battles in America's long line of so-called Indian Wars occurred soon after World War I. In what ways does King Philip's War linger?

First, violence and hardship still shape the lives of many Native Americans. According to Bureau of Justice statistics, Native Americans are more than twice as likely as the rest of the population to be the victim of a violent crime. The poverty rate among Native Americans is also nearly twice that of the population as a whole. Alcoholism, domestic abuse, obesity, and unemployment are all prevalent in Native communities. Though it is not possible to draw a straight line of causation from one seventeenth-century war to present circumstances, it is easy to see how the actions and policies of white Americans over this long

18. Alberta Pualani Hopkins, "The Challenge of the Future: Creating a Place Called Home," in Treat, *Native and Christian*, 165.

period have contributed to Natives' struggles. Even so, Native Americans face these struggles with dignity, often with the help of traditional and Christian religious resources.[19]

Second, the cultural in-betweenness that cost John Sassamon his life continues to pose challenges for Native Christians. These challenges are reflected in the stories of Charlie Lee, Robert Allen Warrior, William Baldridge, Rosemary McCombs Maxey, and Alberta Pualani Hopkins. Cultural tensions even complicate attempts to count Native American Christians. Estimates of the proportion of Native Americans who identify as Christians today range from 3 percent to more than 30 percent, depending on survey methodology as well as how one defines both "Native American" and "Christian."[20]

Third, competing efforts to narrate Native American history persist, both in obvious places (textbooks, movies, the National Museum of the American Indian) and in surprising places. In 2010, James Poniske, a middle-school history teacher, published a board game called King Philip's War in which players representing Metacom's forces and the English colonists rolled dice to inflict damage on each other's armies and settlements. Activists led by Julianne Jennings, a member of the Nottoway Tribal Community in Virginia, protested the game with signs reading, "Stop Playing the Genocide Game" and "Would a Holocaust Game Be OK?" Where Poniske saw an opportunity to help people understand an obscure episode in military history, Jennings saw a symbolic attack on her heritage.[21]

William Faulkner famously wrote, "The past is never dead. It's not even past." Applied to King Philip's War, this dictum illustrates a crucial difference between Anglo and Native Americans. For most Anglo-Americans, the war is long dead, long past. They can afford to forget it. For Native Americans, though, the fight for personal and cultural survival continues, weighted rather than lightened by the passage of time.

---

19. Steven W. Perry, *American Indians and Crime: A BJS Statistical Profile, 1992–2002* (Washington, DC: US Department of Justice, Office of Justice Programs, Bureau of Justice Statistics, 2004); US Census Bureau, "Facts for Features: American Indian and Alaska Native Heritage Month, November 2013," October 31, 2013, https://www.census.gov/newsroom/facts-for-features/2013/cb13-ff26.html.

20. Nikki Tundel, "American Indians Balance Native Customs with Christianity," Minnesota Public Radio News, November 13, 2013, http://www.mprnews.org/story/2013/11/13/arts/native -spirituality-christianity; Donald E. Pelotte et al., "Native American Catholics at the Millennium: A Report on a Survey by the United States Conference of Catholic Bishops' Ad Hoc Committee on Native American Catholics" (Washington, DC: US Conference of Catholic Bishops, 2002), https://www.usccb.org/issues-and-action/cultural-diversity/native-american/resources/upload /NA-Catholics-Millennium.pdf.

21. Matthew Kirschenbaum, "Contests for Meaning: Playing King Philip's War in the Twenty-First Century," in *Pastplay: Teaching and Learning History with Technology*, ed. Kevin Kee (Ann Arbor: University of Michigan Press, 2014), 198–213.

Catharine Brown (1800?–1823), a member of the Cherokee Nation, was educated at Brainerd Mission School in Chattanooga, Tennessee. She became a Christian and then a missionary teacher among the Cherokee before her early death from tuberculosis. Excerpts from this March 8, 1820, letter to her missionary friend Isabella Hall mingle Catherine's thoughts on prayer with her prayerful hopes for the people she loved.

> We know the Lord is good and all things will work together for good to those that love him and put their whole trust in him. And O now, dear ever dear sister, what shall I say to you? How can I possibly express my feelings—could we see each other, we would talk and weep and sing and pray together almost without ceasing. But our Heavenly Father has separated us. . . . Still, dear sister, we can pray for each other. Don't you think our prayers often meet at the same time at the Throne of Grace? Our Heavenly Father will grant all our requests. Yes, he will do it for Jesus, his dear son's sake. O, then, let us pray on and never cease to pray for each other while he lends us breath, and when in heaven we meet [we] shall see him whom our soul loveth. . . . O, let us rejoice continually and praise the Lord for what He is doing among this people.[22]

FURTHER READING

Archuleta, Margaret L., Brenda J. Child, and K. Tsianina Lomawaima, eds. *Away from Home: American Indian Boarding School Experiences, 1879–2000*. Phoenix: Heard Museum, 2002.

Bender, Norman J. *Winning the West for Christ: Sheldon Jackson and Presbyterianism on the Rocky Mountain Frontier, 1869–1880*. Albuquerque: University of New Mexico Press, 1996.

Bowden, Henry Warner. *American Indians and Christian Missions: Studies in Cultural Conflict*. Chicago: University of Chicago Press, 1981.

Cogley, Richard W. *John Eliot's Mission to the Indians before King Philip's War*. Cambridge, MA: Harvard University Press, 1999.

Fisher, Linford. *The Indian Great Awakening: Religion and the Shaping of Native Cultures in Early America*. New York: Oxford University Press, 2012.

Graber, Jennifer. *The Gods of Indian Country: Religion and the Struggle for the American West*. New York: Oxford University Press, 2018.

---

22. Theresa Strouth Gaul, ed., *Cherokee Sister: The Collected Writings of Catharine Brown, 1818–1823* (Lincoln: University of Nebraska Press, 2013), 74–75. Spelling and punctuation have been modified for readability.

Juster, Susan. *Sacred Violence in Early America*. Philadelphia: University of Pennsylvania Press, 2016.

Lepore, Jill. *The Name of War: King Philip's War and the Origins of American Identity*. New York: Vintage, 1998.

Lewis, Bonnie Sue. *Creating Christian Indians: Native Clergy in the Presbyterian Church*. Norman: University of Oklahoma Press, 2003.

Silver, Peter. *Our Savage Neighbors: How Indian War Transformed Early America*. New York: Norton, 2008.

Tarango, Angela. *Choosing the Jesus Way: American Indian Pentecostals and the Fight for the Indigenous Principle*. Chapel Hill: University of North Carolina Press, 2014.

Treat, James, ed. *Native and Christian: Indigenous Voices on Religious Identity in the United States and Canada*. New York: Routledge, 1996.

4

Evangelicalism Sweeps America

George Whitefield Sparks the First Great Awakening, 1740

In the 1730s and 1740s, revivals on both sides of the Atlantic radically altered worship practices. As sermons grew more emotional and dramatic, filled with images designed to help listeners experience spiritual realities, hymns with the same vibrant imagery surged in popularity.

The most prominent writer of these hymns was Isaac Watts (1674–1748), a theologian and minister often called the "Father of English Hymnody." Watts wrote hundreds of hymns, including "Joy to the World," "O God, Our Help in Ages Past," and the evocative Communion hymn "When I Survey the Wondrous Cross."

> When I survey the wondrous cross
> On which the Prince of glory died,
> My richest gain I count but loss,
> And pour contempt on all my pride.
>
> Forbid it, Lord, that I should boast,
> Save in the death of Christ, my God!
> All the vain things that charm me most,
> I sacrifice them through his blood.

See, from his head, his hands, his feet,
sorrow and love flow mingled down.
Did e'er such love and sorrow meet,
Or thorns compose so rich a crown?

Were the whole realm of nature mine,
that were a present far too small.
Love so amazing, so divine,
demands my soul, my life, my all.[1]

Imagine a preacher so famous that crowds of thousands stood outside for hours to hear him. A man whose travels, personal journals, sermons, and controversies filled half of all the printed pages in America. A man called "Son of Thunder" and "the Wonder of the Age," far and away the biggest celebrity of his era. That man was George Whitefield.

Born in Gloucester, England, in 1714, and reared by a single mother who owned an inn frequented by actors, the young Whitefield exhibited a knack for theater. His mother, however, encouraged him to pursue a more stable and respectable career in the Church of England. Upon discovering that poor students could attend Oxford while working as their richer classmates' servants, Whitefield got serious about his college-prep academics and about the state of his soul. In 1732, he entered Oxford's aristocratic Pembroke College as a servitor, willing to work hard but feeling very lonely.

At Oxford, Whitefield came into the orbit of brothers John and Charles Wesley, whose unusually rigorous attention to spiritual disciplines had earned them the derisive nickname "Methodists." Whitefield readily took to the Methodists' intense practices of prayer and self-discipline—too readily, in fact. Prolonged fasts eroded his health, and charitable work edged out his studies, to the point that Whitefield was threatened with expulsion from school. During a subsequent leave of absence from Oxford, he threw himself on God's mercy and received an outpouring of grace that he understood as the "New Birth." Soon afterward, he preached his first sermons to prisoners at the county jail.

In short order, Whitefield returned to Oxford, graduated, and was ordained a deacon in the Church of England. In a letter to a friend, he described his first sermon after his 1736 ordination, which he preached in his boyhood church.

Curiosity, as you may easily guess, drew a large congregation together upon the occasion. The sight at first a little awed me; but I was comforted with a heartfelt sense of the divine presence, and soon found the unspeakable advantage of having been accustomed to public speaking when a boy at school, and of exhort-

---

1. This version is from the *Psalter Hymnal* (Grand Rapids: CRC Publications, 1987), no. 384.

ing and teaching the prisoners and poor people at their private houses, whilst at university. By these means I was kept from being daunted over much. As I proceeded, I perceived the fire kindled, till at last, though so young, and amidst a crowd of those, who knew me in my infant childish days, I trust I was enabled to speak with some degree of gospel authority. Some few mocked, but most for the present seemed struck; and I have since heard that a complaint had been made to the bishop, that I drove fifteen mad the first sermon. The worthy prelate, as I am informed, wished that the madness might not be forgotten before next Sunday.[2]

George Whitefield was famous for his dramatic preaching style. He drew crowds of thousands on both sides of the Atlantic.

All the elements of Whitefield's legendary preaching were present from the start of his public ministry. Curiosity drew a crowd. Whitefield sensed God's presence and also drew on his own skills, including the stage acting he had practiced at school. He kindled a fire in his audience that, in a few hearts, flamed out of control, generating controversy. Yet a church authority was pleased with the result and hoped that Whitefield would return to ignite the congregation again.

Instead of settling into a pastorate, Whitefield responded to John Wesley's call for preachers in America. Both Wesley brothers had attempted to minister in the new, sparsely settled colony of Georgia, but Charles's ill health and John's failed romance with a parishioner chased them back home to England. For various reasons, Whitefield did not leave for America until early in 1738. In the interim, he honed his preaching craft, learning to speak with emotion and without notes—a sharp contrast to the standard style of the day, in which the preacher read from a long, erudite manuscript. Whitefield also became skilled at public relations, feeding stories of his successes to the London press and finding publishers to print and distribute written versions of his popular sermons.

Whitefield needed all these skills and more in Georgia. The colony was poor, and poorly managed. Its varied population of landowners, laborers, and Native

2. George Whitefield to Mr. H., June 30, 1736, in *Letters of George Whitefield for the Period 1734–1742* (Carlisle, PA: Banner of Truth Trust, 1976), 18–19. Whitefield would be ordained to the Anglican priesthood in 1739.

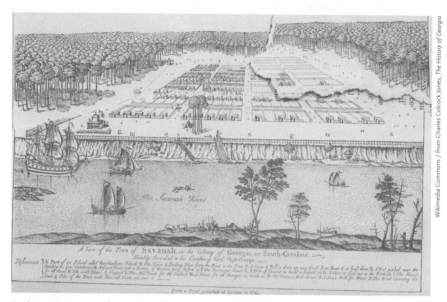

As this early drawing of the town of Savannah shows, almost nothing had been built in the colony of Georgia when John and Charles Wesley and, later, George Whitefield attempted to minister there in the 1730s.

Americans (though not slaves; slavery was outlawed in Georgia until 1750) lacked churches, schools, and charitable institutions. Whitefield decided that he could best serve the colony's needs, spread the message of the New Birth, and attract the crowds whose energy kept him going by becoming a fundraiser. He would travel widely, preaching and collecting donations for an orphanage.

After just three months in Georgia, Whitefield sailed to England to begin his campaign. When pastors refused him access to their pulpits—a move he interpreted as persecution for the sake of the gospel—he preached outdoors instead, to larger and less inhibited audiences. November 1739 found him back in America, kicking off a colonial tour in Philadelphia. While there, he favorably impressed a young printer named Benjamin Franklin, who never adopted Whitefield's religion but nonetheless considered the preacher a friend, as well as a lucrative source of print materials, ever after.

Following ten days of private and public meetings in Philadelphia, Whitefield traveled through New Jersey to New York City, then back to Philadelphia before embarking on an overland journey to Georgia. He preached in Delaware, Maryland, Virginia, and North Carolina before crossing into South Carolina on January 1, 1740. After stints in Savannah and Charleston, he sailed to Delaware in April, spent more time in Pennsylvania and New Jersey, and eventually worked his way up through New England. By his own (possibly

Benjamin Franklin on George Whitefield

In 1739 arriv'd among us from England the Rev. Mr. Whitefield, who had made himself remarkable there as an itinerant Preacher. He was at first permitted to preach in some of our Churches; but the Clergy taking a Dislike to him, soon refus'd him their Pulpits and he was oblig'd to preach in the Fields. The Multitudes of all Sects and Denominations that attended his Sermons were enormous and it was [a] matter of Speculation to me who was one of the Number, to observe the extraordinary Influence of his Oratory on his Hearers, and how much they admir'd and respected him, notwithstanding his common Abuse of them, by assuring them they were naturally half Beasts and half Devils. It was wonderful to see the Change soon made in the Manners of our Inhabitants; from being thoughtless or indifferent about Religion, it seem'd as if all the World were growing Religious; so that one could not walk thro' the Town in an Evening without Hearing Psalms sung in different Families of every Street. . . .

I happened soon after to attend one of his Sermons, in the Course of which I perceived he intended to finish with a Collection, and I silently resolved he should get nothing from me. I had in my Pocket a Handful of Copper Money, three or four silver Dollars, and five Pistoles [Spanish coins] in Gold. As he proceeded I began to soften, and concluded to give the Coppers. Another Stroke of his Oratory made me asham'd of that, and determin'd me to give the Silver; and he finish'd so admirably, that I emptied my Pocket wholly into the Collector's Dish, Gold and all.

Benjamin Franklin's Autobiography: An Authoritative Text, Backgrounds, Criticism, ed. J. A. Leo Lemay and P. M. Zall (New York: Norton, 1986), 87–88.

inflated) count, on one day in October he spoke to twenty thousand people at Boston Common. That would have been the largest crowd ever assembled in the American colonies, well over the city's estimated population of sixteen thousand.

As Whitefield crossed all these geographical boundaries, the religious movement he represented—evangelicalism—eroded many cultural boundaries while building up new ones. Denominations collaborated and split. New opportunities arose for women and minorities, but traditional elites reasserted their grip on power. Through it all, Whitefield and the other revivalists of the First Great Awakening pioneered a new way of being Christian that was particularly suited to what would become, a generation later, a new nation, the United States.

The Landscape

The many places Whitefield visited differed as much in religious climate as they did in temperature and topography. A brief tour of these areas gives a sense of the landscape that evangelicalism built upon or bulldozed through.

In England, the Church of England enjoyed the benefits of establishment, including legal privileges and public funding. With the 1689 Act of Toleration, however, conditions for Dissenters had improved. Puritans (whom we met in chap. 2), Presbyterians, and Baptists no longer had to flee to the colonies to practice their religion freely, though they still faced barriers in England, such as being denied entry to most of the colleges in Oxford and Cambridge. Toleration did not extend to Catholics—except in Maryland, a colony founded as a haven for Catholics in 1632.

Methodism began as a renewal movement within the Church of England. John Wesley, Charles Wesley, and George Whitefield were all ordained in the Anglican Church, and none of the three ever sought to leave it. But the emphases of Methodism, including intense piety, emotional worship, and very high behavioral expectations for members and clergy, bothered many genteel Anglicans. A major rupture occurred around the time of the American Revolution, when John Wesley, seeking to remedy a shortage of ministers in America, sidestepped the Church of England hierarchy to ordain preachers for the colonies on his own authority. The split between Anglicans and Methodists was finalized after Wesley's death in 1791.

Theologically, the Church of England was fairly broad, accommodating a range of viewpoints on such subjects as the human condition and the nature of salvation. Initially, Methodism was theologically mixed too. John Wesley, following Dutch theologian Jacobus Arminius, believed that anyone could repent and be saved. Other early Methodists, notably Whitefield, followed French theologian John Calvin in believing that God had elected only some people for salvation. This disagreement soured the relationship between Wesley and Whitefield, though not so badly as to prevent Wesley from delivering a warm eulogy upon Whitefield's death in 1770. Wesley's Arminian theology came to dominate the Methodist Church and its offshoots, including the Wesleyan Church (founded 1843), the Free Methodist Church (1860), and the Church of the Nazarene (1908).

In New England, Congregationalism, though born of Puritan dissent, functioned as the religious establishment. Ministers held tremendous cultural authority, and a Congregational church stood both literally and symbolically at the center of most towns. Nonetheless, Congregationalism hardly enjoyed universal support. Baptists, Presbyterians, Quakers, Huguenots, and even Anglicans had

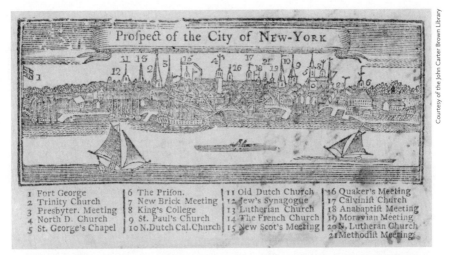

Prospect of the City of NEW-YORK

1 Fort George	6 The Prison.	11 Old Dutch Church	16 Quaker's Meeting
2 Trinity Church	7 New Brick Meeting	12 Jew's Synagogue	17 Calvinist Church
3 Presbyter. Meeting	8 King's College	13 Lutherian Church	18 Anabaptist Meeting
4 North D. Church	9 St. Paul's Church	14 The French Church	19 Moravian Meeting
5 St. George's Chapel	10 N.Dutch Cal.Church	15 New Scot's Meeting	20 N. Lutheran Church
			21 Methodist Meeting

The Middle Colonies, which included the bustling, cosmopolitan city of New York, had the highest number and greatest diversity of churches in colonial America. This 1771 woodcut identifies seventeen churches and a synagogue in lower Manhattan.

built churches in New England by the time of Whitefield's visit. Additionally, Indigenous religions and European folk practices, sometimes labeled "witchcraft," persisted. Plenty of people simply did not go to church at all. Thanks to the Half-Way Covenant, there was also a substantial group of people who attended Congregational churches but could not become full members because they had not publicly testified to personal conversion. People in this category were especially responsive to the revival preaching of the Great Awakening.

In Southern colonies, the Church of England was established, but not very well. Few Anglican ministers desired posts in the swampy, sweaty South, and an economy based on plantation agriculture made for long distances between households. A handful of the region's settlements became centers for trade in goods and enslaved people, but there were not many of the church-centered towns that dotted New England. By 1750, the Chesapeake and Southern colonies combined had only one church for every 1,046 white inhabitants, compared to one church for every 606 white inhabitants in New England.[3]

The Middle Colonies had both the highest concentration of churches—one for every 467 white inhabitants—and the greatest variety. New York, originally a Dutch colony, retained a strong Dutch Reformed presence but also attracted a wide variety of immigrants and their faiths to the commercial hub of New York City. Presbyterians predominated in New Jersey, followed by Quakers,

3. Patricia U. Bonomi and Peter R. Eisenstadt, "Church Adherence in the Eighteenth-Century British American Colonies," *William and Mary Quarterly* 39, no. 2 (April 1982): 273.

A Faithful Narrative of the Surprising Work of God, 1737

Jonathan Edwards (1703–58), a Congregational minister and a brilliant theologian, set the pattern for evangelical revival in his widely disseminated "Faithful Narrative" of a spiritual outpouring in Massachusetts. This excerpt describes how the awakening spread and what effects it had on the community.

> When this work of God first appeared, and was so extraordinarily carried on amongst us in the winter, others round about us seemed not to know what to make of it; and there were many that scoffed at and ridiculed it; and some compared what we called conversion to certain distempers. But it was very observable of many that occasionally came amongst us from abroad, with disregardful hearts, that what they saw here cured them of such a temper of mind: strangers were generally surprised to find things so much beyond what they had heard, and were wont to tell others that the state of the ▶

Anglicans, Dutch Reformed, and Baptists. Pennsylvania, founded by Quaker William Penn, embraced religious tolerance and therefore attracted followers of persecuted faiths such as the Amish, Mennonites, and Moravians. These Anabaptists were outnumbered, though, by Quakers, German Reformed, Lutherans, Anglicans, and Presbyterians. Delaware, which initially was settled by Swedish Lutherans and Dutch Reformed, became home to increasing numbers of Anglicans in the early eighteenth century.

When Whitefield arrived in a city, he often met first with Anglican leaders, his clerical brethren. Otherwise, though, denominational boundaries mattered little to him. When the Anglican Commissary, or bishop's representative, in Boston asserted that the Church of England was the only true church, the evangelist replied, "I saw regenerate souls among the Baptists, among the Presbyterians, among the Independents, and among the Church [of England] folks—all children of God, and yet all born again in a different way of worship: and who can tell which is the most evangelical?"[4] Whitefield would preach wherever his message was welcome, and he would keep preaching no matter who opposed him.

While Whitefield's preaching tour was not limited by colonial or denominational boundaries, he did follow paths mapped out by earlier developments.

4. George Whitefield, *George Whitefield's Journals* (London: Banner of Truth Trust, 1960), 458.

town could not be conceived of by those that had not seen it. The notice that was taken of it by the people that came to town on occasion of the Court, that sat here in the beginning of March, was very observable. And those that came from the neighborhood to our public lectures, were for the most part remarkably affected. Many that came to town, on one occasion or other, had their consciences smitten and awakened, and went home with wounded hearts and with those impressions that never wore off till they had hopefully a saving issue; and those that before had serious thoughts had their awakenings and convictions greatly increased. And there were many instances of persons that came from abroad on visits or on business, that had not been long here before to all appearance they were savingly wrought upon, and partook of that shower of divine blessing that God rained down here, and went home rejoicing; till at length the same work began evidently to appear and prevail in several other towns in the county.

Jonathan Edwards, "A Faithful Narrative of the Surprising Work of God," in *A Jonathan Edwards Reader*, ed. John E. Smith, Harry S. Stout, and Kenneth P. Minkema (New Haven: Yale University Press, 1995), 64.

Among Lutherans and continental Reformed bodies, a renewal movement called Pietism had been nurturing heartfelt, activist Christianity since the 1630s. Scots-Irish Presbyterians had a tradition of "holy fairs," regional gatherings for preaching, prayer, and confession leading up to the once- or twice-yearly taking of Communion. New England Congregationalists experienced many waves of revival before and after Whitefield's tour, so many that some scholars question whether the "Great Awakening" of 1740–43 deserves its own special designation. All of these factors primed ministers and congregations to respond to the famous evangelist.

New Divisions

As thousands of people listened to Whitefield and other itinerant evangelists, hundreds were added to church rolls. Accounts of the revivals filled letters and newspapers throughout the colonies and in England, Scotland, and Wales, which experienced their own revivals in the same era. Inevitably, all of this fervor provoked skepticism and even outright hostility, though not necessarily along the lines one might expect.

As mentioned earlier in this chapter, Protestantism encompassed two large schools of thought regarding salvation. Arminians, appealing to texts such as

2 Peter 3:9 (God is "not willing that any should perish"), believed that salvation was available to anyone who confessed their sin and received God's grace. The choice was up to the individual. Calvinists, appealing to such texts as Romans 8:29 ("For whom he did foreknow, he also did predestinate"), believed that only the elect could receive God's grace. The choice was up to God, based on his sovereign will alone.

Because the aim of revival preaching was to convict listeners of sin and bring them to salvation, it might seem to be a more Arminian than Calvinist practice. If God has already decided who will be saved and who will not, what is the point of trying to change anyone's heart? In fact, many Calvinists—including Whitefield and Jonathan Edwards—avidly preached revival, believing that activities such as praying, reading Scripture, and hearing sermons could prepare hearts to receive saving grace. Rather than feeling disempowered by the mystery of election, these preachers advised people to keep a sharp watch for signs of God's renewing work.

Another potential dividing line would pit those who prized rationality against those who valued emotional experience. The intellectual movement known as the Enlightenment hit its stride in the American colonies in the mid to late eighteenth century, and its emphases included the search for verifiable facts, skepticism toward religion, and disdain for outbursts of enthusiasm. Revivalism earned poor marks on all of these measures, and some critics (called "Old Lights") opposed the revivals for these reasons. For example, the Old Lights leader Charles Chauncy, minister at Boston's First (Congregational) Church from 1727 to 1787, asserted, "Tis not evident to me that Persons, generally, have a better Understanding of Religion, a better Government of their Passions, a more Christian Love to their Neighbour, or that they are more decent and regular in their Devotions towards God" as a result of the revivals.[5] Chauncy also averred, "The plain Truth is, an enlightened Mind, and not raised Affections, ought always to be the Guide of those who call themselves Men."[6]

It is misleading, though, to view the Great Awakening and the evangelical tradition it spawned as antithetical to the Enlightenment. Edwards, a leader of the "New Lights," or pro-revival faction, took pains in his "Faithful Narrative of the Surprising Work of God" (1737) to document his local awakening with dates, places, and descriptions of individuals whose lives were transformed. (Pastoral discretion prevented him from naming names, unless the people were very young or were dead.) Furthermore, *experience* counted as evidence for

5. Charles Chauncy, *A Letter from a Gentleman in Boston, to Mr. George Wishart, One of the Ministers of Edinburgh, Concerning the State of Religion in New-England* (Edinburgh, 1742), 22.
6. Charles Chauncy, *Seasonable Thoughts on the State of Religion in New England* (1743; repr., Hicksville, NY: Regina Press, 1975), 326–27.

Enlightenment thinkers, and knowledge gained through direct observation was valued above that which was received from books. Rather than dismiss revivalism as mere emotionalism, Edwards argued that the experiences of people touched by revival should be taken every bit as seriously as phenomena observed in nature or the results of a laboratory experiment.

Even those who took the emotional experiences of revival seriously were not always comfortable with everything they saw or heard about, however. Edwards admitted that the revivals produced some "great imprudences" and "sinful irregularities," and he was especially suspicious of anyone who claimed a direct revelation from God. Spiritual dreams and visions were common in this era—Whitefield recounted several in his early life, and Edwards's wife had them frequently—but they were considered trustworthy only if they contained explicitly biblical imagery or affirmed truths already revealed in Scripture. Visions that purported to offer new revelations might be dangerous, even satanic.[7]

People who supported the revivals but questioned some displays of enthusiasm can be called moderate evangelicals. Radical evangelicals had fewer qualms. Another difference between the two emerging camps was their view of ministers who disagreed with them. Moderates, such as Edwards, had harsh words for "Old Lights," who disdained the revivals, but they hesitated to go so far as to declare their opponents unchristian. Radicals, such as the Presbyterian minister Gilbert Tennent (1703–64), pulled no punches. In his most famous sermon, "The Danger of an Unconverted Ministry," Tennent likened revival skeptics to Pharisees and warned of "many Servants of Satan, under a religious Mask."[8]

Most provokingly, Tennent advised parishioners who suspected their minister of being "unconverted" to listen to a different preacher instead. While this advice might seem innocuous in an era of church-shopping, it was deeply unsettling in the eighteenth century. Churches in the Colonial period served as cornerstones of the social order. Leaving your church was akin to, and might entail, disowning your family. Tennent's advice also upset the hierarchy of clergy and laity. If laypeople had the authority to judge their minister's spiritual state, could the collapse of society be far behind? As a May 3, 1742, article in the *Boston Evening Post* fretted, "These Itinerants aim very much at dividing the Churches, and disaffecting People to their faithful Pastors, and what wild Scheme they are pursuing next, God only knows."[9]

---

7. Jonathan Edwards, *The Distinguishing Marks of a Work of the Spirit of God* (Boston, 1741).

8. Gilbert Tennent, "The Danger of an Unconverted Ministry," in *The Colonial Idiom*, ed. David Potter and Gordon L. Thomas (Carbondale: Southern Illinois University Press, 1970), 483. The sermon was published in Philadelphia by Benjamin Franklin in 1740.

9. Quoted in Thomas S. Kidd, *The Great Awakening: The Roots of Evangelical Christianity in Colonial America* (New Haven: Yale University Press, 2007), 137.

For good or for ill, radical evangelicals upended all sorts of hierarchies. They allowed folks without formal training in theology to preach. Some of these "exhorters" (a less exalted title than "minister") were youths, women, enslaved people, and Native Americans. Radical itinerant Daniel Rogers reported that, after he spoke at a church in Kittery, Maine, "a Negroe man [servant] of Col. Pepperell's broke out & spoke in a Wonderfull manner of the Sweet Love of Jesus. . . . He exhorted all to come & taste ye the Love of [Christ]." Though Rogers was himself a Harvard graduate, son of a minister, and former associate of the famous Whitefield, he nonetheless believed that people who lacked any of his privileges could exhort and even prophesy. "We must be willing that God should carry on his Work in his own Way," he declared.[10] On the other hand, radical evangelicals could also be schismatic and arrogant, accusing anyone who criticized them of being opposed to the Spirit of God.

Revival and Revolution

Because of its democratizing impulses, the First Great Awakening is seen by some scholars as a forerunner of the American Revolution. George Whitefield, despite his English roots, has been claimed as an American patriot. Historian Thomas Kidd, who called Whitefield "America's spiritual founding father," recounted the story of a group of soldiers in the Continental Army who stopped by Whitefield's crypt in Newburyport, Massachusetts, in 1775. The soldiers opened the tomb, cut pieces from Whitefield's clothing, and carried these relics as they marched. These soldiers drew a direct connection between the New Birth that Whitefield preached and the new nation they were battling to form.[11]

In some places, pro- and anti-revival factions within denominations gradually morphed into competing political parties. In Connecticut, legislators attempted to curb the awakening by subjecting itinerant ministers to jail, fines, public humiliation, and expulsion from the colony. These draconian policies enacted by wealthy and powerful Old Lights provoked a backlash from the less prominent but more numerous New Lights. This fight subsided by the late 1740s, but the same two sides, battle-hardened and organized, faced off again over the Stamp Act in the 1760s. An Old Light took the post of stamp distributor, which made him the local face of the increasingly detested British government. New Lights rebelled, overthrowing the governor. More wide-

10. Thomas S. Kidd, "Daniel Rogers' Egalitarian Great Awakening," *Journal of the Historical Society* 7, no. 1 (March 2007): 121, 117.

11. Thomas S. Kidd, *George Whitefield: America's Spiritual Founding Father* (New Haven: Yale University Press, 2014), 257.

In 1775 Continental Army troops, roused by a sermon on Exodus 33:15 ("If thy presence go not with me, carry us not up hence"), decided to take George Whitefield's presence with them into battle. They ventured down to the crypt of the Old South Presbyterian Church in Newburyport, Massachusetts, where Whitefield was buried, and cut portions of his clothing as relics.

spread opposition to the Stamp Act yielded the slogan "No taxation without representation," a rallying cry for the revolution.

Less direct connections can also be drawn between the revivals and the revolution. For example, Thomas Paine, though he was no orthodox Christian, dipped into the well of evangelical rhetoric to craft his influential 1776 pamphlet *Common Sense*. The document as a whole read like a secular sermon. Paine's call for the colonists to follow their own political affections in some ways echoed Jonathan Edwards's valuation of religious affections. Paine even used the language of conversion, writing,

> Perhaps the sentiments contained in the following pages, are not YET sufficiently fashionable to procure them general favour; a long habit of not thinking a thing WRONG, gives it a superficial appearance of being RIGHT, and raises at first a formidable outcry in defense of custom. But the tumult soon subsides. Time makes more converts than reason.... The cause of America is in a great measure the cause of all mankind. Many circumstances hath, and will arise, which are not local, but universal, and through which the principles of all Lovers of Mankind are affected, and in the Event of which, their Affections are interested.[12]

12. Thomas Paine, introduction to the third edition of *Common Sense* (Philadelphia, 1776), https://www.ushistory.org/paine/commonsense/sense1.htm. See also Christine Leigh Heyrman, "Religion and the American Revolution," Divining America, TeacherServe©. National Humanities Center, 2014, http://nationalhumanitiescenter.org/tserve/eighteen/ekeyinfo/erelrev.htm.

Paine exhorted American patriots to slough off restrictive customs and open their hearts to self-determination. Revivalists exhorted American sinners to break free from sin and open their hearts to God's salvation. These exhortations were by no means identical, but it is easy to see how they reinforced each other.

Not all historians see strong links between the First Great Awakening and the revolution. The Declaration of Independence, for instance, is devoid of revivalist rhetoric, making reference to "Nature's God" but eschewing mention of Christ or quotation from the Bible. Some preachers in the 1760s and 1770s elevated rebellion to a holy cause, but many refrained from political comment, and a sizable minority remained loyal to England. The religious issue that attracted the most attention in the run-up to the revolution was the proposed appointment of a bishop to preside over the colonies' Anglican churches—a fight that had little if anything to do with revivalists' concerns. None of the Intolerable Acts passed by England in retaliation for the Boston Tea Party even touched on religion.

If the Great Awakening was just one of several developments contributing to the American Revolution, though, there is no doubt that the awakening birthed a religious tradition that has had an immense influence on American history: evangelicalism. The term is a familiar one and has been used throughout this chapter, but its meaning and membership have changed over the centuries, so it merits exploration.

Evangelicalism

Defining evangelicalism is something of a cottage industry among scholars and among evangelicals themselves. The term comes from the Greek *euangelion*, which means "gospel" or "good news." During the Reformation of the sixteenth century, leaders such as William Tyndale and Martin Luther applied the word to their forms of Christianity. The label "Protestant" characterized these Christians by what they opposed—they *protested* the existing Roman Catholic order—whereas "evangelical" characterized them by the message they wished to live and preach.

While "evangelical" (*evangelische*) continued to mean Protestant or non-Catholic in the German-speaking world, the term took on a sharper meaning in the English-speaking world as a result of the revivals of the 1730s and 1740s. When George Whitefield mused to the Anglican Commissary in Boston, "Who can tell which is the most evangelical?" he was not pondering which Christians had achieved maximum distance from Roman Catholicism. He had in mind a more specific set of traits.

British historian David Bebbington defined evangelicalism using four characteristics, known in shorthand as the "Bebbington quadrilateral." First, evangelicals are *biblicist*, holding a high view of the inspiration and authority of Scripture. Second, their faith is *crucicentric*, or centered on the cross as the site of human salvation. Third, evangelicals are *conversionist*, able to articulate their own journey of salvation and eager to bring others along the same path. Fourth, evangelicals are *activist*, convinced that their faith should have a tangible impact on the world around them.

It is difficult to gauge the distinctiveness of these qualities without comparing evangelicals to other Christian traditions. For example, since the time of Martin Luther, Protestants have upheld the principle of *sola scriptura*—the Bible alone—in contrast to Roman Catholics and the Orthodox, who consider some teachings of church leaders authoritative as well. But many Protestants also look to confessions of faith (e.g., the Book of Concord for Lutherans, the Westminster Confession of Faith for Presbyterians) or other founding documents to guide biblical interpretation and circumscribe the boundaries of the church. Evangelicals, by and large, reject such extrabiblical texts, or at most consider them informative but nonbinding. When evangelicals use the works of their favorite pastors or theologians as guides to biblical interpretation, however, they are doing much the same thing as other Christians do with their creeds and confessions, though evangelicals think of themselves as uniquely committed to the Bible.

In the same vein, Christ's death on the cross holds significance for all Christians, but theories of atonement have varied over time. Some ancient theologians saw Christ's incarnation as a second creation, restoring the intended relationship between humanity and God. To these theologians, Christ's life mattered as much as his death. Medieval theologian Peter Abelard understood Christ as a moral exemplar, teaching humans how to obey God. In this view, Christ's primary work was pointing humans toward the good rather than saving them from the bad.

Evangelicals did not embrace these "recapitulation" or "moral influence" theories. They favored a theology known as penal substitution, according to which Christ on the cross paid the penalty of sin for Christians, absorbing God's wrath on their behalf. It is in this way that evangelical faith was crucicentric, focused more on the cross than on any other aspect of Christ's time on earth. The earliest form of the Wordless Book, a witnessing tool first used by evangelical preacher Charles Haddon Spurgeon in the 1860s, captured the essence of this theology of atonement. The book consisted simply of blank pages of different colors, used to present the gospel message. The first color, black, represented the soul's sinful condition. The second color, red, represented Christ's blood shed on the cross. The third color, white, represented the cleansed soul. Later versions of the Wordless Book added blue for baptism, green for spiritual growth, and gold for heaven, but for evangelicals, nothing mattered as much as a person's transition from a sinful to a saved condition, effected by the power of Christ's blood. A Roman Catholic church with a large crucifix at the front is also crucicentric, but in a very different way.

Evangelical conversionism was especially distinctive during the First Great Awakening and remains especially distinctive today. Whether operating in a Calvinist or Arminian framework, revivalists in the 1730s and 1740s believed that *something* happened to people when they received the New Birth, and that same *something* had to happen to anyone who hoped to be saved. By contrast, Roman Catholics, the Orthodox, and nonrevivalist Protestants expected salvation to come, by God's grace, through ongoing participation in the sacramental life of the church. Evangelicals' expectation that conversion would be a one-time, emotionally fraught event and their enduring efforts to convince others to experience this event are well-known hallmarks of the tradition.

Activism is perhaps the most nebulous of these allegedly evangelical qualities. There was an expectation in the First Great Awakening that persons touched by revival would change their behaviors and their communities in noticeable ways. Jonathan Edwards watched for people to obey church and familial authorities, to stop chattering frivolously, and to exchange melancholy for joy. A century later, during what is often called the Second Great Awakening, revivalist Charles Finney equated true religion with "disinterested benevolence," meaning a desire to seek justice, mercy, and goodness for all people without any selfish motive. Some especially active nineteenth-century evangelicals shut down saloons, founded orphanages, started rescue missions in urban slums, or fought to abolish slavery. (We will meet some of these people in chap. 7.)

Evangelicals' conversionism has, however, sometimes worked against social activism. Take the example of twentieth-century evangelical revivalist Billy Graham. His answer to the social problems of his era, from racism to divorce to nuclear proliferation, was to transform one soul at a time, and then to trust born-again believers to do right by their fellow beings. Graham's approach seemed like the opposite of activism to the thousands of Americans, many of them Black, who were marching in the streets demanding systemic change. Activism, like every point of the Bebbington quadrilateral, is in the eye of the beholder, making this definition of evangelicalism less stable than it appears.

Another definition of evangelicalism, offered by historian Catherine Brekus, goes beyond the quadrilateral and helps explain why this form of Protestantism was uniquely poised to flourish as the American colonies became the United States. Brekus wrote,

In order to meet the new spiritual needs of their age, evangelicals also set themselves apart from earlier Protestants in several crucial ways: they placed more trust in the reliability of firsthand experience; they expressed greater assurance about their ability to know whether they had been "saved"; they made the converted individual, not the community or the church, the main locus of authority; they emphasized that all Christians were called to spread the gospel through missions and evangelism; they defined true religion as a matter of the heart or affections; they had a robust faith in progress; and they borrowed the techniques of the consumer revolution to spread the gospel.[13]

Individualism and self-determination suited a nation moving toward democracy and a consumer economy. A downside to the explosion of political and economic choices, though, was a nagging fear that one could never be sure of making the *right* choice. Here, evangelicalism offered assurance backed by the emotional experience of conversion. The heart knew the truth, evangelicals claimed, and this truth was reinforced every time an evangelical shared his testimony or heard the testimony of a fellow believer. Evangelical faith was personal, portable, and powerful, even when the nearest church was miles away—a common circumstance on the expanding American frontier.

The Aftermath

The First Great Awakening undeniably influenced American political and religious history, but it did not create a Christian nation. On the eve of the revolution, by scholars' best estimates, fewer than 20 percent of Americans were church members. The average size of a congregation was probably 75. At the risk of conflating apples and oranges, it is intriguing to note that in the early twenty-first century, about 20 percent of Americans attended church on any given Sunday, and the median size of a congregation was 75. (The average American congregation size had grown to 185, but this number reflected massive attendance at a small number of very large churches. A median of 75 means that half of American churches had fewer than 75 regular participants, and half had more.)

The 20 percent membership statistic held fairly consistent across the colonies.[14] All of the New England colonies were in that range, except for Vermont, where only 9 percent of residents were church members. The Middle Colonies hovered around 20 percent as well. In the Southern Colonies, very few enslaved

13. Catherine A. Brekus, *Sarah Osborn's World: The Rise of Evangelical Christianity in Early America* (New Haven: Yale University Press, 2013), 11.

14. Criteria for membership in some churches was quite strict, so membership numbers often undercounted church participation.

people were church members, so while church adherence for whites averaged around 20 percent, church adherence as a percentage of total population was much lower, around 12 percent. (The slow, then skyrocketing, growth of early African American Christianity is the subject of chap. 5.)

There was significant church growth in the period 1740–70, some of it related to the revivals and some not. Presbyterians, who were divided about the revival, and Baptists, who generally favored it, started at least 400 new churches, total, in these decades. Meanwhile, the Society for the Propagation of the Gospel, an Anglican mission agency not friendly to revival, started nearly 150 churches. Quakers and various German ethnic churches were also busy planting churches, mainly in Pennsylvania. All of these efforts, though, struggled to keep pace with the population of the colonies, which swelled from just under one million to more than two million in this period and continued to spread westward from the Atlantic Coast.

Demographics tell one kind of story about religious change over time. The life of one person tells another kind of story, less linear and more illuminating.

Sarah Osborn (1714–96) grew up poor in the bustling shipping town of New-port, Rhode Island. According to her 1743 memoir, her youth was marked by sinfulness, guilt, anger toward her parents, and thoughts of suicide. Then, in 1740, "God in mercy sent his dear servant Whitefield here, which something stirred me up." Osborn was not, however, immediately converted. She next heard Gil-bert Tennent preach, and her heart was moved again, but her "dreadful" doubts continued. "I questioned the truth of all I had experienced and feared I had never yet passed through the pangs of the new birth nor never had one spark of grace," she wrote. After a few days of Bible study, she became convinced that her doubts were just one of the common temptations from which God promised deliverance in 1 Corinthians 10:13. This realization yielded a breakthrough: "God was pleased that moment, I see it, to give me faith, to lay hold on it and claim it as my own."[15]

We know about Osborn's life because she became a revival leader in her own right and, consequently, one of few published female writers in the Colonial period. Osborn's experience of faith and success at passing that faith along to others served as her credentials even though she lacked education, wealth, or legal rights. Evangelicalism opened these possibilities for her, within limits. In the 1760s, as her local pastor descended into drunkenness, Osborn began hold-ing religious meetings in her home for women, enslaved people, and, eventually, some young men. A woman of strong religious character teaching other women and enslaved people was fine, but a woman purporting to exercise leadership over men caused scandal. Only when Osborn's failing pastor was replaced with a

15. Brekus, *Sarah Osborn's World*, 93, 111.

solidly New Lights student of Jonathan Edwards, at Osborn's behest and against fierce opposition, was her leadership acknowledged.

After the new pastor, Samuel Hopkins, took over Newport's First Church of Christ, Osborn stopped most of her home meetings. Her health was also declining. Illness, poverty, and fear characterized her experience of the American Revolution, along with a millennial hope that the new nation would become God's unique instrument to bless humankind. Osborn died with a vision of heaven as a boundless ocean devoid of pride, idleness, or unbelief.

Osborn's story reminds us that early evangelicalism was marked by faith and doubt, by freedom and restrictions. It was led by both men and women, and it touched Black, Indigenous, and white. Sometimes revivalism strengthened churches, and sometimes it nearly destroyed them. It was in some ways similar to twenty-first-century evangelicalism and in other ways quite different. Evangelicals still sing the hymns of Isaac Watts and wait to be electrified by the next George Whitefield. They still have high hopes for their nation and an angular relationship to its social order. They remain both influential and controversial.

In this passage from Sarah Osborn's diary, here edited for readability, she thanks God for those who helped her in the past and asks for strength to pay the blessings forward.

O let us build upon the dear, the sure foundation, Christ Jesus, all the good works we can. O let this be ever as oil to our wheels to make them run swift. "Inasmuch as ye did unto them, ye did it unto me." O may God reward every kind benefactor he has raised to me in every time of distress. O may they never lose their reward, though they did it to the least of thine. Let them hear thee say, dear Lord, to them, "Precious souls, even herein as much as ye did it unto me." O reward them a thousandfold! . . . As I have freely received in times of my distress, so let me freely give as God enables and occasion offers. Lord, ever open my hand and heart to the sick, poor, and needy, and make me a blessing in my day. O make me extensively useful in my family, in my school, in the dear, dear society, to all around me. O let the Lord God almighty delight to own me, to use me, to set me apart for himself in secret, in private, and in every way my proper station admits.[16]

FURTHER READING

Bonomi, Patricia. *Under the Cope of Heaven: Religion, Society, and Politics in Colonial America*. New York: Oxford University Press, 2003.

16. Brekus, *Sarah Osborn's World*, 217.

Brekus, Catherine A. *Sarah Osborn's World: The Rise of Evangelical Christianity in Early America*. New Haven: Yale University Press, 2013.

Butler, Jon. *Awash in a Sea of Faith: Christianizing the American People*. Cambridge, MA: Harvard University Press, 1992.

Carté, Kate. *Religion and the American Revolution: An Imperial History*. Chapel Hill: University of North Carolina Press, 2021.

Finke, Roger, and Rodney Stark. *The Churching of America, 1776–2005: Winners and Losers in Our Religious Economy*. New Brunswick, NJ: Rutgers University Press, 2005.

Kidd, Thomas S. *The Great Awakening: The Roots of Evangelical Christianity in Colonial America*. New Haven: Yale University Press, 2007.

Marsden, George M. *A Short Life of Jonathan Edwards*. Grand Rapids: Eerdmans, 2008.

Noll, Mark. *The Rise of Evangelicalism: The Age of Edwards, Whitefield and the Wesleys*. Downers Grove, IL: InterVarsity, 2003.

Stout, Harry S. *The Divine Dramatist: George Whitefield and the Rise of Modern Evangelicalism*. Grand Rapids: Eerdmans, 1991.

———. *The New England Soul: Preaching and Religious Culture in Colonial New England*. 2nd ed. New York: Oxford University Press, 2011.

5

A Faith for Enslaved and Free

*First African American Church Founded
at Silver Bluff, South Carolina, 1773*

The spirituals now featured in most American hymnbooks are typically listed without authors or composers, because nobody knows their exact origins. Marked by rolling melodies, emotional lyrics, and striking biblical imagery, the songs developed organically in a culture influenced by African traditions and revivalist Christianity. The well-known spiritual "There Is a Balm in Gilead," which probably evolved to its current form in the early nineteenth century, evokes Jeremiah 8:22, the experience of wearying work, and a simple gospel message. The phrase "sin-sick soul" might have been borrowed from a 1779 lyric by John Newton, the slave-ship captain turned evangelical abolitionist who is better known for the hymn "Amazing Grace."

> There is a balm in Gilead
> To make the wounded whole;
> There is a balm in Gilead
> To heal the sin-sick soul.
>
> Sometimes I feel discouraged,
> And think my work's in vain,
> But then the Holy Spirit
> Revives my soul again.

If you cannot preach like Peter,
If you cannot pray like Paul,
You can tell the love of Jesus,
And say He died for all.[1]

In 1773, Phillis Wheatley, an enslaved woman in Boston, became the first published African American writer when her *Poems on Various Subjects, Religious and Moral* appeared in London. In addition to an elegy for George Whitefield—the poem that first made Wheatley famous—the volume included the short but thorny verse "On Being Brought from Africa to America."

'Twas mercy brought me from my *Pagan* land,
Taught my benighted soul to understand
That there's a God, that there's a *Saviour* too:
Once I redemption neither sought nor knew.
Some view our sable race with scornful eye,
"Their colour is a diabolic die."
Remember, *Christians, Negros,* black as *Cain,*
May be refin'd, and join th' angelic train.[2]

The first four lines of this poem rehearse a favorite slaveholders' claim: Africans were better off enslaved in America than free in Africa because in America they could become Christians and escape hell. There is no way to know whether Wheatley agreed with this problematic argument or included it for some more subtle reason. The next two lines challenge racism, mocking the association of dark skin with moral inferiority. The last two lines are ambiguous. Was Wheatley boldly arguing that Black Americans could become the spiritual equals of whites? Or was she suggesting that the "sable race" needed to be more refined—more civilized, more like whites—in order to be saved?

Wheatley's poem introduces some of the complexities navigated by Black Christians in the eighteenth century. The story of a Black church founded at Silver Bluff, South Carolina, in the same year illuminates even more complexities and highlights some of the ways in which Wheatley's contemporaries transformed the religion of their oppressors into a source of comfort and strength—a turning point not just for African American Christians but for Christianity as a global faith.

In the early 1770s, Wait Palmer, a white Baptist minister from Connecticut, brought revivalistic preaching to the estate of George Galphin, which lay on the

---

1. This version is from the *Psalter Hymnal* (Grand Rapids: CRC Publications, 1987), no. 494.
2. Phillis Wheatley, *Poems on Various Subjects, Religious and Moral* (London: A. Bell, 1773), 18.

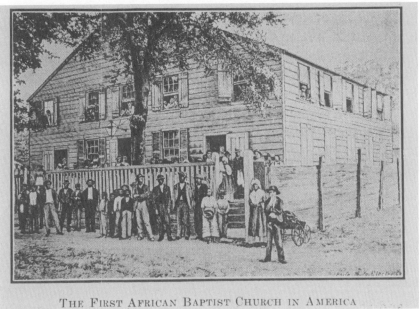

THE FIRST AFRICAN BAPTIST CHURCH IN AMERICA

Although a few other churches also vie for the title, pioneering Black historian Carter G. Woodson awarded Silver Bluff the distinction of being the first Black Baptist church in America.

South Carolina side of the Savannah River about twelve miles from Augusta, Georgia. Galphin, an Irishman by birth, had made his fortune trading goods with local Native Americans. By his death in 1780, Galphin owned more than 40,000 acres of land and 128 enslaved persons.

By all available accounts, Galphin maintained cordial relations with African Americans and Native Americans. (He is also known to have fathered children with two Native American women and an enslaved Black woman, evidence of a different kind of relations.) So when Brother Palmer asked Galphin if he could preach to the enslaved individuals on his estate, Galphin agreed. Many planters would have said no out of fear that those who became Christians would demand to be treated as human beings rather than as property. A group of enslaved Black Christians had made precisely that argument to the Anglican bishop in Virginia in 1723, unsuccessfully. Other enslavers feared any gathering of enslaved men and women, especially one that might combine religious fervor with drastic action. Those elements produced the Stono Rebellion in South Carolina in 1739, when a group of enslaved Black Catholics—who had brought their faith with them from the Catholic African kingdom of Kongo— killed twenty whites in a failed attempt to flee to Spanish Florida. But Galphin let Palmer preach.

Though Palmer is often cited as the first preacher at Silver Bluff, another preacher, George Liele, had already made contact with the enslaved population there. Liele, born into slavery in about 1751, recalled in a 1791 letter that he "always had a natural fear of God from my youth," a legacy from the godly Black father he never knew.[3] Though Liele dated his conversion to 1774 and credited the influence of a white Baptist minister, Liele himself had preached as early as 1770, according to Galphin's personal servant, David George, who remembered Liele's sermon. Dates and details are hard to nail down, but it is important to note that Christianity was not just an idea introduced to Black Americans by white preachers. A few enslaved individuals had Christian, African ancestry, while others were developing an understanding of Christianity with only sporadic influence from white enslavers or ministers.

The most complete account of the founding of the Silver Bluff church comes from David George, who told the story in the early 1790s to British Baptists who were supporting his later missionary work. George described a young adulthood marked by moderately bad behavior, a conviction of sinfulness, and uncertainty what to do about it. His narrative continues:

> Soon after I heard Brother George Liele preach. . . . His sermon was very suitable, on *Come unto to me all ye that labour, and are heavy laden, and I will give you rest*. When it was ended, I went to him and told him I was so; that I was weary and heavy laden, and that the grace of God had given me rest. Indeed his whole discourse seemed for me. Afterwards Brother Palmer, who was pastor at some distance from Silver Bluff, came and preached to a large congregation at a mill of Mr. Galphin's. He was a very powerful preacher, and as he was returning home Lord's-day evening, I went with him two or three miles, and told him how it was with me. About this time more of my fellow-creatures began to seek the Lord. Afterwards Brother Palmer came again and wished us to beg Master to let him preach to us; and he had leave, and came frequently. There were eight of us now who had found the great blessing and mercy from the Lord, and my wife was one of them, and brother Jesse Galphin that you mention in the history of us poor slaves, was another. Brother Palmer appointed a Saturday evening to hear what the Lord had done for us, and the next day he baptized us in the mill-stream. . . . Brother Palmer formed us into a church, and gave us the Lord's supper at Silver Bluff. Then I began to exhort in the church, and learned to sing hymns.

Members of the church urged George to become their preacher, and although George felt unworthy, Palmer encouraged him.

3. John Rippon, *The Baptist Annual Register for 1790, 1792, 1792, and Part of 1793* (London, 1793): 1: 332–33, cited in Noel Leo Erskine, "George Liele: Liberated Slave and African American Baptist Missionary to Jamaica," *Missiology: An International Review* 50, no. 1 (2022): 27–40, https://doi.org/10.1177/00918296211043527.

So I was appointed to the office of an Elder and received instruction from Brother Palmer how to conduct myself. I proceeded in this way till the American war was coming on, when the Ministers were not allowed to come amongst us lest they should furnish us with too much knowledge. The Black people all around attended with us, and as Brother Palmer must not come, I had the whole management, and used to preach among them myself. Then I got a spelling book and began to read. . . . I continued preaching at Silver Bluff, till the church, constituted with eight, increased to thirty or more, and till the British came to the city [of] Savannah and took it.[4]

Three important lessons stand out in this account. The first is the collaboration between white and Black church leaders. Palmer administered baptism and the Lord's Supper, formally inaugurating the church, then George continued as its presiding elder, preaching and bringing in new members. The second is George's declaration of his authority: "I had the whole management" of the church. In part, George assumed this role because a crackdown on itinerant preaching prevented Palmer from visiting Silver Bluff. However he came by the position, though, George probably had become the first Black minister leading a Black congregation in the United States. The American Black church tradition was born.

The third lesson pertains to how the Revolutionary War affected Black Americans, and it requires a fuller explanation.

Slavery and the War of Independence

In November 1775, the Earl of Dunmore, royal governor of the colony of Virginia, issued a proclamation freeing any enslaved persons who left their masters to fight for the British. Antislavery sentiment was growing in England, and the British also needed all the allies they could muster against the rebellious colonists. Galphin, however, was a patriot, who even used his influence with the Creek Nation and other Native Americans to deter them from aiding the British. The multiracial, mixed-status community at Silver Bluff fractured under the political strain.

During the war, Galphin left his estate, and the people who had been enslaved there scattered. George and about fifty others relocated to the area around Savannah, Georgia, which was captured by the British in 1778. For a short time,

4. "An Account of the Life of Mr. David George, from Sierra Leone in Africa; Given by Himself in a Conversation with Brother Rippon of London, and Brother Pearce of Birmingham," in John Rippon, *The Baptist Annual Register for 1790, 1791, 1792, and Part of 1793* (London, 1793), 475–76 (lightly edited for readability).

George preached and farmed alongside his old friend George Liele. Life was difficult, though, and George was nearly killed by a cannonball, then smallpox, then starvation. When British control in the area faltered a few years later, a British commander advised George to move to Halifax, Nova Scotia, far from the risk of re-enslavement. A few thousand Black loyalists made this journey to a place colder than any place they had ever lived. George founded an integrated church at Halifax but faced opposition from many white residents, so when the opportunity arose to settle in the newly founded African colony of Sierra Leone, he took it. With support from Baptists in England, he ministered there until his death in 1810.

The man who owned Liele, Henry Sharp, had recognized Liele's gifts as a preacher and given him his freedom. Then Sharp, a loyalist, joined the British army. When Sharp died in battle, his heirs sought to re-enslave Liele, and Liele ended up in jail. Free Blacks persistently faced the risk of being captured as "runaways" in the slaveholding American South. Liele was able to produce his manumission papers and leave jail, but for greater safety he attached himself as an indentured servant to a British colonel. Following the British evacuation of Savannah in 1782, the colonel moved to Jamaica, taking Liele and his family with him.

Liele spent his first two years in Jamaica working for the colony's governor, and then he earned his freedom a second time. He began preaching to a congregation that grew from four previously enslaved Black Americans to several hundred members, mostly enslaved persons and a few white people. The ministry eventually extended to multiple locations under Liele's leadership. He described his work to the same English Baptists who supported George, writing, "I have deacons and elders, a few; and teachers of small congregations in the town and country, where convenience suits them to come together; and I am pastor. I preach twice on the Lord's Day, in the forenoon and afternoon, and twice in the week, and have not been absent six Sabbath Days since I formed the church in this country."[5]

William Carey, the English founder of the Baptist Missionary Society, is often recognized as the father of modern Protestant missions, but he did not sail for India until 1793—nearly a decade after George began preaching in Nova Scotia and Liele in Jamaica. Granted, the circumstances were different. Carey first laid out his plan for missionary work in a treatise on the "conversion of the heathens," and then he traveled to a foreign country for the purpose of evangelism. George and Liele traveled to foreign lands for the purpose of

---

5. "Letters Showing the Rise and Progress of the Early Negro Churches of Georgia and the West Indies," *Journal of Negro History* 1, no. 1 (January 1916): 72.

survival and then started churches there, much as they had back in America. But the forced nature of George's and Liele's journeys does not disqualify them as pioneering missionaries. All three men left their homes and brought the Baptist faith to the far corners of the British Empire. The two Black men did it first.

One of the early leaders of the Silver Bluff church, Jesse Galphin, also known as Jesse Peters, stayed to minister in what became the United States. After the British left Savannah, he and other remaining members of the congregation moved back to Silver Bluff and then to Augusta, Georgia, where they established Springfield Baptist Church. That church grew to around five hundred members before Galphin's death, and it became the birthplace of Morehouse College after the Civil War. Because of its Silver Bluff roots, Springfield Baptist can claim to be the oldest Black church in America.

The Revolutionary War did not grant independence to Black Americans. Perhaps as many as one hundred thousand enslaved individuals escaped from their plantations during the war, hoping to accept the crown's offer of emancipation, but only about two thousand ever joined the royal army, and loyalists who wished to keep their freedom, like George and Liele, needed to move to other colonies following the British defeat. Taking the patriot side did not hasten freedom for most Black Americans either. Around nine thousand Black Americans fought for the Continental army or navy, and while some of them earned liberty this way, many were subsequently re-enslaved or denied the payment promised to them for their service.

The US Constitution ensured that slavery would be the default status for Black Americans until the Civil War. As a compromise between Northern and Southern delegates, each one seeking to maximize his region's political influence, an enslaved person counted as three-fifths of a person in calculating congressional representation. The so-called Fugitive Slave Clause declared that anyone legally enslaved in one state could not gain freedom by escaping to another state but must be returned to the person who owned them. Another clause prevented Congress from ending the importation of Black people captured for the slave trade before 1808. American participation in the foreign slave trade did cease that year, but because enslaved persons in the United States (unlike those in the Caribbean, Dutch Guiana, and Brazil) had a higher birth rate than death rate, the American population of enslaved persons continued to grow, from 1.2 million in 1810 to 4 million in 1860. Ending the international slave trade only made the domestic trade in human bodies more profitable because it decreased supply without decreasing demand.

The much smaller free Black population also increased in the years after the revolution. By 1810, more than 186,000 free Blacks lived in the United

States, about 13.5 percent of the total Black population. In the North, where several states had begun phasing out slavery in the 1780s, three-fourths of African Americans were free by 1810, and virtually all were free by 1840. About the same number of free Blacks lived in the upper South as in the North in 1810, but they constituted only 10 percent of the Black population there. Free Blacks were rare in the lower South, constituting just 4 percent of the Black population for the region, and only 2 percent in Georgia and South Carolina.[6]

Visible Institutions

As the country separated into slave and free states, Black Christianity developed along two trajectories. Free Blacks, mostly in the North, established their own churches and denominations, which became cornerstones of Black society. Enslaved persons, meanwhile, developed an "invisible institution"—a network of secret meetings, away from white control, where worshipers could sing, pray, and explore the Bible's message for their lives.

The foremost Black denomination, the African Methodist Episcopal Church, was founded by Richard Allen. Born into slavery in Delaware in 1760, Allen became a Methodist at age seventeen and immediately began preaching to his fellow captives, irritating some of their owners. Allen's enslaver, though, influenced by the white Methodist preacher Freeborn Garretson, became convinced that slavery was wrong, and he allowed all of the people he owned to purchase their freedom. Antislavery preaching by Methodists and Baptists in the years right after the revolution caused a few white enslavers to free those they had enslaved, while many others began looking for a way to be "good Christians" and enslavers at the same time.

After Allen bought his freedom in 1780, he moved to Philadelphia, a city with many job opportunities and a growing free Black community. He continued to preach, traveling widely on his often sore feet. In 1784, he was one of two Black attendees at the Christmas Conference in Baltimore, which established the Methodist Episcopal Church in America. John Wesley, the founder of the Methodist tradition, never intended to separate Methodists from the Anglican Church, but the revolution had frayed transatlantic ties, and American Methodists needed their own hierarchy (as did the American Anglicans who had not fled to Canada but remained to form the Protestant Episcopal Church in 1789). "Many of the ministers were set apart in holy orders at this Conference, and were said to be entitled to the gown," Allen recounted, though apparently

6. Peter Kolchin, *American Slavery, 1619–1877* (New York: Hill & Wang, 1993), 81.

he did not receive this honor himself.[7] Allen and the other African American attendee, "Black Harry" Hosier, also were not allowed to vote at the meeting.

Around this time Allen received another racial insult. The leader of American Methodism, Francis Asbury, invited Allen to travel with him but warned that, in slave states, Allen would have to sleep in the carriage. As was common for Methodist itinerants at the time, Allen also would receive no compensation beyond food and clothing. Allen refused this offer, afraid that if he fell ill (a strong possibility because he suffered from rheumatism), no one would take care of him. Instead, in 1786, Allen became a regular preacher at St. George's Methodist Episcopal Church in Philadelphia. He preached at other Philadelphia locations as well, sometimes four or five times a day.

Then, one final insult convinced Allen to start his own church. He wrote:

> A number of us usually attended St. George's Church in Fourth street; and when the coloured people began to get numerous in attending the church, they moved us from the seats we usually sat on, and placed us around the wall, and on Sabbath morning we went to church and the sexton stood at the door, and told us to go in the gallery. He told us to go, and we would see where to sit. We expected to take the seats over the ones we formerly occupied below, not knowing any better. We took those seats. Meeting had begun, and they were nearly done singing, and just as we got to the seats, the elder said, "Let us pray." We had not been long upon our knees before I heard considerable scuffling and low talking. I raised my head up and saw one of the trustees, H—M—, having hold of the Rev. Absalom Jones, pulling him up off of his knees, and saying, "You must get up—you must not kneel here." Mr. Jones replied, "Wait until prayer is over." Mr. H—M— said, "No, you must get up now, or I will call for aid and I force you away." Mr. Jones said, "Wait until prayer is over, and I will get up and trouble you no more." With that he beckoned to one of the other trustees, Mr. L—S—, to come to his assistance. He came, and went to William White to pull him up. By this time prayer was over, and we all went out of the church in a body, and they were no more plagued with us in the church.[8]

Allen and Absalom Jones, another Black minister, turned from the unwelcoming church to the Free African Society, a mutual-aid organization they had founded to serve the free Black community in Philadelphia. Members of that group agreed that they needed their own church but could not agree on which denomination to affiliate with. The majority chose the Episcopal Church, having become familiar with Anglicanism when they lived in the South, but

---

7. Richard Allen, *The Life, Experience, and Gospel Labours of the Rt. Rev. Richard Allen* (Philadelphia: Martin & Boden, 1833), 10.

8. Allen, *Life, Experience, and Gospel Labours*, 13 (lightly edited for readability).

Richard Allen, the founder of the African Methodist Episcopal Church, is surrounded by portraits of other AME bishops and images of AME ventures and institutions, such as Wilberforce University (upper left) and missions to Haiti (middle right).

Allen remained committed to Methodism. "I was confident that there was no religious sect or denomination would suit the capacity of the coloured people as well as the Methodist," he wrote, "for the plain and simple gospel suits best for any people; for the unlearned can understand, and the learned are sure to understand."[9] This disagreement led to the formation of two churches in 1794, the African Episcopal Church of St. Thomas, pastored by Jones (who in 1804 became the first African American ordained to the Episcopal priesthood), and Bethel African Methodist Episcopal Church, pastored by Allen.

Francis Asbury dedicated the Bethel Church and received it into the Methodist fellowship, but Allen's frustrations with the white Methodist leadership continued. The Philadelphia Annual Conference angled for ownership of the church property, and St. George's Church demanded a high payment for occasional preaching services. A succession of white elders asserted control over the congregation, and one sued the church after members prevented him from preaching there. Finally, in 1816, Bethel joined four other Black churches to form a new denomination, the African Methodist Episcopal (AME) Church, with Allen as bishop.

9. Allen, *Life, Experience, and Gospel Labours,* 16.

Bethel grew under Allen's leadership, adding members and ministries. It offered day school for children and night school for adults. Continuing the work of the Free African Society, it helped newcomers to the community find employment and housing. Allen also fought slavery by publishing pamphlets, signing petitions, and raising money to help enslaved individuals escape. The basement of the church served as a stop on the Underground Railroad, the clandestine transit network that helped those who were fleeing north to freedom.

The AME Church grew in these years as well, adding churches in major cities across the North and upper South. With growth, unfortunately, came dissension. Allen and Daniel Coker, a church leader in Baltimore, disagreed on the merits of a new national movement to alleviate racial tensions by sending Black Americans to Africa. Coker favored this colonization plan and traveled to Africa as a missionary. Allen wanted to press for full recognition in the United States of people who were both African and American. Allen's view prevailed in the denomination.

Gender also proved to be a divisive issue. Jarena Lee, a member of Allen's congregation, felt called to preach a message of personal holiness. Allen authorized her as an exhorter—a lesser rank of preacher—but refused to ordain her as a minister. Allen, like his white Methodist contemporaries, felt that educated men made the best ministers and would be most likely to earn society's respect. Lee countered with Joel 2:28: "And it shall come to pass . . . that I will pour out my Spirit upon all flesh; and your sons and your *daughters* shall prophesy" (emphasis added). Even without Allen's support, Lee journeyed thousands of miles, preached hundreds of sermons, and recorded her efforts in the first autobiography published by an African American woman. Women were finally ordained as ministers in the AME Church in 1960.

Internal divisions and a persistent lack of funds hampered the early AME Church, but external opposition was more damaging, especially in the South, where the church's expansion was stopped by violence. In 1822, Denmark Vesey, one of the leaders of the large AME Church in Charleston, South Carolina, was accused of plotting a slave rebellion. The plot was betrayed before any harm was done, but white citizens in Charleston responded swiftly, condemning Vesey in a secret court, executing him and dozens of alleged coconspirators, and burning down the church. The city went further a few years later and outlawed all Black churches, forcing members to worship in secret.

Vesey's church, reconstituted as Mother Emanuel AME Church, rebuilt after the Civil War. When an earthquake destroyed the building in 1886, the church rebuilt again. This is the same church where, in 2015, a white supremacist shot and killed senior pastor Clementa Pinckney and eight other people at a Wednesday evening Bible study. The killer expressed a dim knowledge of the site's history. President Barack Obama, in his stirring eulogy for Rev. Pinckney, professed a profounder knowledge and respect, calling Mother Emanuel "a church built by blacks seeking liberty, burned to the ground because its founder sought to end slavery, only to rise up again, a phoenix from these ashes." He called the Black church "our beating heart."[10]

"The Black church" is a label with its own history. In 1903, the pioneering Black sociologist and activist W. E. B. Du Bois published a report on "The Negro Church," which featured charts and local studies of churches in Baptist, AME, AME Zion, Methodist, Episcopal, and Presbyterian denominations. A 1990 book by scholars C. Eric Lincoln and Lawrence H. Mamiya, *The Black Church in the African American Experience*, identified a somewhat different list of "seven major historic Black denominations": AME; AME Zion; Christian Methodist Episcopal (CME) Church; National Baptist Convention, USA, Incorporated (NBC); National Baptist Convention of America, Unincorporated (NBCA); Progressive National Baptist Convention (PNBC); and Church of God in Christ (COGIC). There are many Black American Christians, and Black-majority congregations, outside these denominations, and there are significant variations within and among them. Generally speaking, "the Black church" can be described as denominational (as opposed to independent or nondenominational), hierarchical, theologically conservative, and politically progressive. Black-majority *churches* in the United States, especially those whose membership includes a lot of more recent African immigrants, might be quite different.

The Invisible Institution

Few independent Black churches were established in the South before the Civil War. There were two orders of Black Roman Catholic nuns founded: the Oblate Sisters of Providence in Baltimore in 1829, and the Holy Family Sisters in New Orleans in 1842. There was also a Black Catholic parish established in 1858 near the border of what became the Union and the Confederacy: St. Augustine in Washington, DC, known as the Mother Church of Black Catholics. Across most of the antebellum South, however, a typical Sunday morning found enslaved persons sitting in a restricted section of the local church, above or behind the seats reserved for whites. Sometimes enslaved persons were forced to attend, but many came willingly, and it was not uncommon for the Black members

10. "Remarks by the President in Eulogy for the Honorable Reverend Clementa Pinckney," June 26, 2015, https://obamawhitehouse.archives.gov/the-press-office/2015/06/26/remarks-president-eulogy-honorable-reverend-clementa-pinckney.

Though published after the Civil War, this engraving by a former Confederate soldier conveys white wariness regarding the religious expressions of enslaved persons. It was labeled "The sunny South—a negro revival meeting—a seeker 'getting religion.'"

of the congregation to outnumber the whites. Additionally, on a large plantation, the enslaver might build a chapel where a white minister could preach periodically. Colossians 3:22, "Slaves, obey your earthly masters in everything," was a common text at these services. The goal, for the enslaver, was to render those enslaved more compliant while demonstrating his own paternal benevolence. How could slavery be bad, enslavers asked, if it produced such Christian devotion?

In the early 1800s, enslaved persons also often accompanied their enslavers to the camp meetings that were a key feature of what some historians call the Second Great Awakening. There, the mood was more relaxed, the seating arrangements more fluid, the music more rollicking, and the message apt to emphasize liberty rather than control. For whites, including poor whites marginalized by the planter aristocracy, camp meetings offered unprecedented opportunities for free assembly and a free response to the preacher's invitation to come forward and be saved. Unlike the First Great Awakening, which was dominated by Calvinists, the Second Great Awakening was strongly Arminian, with a corresponding shift in emphasis from God's sovereignty to human agency and responsibility. This democratization of faith resonated with the (incremental) democratization of American politics in the early republic.

Enslaved persons at the camp meetings breathed in these ideas and practices. Some of these people subsequently held their own backwoods meetings, with their own preachers, songs, and rituals. To the white community's dismay, these gatherings combined the exuberance of Christian revivals with African elements that seemed foreign and frightening. One example was the "ring shout," a circular dance characterized by stomping, clapping, and phrases repeated in a call-and-response pattern. A white observer in 1862 scoffed, "I never saw anything so savage. They call it a religious ceremony, but it seems more like a regular frolic to me."[11]

White critics missed the ways that shouts, work songs, and the spirituals into which they evolved embodied a remarkable adaptation of Christianity. Enslaved persons browbeaten by sermons on obedience might well have rejected Christianity entirely, but instead they mined it for stories that gave them hope. The exodus narrative was especially meaningful, as in the shout song "Pharaoh's Host Got Lost":

> Moses, Moses lay your rod
> > In that Red Sea.
> Lay your rod, let the children cross
> > In that Red Sea.
> Ol' Pharaoh's hos' got los', los', los',
> Ol' Pharaoh's hos' got los',
> > In that Red Sea.
> They shout when the hos' got los', los', los',
> They shout when the hos' got los',
> > In that Red Sea.[12]

African and Christian elements also blended in the enslaved population's understanding of supernatural power. In African traditions, broadly speaking, good and evil spirits were very real, and either could take possession of a person. Evil could be warded off (or directed toward an enemy) with conjure, or hoodoo, a type of magic usually performed with bundles of ritual objects. Enslaved persons who encountered Christianity sometimes practiced the new religion alongside conjure, seeking whatever supernatural help they could get. They also overlaid Christian definitions on older beliefs. The evil spirit became the devil. Visions merged with prayer. And the trickster figure that was, in the

---

11. Laura M. Towne, *The Letters and Diary of Laura M. Towne: Written from the Sea Islands of South Carolina, 1862–1884*, ed. Rupert Sargent Holland (Cambridge: Riverside, 1912), 20.

12. Art Rosenbaum, Margo Newmark Rosenbaum, and Johann S. Buis, *Shout Because You're Free: The African American Ring Shout Tradition in Coastal Georgia* (Athens: University of Georgia Press, 1998), 130–31.

old myths, a small, weak animal who overcame a larger foe through cleverness became the meek but triumphant Christian Savior, Jesus.

White Southerners' worst fears about African American religion were realized in the person of Nat Turner, a man enslaved in southeastern Virginia. By his own account, as recorded by a white interviewer, he was born with unusual marks on his head and unusual intelligence, which caused other enslaved persons to expect great things from him. His grandmother was "very religious," and he became so too. Then, in early adulthood, he had a series of visions, including one of dewdrops like blood:

> The Holy Ghost was with me, and said, "Behold me as I stand in the Heavens"—and I looked and saw the forms of men in different attitudes—and there were lights in the sky to which the children of darkness gave other names than what they really were—for they were the lights of the Saviour's hands, stretched forth from east to west, even as they were extended on the cross on Calvary for the redemption of sinners. And I wondered greatly at these miracles, and prayed to be informed of a certainty of the meaning thereof—and shortly afterwards, while laboring in the field, I discovered drops of blood on the corn as though it were dew from heaven—and I communicated it to many, both white and black, in the neighborhood—and I then found on the leaves in the woods hieroglyphic characters, and numbers, with the forms of men in different attitudes, portrayed in blood, and representing the figures I had seen before in the heavens. And now the Holy Ghost had revealed itself to me, and made plain the miracles it had shown me—For as the blood of Christ had been shed on this earth, and had ascended to heaven for the salvation of sinners, and was now returning to earth again in the form of dew—and as the leaves on the trees bore the impression of the figures I had seen in the heavens, it was plain to me that the Saviour was about to lay down the yoke he had borne for the sins of men, and the great day of judgment was at hand.[13]

Turner determined that he was God's chosen instrument of judgment. He shared his visions with a few other men and made plans. In August 1831, in the middle of the night, they hacked to death Turner's enslaver and his family and took the family's guns. The group proceeded from farm to farm on a campaign of apocalyptic violence, murdering white people and gathering more followers and weapons. By the time white militias stopped the group, about fifty-five white people had died. In the course of the conflict, white militias killed dozens of alleged conspirators and scores of other African Americans who had nothing to do with the revolt. Turner escaped but was eventually caught, tried, and hanged in the city of Jerusalem, Virginia.

13. Nat Turner, *The Confessions of Nat Turner* (Baltimore: Thomas R. Gray, 1831), 10–11.

Turner's published confession included descriptions of his youth, his visions, and the violence. It did not include repentance. To the end, Turner remained convinced that God's Spirit had told him that "the Serpent was loosened, and Christ had laid down the yoke he had borne for the sins of men, and that I should take it on and fight against the Serpent, for the time was fast approaching when the first should be last and the last should be first." His interrogator asked, "Do you not find yourself mistaken now?" Turner replied, "Was not Christ crucified?"[14]

Religious gatherings of Black Americans had been tolerated by enslavers before, but after Turner's rebellion, whites across the South panicked. Virginia governor John Floyd declared in a speech, "The public good requires the negro preachers to be silenced, who, full of ignorance, are incapable of inculcating any thing but notions of the wildest superstition: thus preparing fit instruments in the hands of the crafty agitators to destroy the public tranquility."[15] New laws targeted Black churches, Black preachers, and anyone who would teach enslaved persons to read or write. In North Carolina, for example, an enslaved or free Black caught preaching could be subject to thirty-nine lashes. At the same time, white evangelists were mobilized to teach a tamer form of Christianity. Enslavers who were previously indifferent to the spiritual condition of those enslaved took a sudden and controlling interest.

Black Christianity continued but was forced deeper into hiding. A formerly enslaved man by the name of Wash Wilson recalled, "When de n—s go round singin' 'Steal Away to Jesus,' dat mean dere gwine be a 'ligious meetin' dat night. De masters . . . didn't like dem 'ligious meetin's, so us natcherly slips off at night, down in de bottoms or somewhere. Sometimes us sing and pray all night."[16] Secrecy mattered because those caught at these meetings in the "hush harbor" faced flogging. Secrecy was especially important if the gathering was, as enslavers feared, connected to the pursuit of physical as well as spiritual freedom. Coded messages in songs might alert fellow enslaved persons to a prayer meeting or an escape attempt. The same sign that pointed to the hush harbor, such as a broken branch, might also mark the Underground Railroad route to the North.

Connections between Black Christianity, the Underground Railroad, and the long movement toward freedom that continued after the Civil War were visible in the life of Harriet Tubman. Her faith was in some ways similar to

14. Turner, *Confessions*, 11.

15. "Excerpts from Governor John Floyd's Message to the General Assembly (December 6, 1831)," *Encyclopedia Virginia*, https://encyclopediavirginia.org/entries/excerpts-from-governor-john-floyds-message-to-the-general-assembly-december-6-1831/.

16. Quoted in Albert J. Raboteau, *Slave Religion: The "Invisible Institution" in the Antebellum South* (New York: Oxford University Press, 1978), 213.

Frederick Douglass on False and True Christianity

Frederick Douglass (ca. 1818–95), who was born into slavery, escaped, and became an abolitionist, eloquently contrasts the false Christianity he despised with the true Christianity he valued.

What I have said respecting and against religion, I mean strictly to apply to the *slaveholding religion* of this land, and with no possible reference to Christianity proper; for, between the Christianity of this land, and the Christianity of Christ, I recognize the widest possible difference—so wide, that to receive the one as good, pure, and holy, is of necessity to reject the other as bad, corrupt, and wicked. To be the friend of the one, is of necessity to be the enemy of the other. I love the pure, peaceable, and impartial Christianity of Christ: I therefore hate the corrupt, slaveholding, women-whipping, cradle-plundering, partial and hypocritical Christianity of this land. Indeed, I can see no reason, but the most deceitful one, for calling the religion of this land Christianity. I look upon it as the climax of all misnomers, the boldest of all frauds, and the grossest of all libels. Never was there a clearer case of "stealing the livery of the court of heaven to serve the devil in." I am filled with unutterable loathing when I contemplate the religious pomp and show, together with the horrible inconsistencies, which every where surround me. . . . The slave auctioneer's bell and the church-going bell chime in with each other, and the bitter cries of the heart-broken slave are drowned in the religious shouts of his pious master. Revivals of religion and revivals in the slave-trade go hand in hand together. The slave prison and the church stand near each other. The clanking of fetters and the rattling of chains in the prison, and the pious psalm and solemn prayer in the church, may be heard at the same time. The dealers in the bodies and souls of men erect their stand in the presence of the pulpit, and they mutually help each other. The dealer gives his blood-stained gold to support the pulpit, and the pulpit, in return, covers his infernal business with the garb of Christianity. Here we have religion and robbery the allies of each other— devils dressed in angels' robes, and hell presenting the semblance of paradise.

Frederick Douglass, *Narrative of the Life of Frederick Douglass* (Boston, 1845), 118–20.

Nat Turner's: she had visions (which might have been caused or enhanced by a severe head wound she sustained as a young woman) and believed that God had empowered her to deliver her people. But where Turner committed acts of violence, Tubman, in the trickster tradition, worked by stealth.

Harriet Tubman earned the nickname "Moses" for her work leading her people to freedom on the Underground Railroad.

Tubman escaped slavery in 1849 and then became a conductor on the Underground Railroad, slipping back into the South repeatedly to lead dozens of family members and other escapees to freedom. For this work, she earned the nickname "Moses." In 1858, she shared logistical knowledge with radical abolitionist John Brown as he plotted his raid on Harpers Ferry. During the Civil War, she served as a nurse, spy, and scout for Union forces. Although Southern planters offered a $40,000 reward for her capture, dead or alive, the short, dark-skinned woman moved unseen.

Eventually, Tubman settled in Auburn, New York, which had been a center of abolitionist sentiment. She obtained a pension from Congress and a plot of land from Senator William Seward (who later became Abraham Lincoln's secretary of state), both of which she used to found a Home for Aged and Indigent Negroes. Leaders of Black churches and activists in a variety of causes sought her out, including suffragist Susan B. Anthony and Black educator Booker T. Washington. "Aunt Harriet" was mourned widely upon her death in 1913, but her hopes for extending services to more formerly enslaved persons went unfunded, and her small Home for the Aged became the property of the AME Zion Church. Her recorded last words echoed Jesus: "I go to prepare a place for you." Like many civil rights leaders across the years, she was more celebrated than supported.

Of all the striking aspects of antebellum Black Christianity, perhaps what is most amazing is that it developed at all. Christianity was the religion of the oppressors, who used it very consciously as a tool of oppression. Yet Black Americans found depths of hope and consolation in the faith that their white enslavers missed entirely. By the dawn of the twenty-first century, Black Americans remained the most religiously committed group in the United States, significantly more likely than any other group to attend church weekly, pray daily, and express absolute certainty that God exists.[17] Their faith, born in turmoil, held firm.

17. Neha Sahgal and Greg Smith, "A Religious Portrait of African-Americans," Pew Research Center, January 30, 2009, http://www.pewforum.org/2009/01/30/a-religious-portrait-of-african-americans/.

On January 1, 1808, Rev. Absalom Jones (1746–1818) preached a thanksgiving sermon at St. Thomas's African Episcopal Church in Philadelphia. He chose as his text Exodus 3:7–8: "And the LORD said, I have surely seen the affliction of my people which are in Egypt, and have heard their cry by reason of their taskmasters; for I know their sorrows; and I am come down to deliver them out of the hand of the Egyptians." Jones's concluding prayer, excerpted here, expressed joy for the end of the foreign slave trade while recognizing the continuing travails of his people.

Oh thou God of all the nations upon the earth! We thank thee, that thou art no respecter of persons, and that thou hast made of one blood all nations of men. We thank thee, that thou hast appeared, in the fulness of time, in behalf of the nation from which most of the worshipping people, now before thee, are descended. We thank thee, that the sun of righteousness has at last shed his morning beams upon them. Rend thy heavens, O Lord, and come down upon the earth; and grant that the mountains, which now obstruct the perfect day of thy goodness and mercy towards them, may flow down at thy presence. Send thy gospel, we beseech thee, among them. May the nations, which now sit in darkness, behold and rejoice in its light. May Ethiopia soon stretch out her hands unto thee, and lay hold of the gracious promise of thy everlasting covenant.[18]

FURTHER READING

Carretta, Vincent, ed. *Unchained Voices: An Anthology of Black Authors in the English-Speaking World of the 18th Century.* Expanded ed. Lexington: University Press of Kentucky, 2004.

Dickerson, Dennis. "Richard Allen and the Making of African Methodism." In *Sing Them Over Again to Me: Hymns and Hymnbooks in America*, edited by Mark A. Noll and Edith L. Blumhofer, 175–93. Tuscaloosa: University of Alabama Press, 2006.

Franklin, John Hope, and Evelyn Brooks Higginbotham. *From Slavery to Freedom: A History of African Americans.* 9th ed. New York: McGraw-Hill, 2010.

Gates, Henry Louis, Jr. *The Black Church: This Is Our Story, This Is Our Song.* New York: Penguin, 2021.

Genovese, Eugene D. *Roll, Jordan, Roll: The World the Slaves Made.* New York: Vintage, 1976.

Harvey, Paul. *Through the Storm, Through the Night: A History of African American Christianity.* Lanham, MD: Rowman & Littlefield, 2011.

Kolchin, Peter. *American Slavery, 1619–1877.* New York: Hill & Wang, 1993.

18. Absalom Jones, "A Thanksgiving Sermon," Project Canterbury, http://anglicanhistory.org /usa/ajones/thanksgiving1808.html.

Lincoln, C. Eric, and Lawrence H. Mamiya. *The Black Church in the African American Experience*. Durham, NC: Duke University Press, 1990.

Mitchell, Henry H. *Black Church Beginnings: The Long-Hidden Realities of the First Years*. Grand Rapids: Eerdmans, 2004.

Raboteau, Albert J. *A Fire in the Bones: Reflections on African-American Religious History*. Boston: Beacon, 1995.

———. *Slave Religion: The "Invisible Institution" in the Antebellum South*. New York: Oxford University Press, 1978.

Sernett, Milton C., ed. *African American Religious History: A Documentary Witness*. 2nd ed. Durham, NC: Duke University Press, 2000.

Shannon, David T., ed. *George Liele's Life and Legacy*. Macon, GA: Mercer University Press, 2012.

6

Far from Rome

John Carroll Elected First Roman Catholic Bishop in the United States, 1789

In 1774, John Adams attended worship at the "Romish Chapel" in Philadelphia and recorded in his diary, "The scenery and the music are so calculated to take in mankind, that I wonder the reformation ever succeeded. The paintings, the bells, the candles, the gold and silver, the Saviour on the cross over the altar, at full length, and all His wounds bleeding. The chanting is exquisitely soft and sweet."[1] No Catholic music in English had yet been published in America, but in 1787, also in Philadelphia, engraver John Aitken produced *A Compilation of Litanies and Vesper Hymns and Anthems as They Are Sung in the Catholic Church*. After an introduction to music theory, the book contained Mass settings and other songs in Latin, several songs in English, and a few tunes with German titles but no lyrics. As an example of this mixture of musical influences, the piece titled "Lucis Creator" featured one verse of an English translation of a text attributed to St. Gregory the Great (ca. 540–604), set to an unusual, probably English or

---

1. *The Works of John Adams*, vol. 2, *Diary, Notes of Debates, Autobiography* (Boston: Charles C. Little and James Brown, 1850), 395. Available online at https://oll.libertyfund.org/title/adams-the -works-of-john-adams-vol-2-diary-notes-of-debates-autobiography.

American tune. The 1791 edition of Aitken's collection included additional verses
in English and Latin.

> O Great Creator of the Light,
> Who from the darksome womb of night
> Brought forth new Light at Nature's Birth
> To shine upon the Face of th'Earth.
>
> Who, by the morn and evening ray,
> Hast measured time and called it day;
> Whilst sable night involves the spheres,
> Vouchsafe to hear our pray'rs and tears.
>
> Lucis Creator optime,
> Lucem dierum proferens,
> Primordis lucis novae,
> Mundi parens originem.
>
> Qui mane junctum vesperi,
> Diem vocari praecipis:
> Illabitur tetrum chaos,
> Audi preces cum fletibus.[2]

———————▼———————

The organization of the Roman Catholic Church in the newly formed United
States had a lot to do, strangely, with Benjamin Franklin. In 1776, the Continental Congress sent Franklin to Quebec to try to convince Canadians to
join the patriots in their fight against England. Because Quebec had a lot of
French speakers, and a lot of Catholics, the delegation included Charles Carroll, a prominent Maryland Catholic who had been educated in France. Another Maryland patriot, Samuel Chase, an Anglican, came along to demonstrate
Protestant-Catholic cooperation. To facilitate discussion with Canadian religious authorities, Congress also requested the participation of Carroll's cousin,
John Carroll, a Catholic priest. Father Carroll was not sure that diplomacy was
a suitable occupation for a priest, but he agreed to accompany the delegation.

The priest might have done well to heed his doubts. The diplomatic mission
failed, and the bishop of Quebec censured him, forbidding any Quebec priests
to converse with the meddling Americans. Carroll abandoned the mission to
accompany an ailing Franklin back to Philadelphia.

Carroll's association with Franklin paid off a few years later, however. By
1783, Carroll and the other two dozen Catholic priests in the United States felt

---

2. John Aitken, *A Compilation of the Liturgies and Vespers Hymns and Anthems as They Are Sung
in the Catholic Church* (Philadelphia, 1787), 24.

that they needed to establish a church structure for the new nation. In correspondence with Pope Pius VI, Carroll wrote, "You are not ignorant that in these United States our religious system has undergone a revolution, if possible, more extraordinary than our political one." Catholics in America no longer faced the restrictions on their rights that Catholics in England did, Carroll explained, but legal restrictions on religious practice had been replaced by deep resentment of any foreign authority. Rather than keeping American Catholics under the jurisdiction of the bishop of London, therefore, it would be best if the pope would "place the episcopal powers, at least such as most essential, in the hands of one amongst us, whose virtue, knowledge, and integrity of faith, shall be certified by ourselves."[3] In the spirit of democracy, the American Catholic clergy were asking permission to choose their own leader.

In a separate piece of correspondence, the American priests nominated Rev. John Lewis for the post. Lewis, an Englishman, was already acting on behalf of the bishop of London. Around the same time, though, papal representatives in Europe were discussing the future of the church with an American diplomat, Benjamin Franklin, who was then serving as ambassador to France. Franklin was for a while, and probably unwittingly, entangled in a plan to put American Catholics under French jurisdiction. When the American priests communicated to Franklin that they did not like that idea at all, Franklin began urging the pope to appoint Carroll, whom he remembered fondly. So the American priests did get one of their own selected to head up the Catholic mission to the United States, just not the one they had originally chosen.

Carroll was not, at this point, named a bishop but was given the lesser title of Superior of the American Mission. From Rome's perspective, the United States was a missionary outpost, hardly ready for its own national hierarchy. American Catholics felt themselves to be far out on the missionary frontier as well. Throughout the eighteenth century, Catholics constituted a tiny minority in the English colonies. They numbered no more than forty thousand at the time of the first US census in 1790, less than 1 percent of the population. Spread across a territory larger than England, France, and Germany combined, many of these Catholics went years between visits from a priest. Instead, colonial American Catholicism centered on the home, where heads of households used books like John Gother's *Prayers for Sundays and Festivals, Adapted to the Use of Private Families and Congregations* (1704) to keep the faith. In this way, early American Catholicism continued adaptations that had developed under repressive laws in post-Reformation England while differing sharply from the

3. John Gilmary Shea, *Life and Times of The Most Rev. John Carroll, Bishop and First Archbishop of Baltimore* (New York: John G. Shea, 1888), 211, 212.

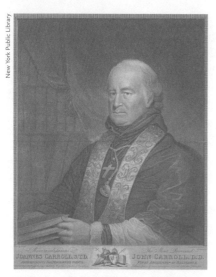

In a nod to his dual identity, this engraved portrait of John Carroll gives his name, title, and academic degree in both Latin (left) and English (right). Elected bishop in 1789, he became archbishop in 1811.

priest- and parish-centered practice in most of Europe.

As one of the only American-born priests of his era, Carroll had unique insight into the American church. Linked through his family to American politics—his cousin Charles was the only Catholic signer of the Declaration of Independence and later served as a Maryland senator—Carroll was also especially attuned to what he called the country's "free and jealous government." To exercise effective church discipline and administer the full array of sacraments, Catholics in the United States needed not just a Superior of Missions but a bishop. To allay suspicion of foreign authorities, that bishop needed to reside in the United States.

Carroll and his colleagues again asked the pope for permission to elect a leader, this time with the title "bishop" attached. The request was granted, according to the pope's representative, "as a special favor and for this first time."[4]

On May 18, 1789, the American priests gathered at Sacred Heart Chapel in White Marsh, Maryland. They celebrated Mass, invoked the guidance of the Holy Spirit, and cast their votes. Carroll garnered twenty-four of twenty-six votes, having cast his own ballot for someone else. After a trip to England to be consecrated, Carroll took up his post as bishop of Baltimore, the principal city of the state with the highest concentration of Catholics in the United States. His diocese, or administrative realm, encompassed the whole country, and his task included charting a path for an ancient church in a new, officially secular nation. What would it mean to be Catholic and American?

Americanization in the Early Republic

A distinctly American Catholicism took root during Carroll's tenure. By design and necessity, it adapted to local conditions, especially in the areas of church governance and religious practice. Laypeople and church leaders shared re-

4. Shea, *Life and Times of The Most Rev. John Carroll*, 333.

sponsibility for cultivating this new branch of global Catholicism, which had both hierarchical European traditions and American democracy in its DNA.

Hierarchy is very important in Roman Catholicism. Certainly, many Catholics would not agree with the bombastic 1302 papal bull *Unam Sanctam*, which declared "that it is absolutely necessary for salvation that every human creature be subject to the Roman Pontiff." Nonetheless, according to Catholic doctrine, salvation proceeds in and through the church, and God's grace is available in and through the sacraments (baptism, confirmation, Eucharist, penance, anointing of the sick, matrimony, and holy orders). Having a church or valid sacraments requires a priest, except in cases of emergency baptism, when the recipient is likely to die before a priest can arrive. Priests, in turn, must be properly educated, ordained, and subject to higher levels of church authority—ultimately, to the pope.

Carroll acknowledged the pope as the spiritual head of the church, but he kept his distance. This was not, initially, very difficult. Correspondence traveled slowly across the Atlantic. It was impractical for Rome to send anyone to investigate the American situation. Additionally, the violently anticlerical French Revolution diverted the attention of European authorities. Carroll and the other American priests were left fairly free to experiment with governance structures. As a measure of the relative unimportance of the pope in Carroll's thinking, he appeared just once in the catechism that Carroll published in 1793. The earliest Catholic prayer books printed in the United States did not mention the pope at all.

The structure that emerged in the American republic, which Catholic historian Jay Dolan called the "congregational parish," strongly resembled Protestantism.[5] Many church properties belonged, legally, to lay trustees rather than to the church or its priests. (Some states mandated this arrangement as a way of maintaining separation between church and state.) These lay trustees, prominent men in their communities, wished to have a say in who led their church and how he did his work. Generally, clergy and laity in the parishes worked together amicably, though there were some conflicts: a pamphlet war in Philadelphia; an exchange of insults in New York; dueling Catholic churches, each claiming to be the true one, in Norfolk, Virginia. Carroll supported the congregational parish model, but he drew the line at allowing trustees to hire and fire priests. That authority belonged to the bishop.

To build up a corps of priests who could work well in this system, Carroll sought to establish a seminary and preparatory academy on American soil.

---

5. Jay Dolan and Jeffrey Burns, "The Parish in the American Past," quoted in Mark Searle, ed., *Parish: A Place for Worship* (Collegeville, MN: Liturgical Press, 1981), 51–62.

Carroll Commends Religious Education

In a 1792 pastoral letter to Roman Catholics in the United States, Bishop Carroll linked the training of children and the beginnings of American Catholic higher education to the welfare of the new nation.

> These being the advantages of a religious education, I was solicitous for the attainment of a blessing so desirable to that precious portion of my flock, the growing generation. A school has been instituted at George-Town, which will continue to be under the superintendence and government of some of my reverend brethren, that is, of men devoted by principle and profession to instruct all, who resort to them, in useful learning, and those of our own religion, in its principles and duties. I earnestly wish, dear brethren, that as many of you, as are able, would send your sons to this school of letters ▶

Both Georgetown Academy (now Georgetown University) and St. Mary's Seminary began holding classes in 1791. Carroll also tried to convince a group of Carmelite nuns who had settled in Maryland to start teaching Catholic girls. He secured Rome's permission for the usually cloistered nuns to engage in this work, but the nuns, whom Carroll had not consulted, refused. "I doubt not the efficacy of their prayers in drawing down blessings on us all," he complained in a letter to a friend, "but their utility to the public goes no farther."[6] A different order, the Visitation sisters, eventually opened the school. Carroll's own "utility to the public" went beyond his explicitly religious duties to include leadership in Baltimore's educational, medical, and humanitarian organizations.

Another notable feature of Carroll's Americanizing project was his support for the use of the English language in worship. Protestants since the time of the Reformation had argued that Christians needed to be able to sing hymns and hear sermons in their everyday language, but Roman Catholics continued to use Latin for their liturgy until the Second Vatican Council in the 1960s. There were, however, exceptions to this long-standing tradition, and Carroll was one of them. "Can there be anything more preposterous than an unknown tongue[?]," he mused in a 1787 letter. Americans did not know Latin and lacked either books or teachers to explain it. In such a situation, Carroll felt that a

---

6. John Carroll to Charles Plowden, September 3, 1800, in R. Scott Appleby, Patricia Byrne, and William L. Portier, eds., *Creative Fidelity: American Catholic Intellectual Traditions* (Maryknoll, NY: Orbis Books, 2004), 61.

and virtue. I know and lament, that the expense will be too great for many families, and that their children must be deprived of the immediate benefit of this institution; but, indirectly, they will receive it; at least, it may be reasonably expected, that some after being educated at George-Town, and having returned into their own neighbourhood, will become, in their turn, the instructors of the youths who cannot be sent from home; and, by pursuing the same system of uniting much attention to religion with a solicitude for other improvements, the general result will be a great increase of piety, the necessary consequence of a careful instruction in the principles of faith, and Christian morality.

> John Carroll, "The Pastoral Letter of 1792," in *The National Pastorals of the American Hierarchy (1792–1919)*, ed. Peter Guilday (Washington, DC: National Catholic Welfare Council, 1923), 4.

refusal to conduct worship in English reflected only "chimerical fears of innovation" or "indolence and inattention" on the part of the clergy.[7] Carroll also avidly promoted sales of a US-printed, English-language, Catholic translation of the Bible.

Even before the end of Carroll's life, though, Americanization began to ebb. After numerical and geographic growth of American Catholicism prompted the creation of four new dioceses in 1808—New York, Boston, Philadelphia, and Bardstown, Kentucky—their bishops were chosen by Carroll (who was elevated to archbishop) rather than by a democratic vote of the clergy. An 1810 council of American Catholic leaders decreed that Latin be used for the entire Mass and all sacraments, though English could still be used for some prayers. In 1818, three years after Carroll's death, Ambrose Maréchal, the new, French-born archbishop of Baltimore, took aim at the lay-trustee system, complaining in correspondence to the Vatican,

The American people clings with the most ardent love to the civil liberty it enjoys. Again it is a primary . . . principle of civil liberty among them, that absolutely all magistrates, whether high or low . . . should be elected by popular vote. Likewise all sects of Protestants, who constitute the greater part of the people, are ruled by the same principles and accordingly elect or dismiss, at their pleasure, their pastors. Now the Catholics living in their society, are evidently exposed to the danger of admitting the same principles of ecclesiastical rule, and by the artifices

7. Quoted in Peter Guilday, *The Life and Times of John Carroll: Archbishop of Baltimore (1735–1815)* (New York: Encyclopedia Press, 1922), 130.

of impious priests, who cater to their pride, are easily led to believe that they also have the right to elect and dismiss their pastors as they please.[8]

For Carroll, Catholic and American identities blended fairly harmoniously. Subsequent generations of American Catholics, especially those born abroad, experienced more dissonance.

Immigrant Influences

American Catholicism trended in a more Old World direction in the middle of the nineteenth century. The American hierarchy asserted itself more forcefully as it sought to maintain order and unity in a country that doubled in size with the Louisiana Purchase in 1803 and stretched to the Pacific Ocean by the late 1840s. Meanwhile, waves of European immigrants brought with them languages, cultures, and ideas about church that did not fit easily into John Carroll's Americanized vision.

John Hughes offered a stark contrast to Carroll as a leader. Born in Ireland in 1797, Hughes moved with his family to the United States in 1817, seeking economic opportunity and freedom from the second-class status imposed on Catholics by English law. Accustomed to farm labor but interested in training for the priesthood, he became a gardener at Mount St. Mary's College and Seminary in Emmitsburg, Maryland, the country's second-oldest Catholic college. When the school's founder, concerned about Hughes's lack of prior education, refused to admit him, Hughes appealed to Mother Elizabeth Bayley Seton, a high-profile convert to Roman Catholicism who would later become the first American-born Catholic saint. Thanks to Seton's advocacy, Hughes enrolled at the seminary in 1820 and was ordained to the priesthood in 1826.

Irish Catholics generally held a very high view of priestly authority, and Hughes entered ministry with an expectation of lay submission. Sent to Philadelphia in 1827, he subdued the fractious trustees at St. Mary's Church. Upon arriving in New York City as coadjutor (assistant) bishop in 1837, he clashed with trustees at Old St. Patrick's Church and then pushed for a resolution that church members should do nothing whatsoever to hinder or prevent the authority of the bishop. "We have brought the trustees so low that they are not able to give a decent kick!" he exulted in a letter.[9] He signed this letter, as he signed all

8. Quoted in Jay Alan Sekulow, *Witnessing Their Faith: Religious Influence on Supreme Court Justices and Their Opinions* (Lanham, MD: Rowman & Littlefield, 2006), 5.

9. John Hughes to Mr. Frenaye, March 20, 1839, in John R. G. Hassard, *Life of the Most Reverend John Hughes, D.D., First Archbishop of New York* (New York: D. Appleton, 1866), 196.

Hughes Laments Biased Education

In a widely printed 1840 speech, Bishop Hughes decried the anti-Catholic bent of the New York public schools as unjust and un-American.

There were in the class books of those schools false (as we believe) historical statements respecting the men and things of past times calculated to fill the minds of our children with errors of fact, and at the same time to excite in them prejudice against the religion of their parents and guardians. These passages were not considered as sectarian, inasmuch as they had been selected as mere reading lessons, and were not in *favor* of any particular sect, but merely *against* the Catholics. We feel it is unjust that such passages should be taught at all in schools, to the support of which we are contributors as well as others. But that such books should be put into the hands of *our own* children, and that in part at our own expense, was in our opinion unjust, unnatural, and at all events to us intolerable. Accordingly, through very great additional sacrifices, we have been obliged to provide schools, under our churches and elsewhere, in which to educate our children as our conscientious duty required. . . .

And although most of us are poor, still the poorest man amongst us is obliged to pay taxes, from the sweat of his brow, in the rent of his room or little tenement. Is it not then hard and unjust that such a man cannot have the benefit of education for his child without sacrificing the rights of his religion and conscience? He sends his child to a school under the protection of his Church, in which these rights will be secure. But he has to support this school also. In Ireland he was compelled to support a church hostile to his religion, and here he is compelled to support schools in which his religion fares but little better, and to support his own school besides.

Is this state of things, fellow-citizens, and especially Americans, is this state of things worthy of *you*, worthy of our country, worthy of our just and glorious constitution?

John Hughes, "Speeches on the School Question," in part 3 of *Life of Archbishop Hughes*, 2nd ed. (New York: The American News Company, 1864), 17.

his letters, with a cross before his name. Both this symbol and his pugnacious spirit earned him the nickname "Dagger John."

Hughes had numerous reasons to get feisty during his years as coadjutor bishop, then bishop, and finally archbishop of New York. Most of New York's Catholics, like Hughes, were Irish, and, also like Hughes, they suffered from a lack of education and opportunity. But the city's taxpayer-supported public

In this infamous 1871 illustration by prolific artist Thomas Nast, Catholic clergymen are depicted as crocodiles crawling out of "The American River Ganges" to prey on American children. Images in the background link the Vatican with New York's political machine, Tammany Hall, and foretell peril to US public schools.

schools did not welcome Catholic children. The curriculum used the King James Bible, a translation that Catholics considered biased, alongside textbooks that celebrated Protestant leaders such as Martin Luther but disparaged Catholics. One such classroom text warned that if the influx of "drunken and depraved" Irish immigrants was allowed to continue, America would soon become a "common sewer." Hughes launched a crusade to scrub the public schools of religious bias, or secure public funds for private education, or both.[10]

The Maclay Bill of 1842 was intended to settle the New York school debate with a compromise: control over the public schools, and the curriculum taught within them, would be made religiously neutral, but no public funds would be used for explicitly Catholic education. By this point, though, the issue was thoroughly politicized, with various factions seeking advantage by pandering to one side of the deepening religious divide while demonizing the other. The very night the Maclay Bill passed, mobs attacked Irish churches and homes, including Hughes's own residence, though he was absent at the time.

10. John Hughes, "Speeches on the School Question," in part 3 of *Life of Archbishop Hughes*, 2nd ed. (New York: American News Company, 1864), 7.

Anti-immigrant sentiment, also called nativism, soon grew much worse. A lurid book purporting to reveal atrocities committed in convents, titled *Awful Disclosures of Maria Monk* (1836), inflamed anti-Catholic rumors. In 1845, the potato crop in Ireland failed, initiating several years of devastating famine. Perhaps one million Irish died in the famine, while another one million emigrated, often packed onto vessels dubbed "coffin ships" because of their tight conditions and high mortality rates. About three-fourths of the emigrants came to the United States, where they tended to settle in large Eastern seaboard cities. By 1850, one-fourth of the population of Boston, Philadelphia, New York, and Baltimore was Irish, virtually all of them Catholic. Impoverished, poorly educated, and crammed into urban slums, the immigrants needed a lot of help. The situation roused Catholic leaders to action and nativists to revulsion.

Hughes's fierce advocacy helped Irish Catholics in America but also gave fodder to rising, sometimes violent anti-Catholic hostility. His 1850 address "The Decline of Protestantism" predicted the "wreck" of Protestantism within a hundred years and declared it Catholics' mission "to convert the world, including the inhabitants of the United States, the people of the cities, and the people of the country, the officers of the navy and the marines, commanders of the army, the Legislatures, the Senate, the Cabinet, the President, and all!"[11] Protestants were enraged by such rhetoric. Protestant clergymen published point-by-point rebuttals to Hughes's speech, while conspiracy theorists formed secret societies and a political party, formally known as the American Party, to combat the purported Catholic menace. The political party was better known as the Know-Nothings, because, if asked about activities that included voter intimidation and ballot-rigging, its members were instructed to reply that they knew nothing. Operatives in Catholic political machines, such as New York's Tammany Hall, sometimes engaged in reciprocal skulduggery. It was an ugly, dangerous time.

Ethnic divisions created tensions between Catholics and other Americans, but they also created tensions within the Catholic Church. Because of their massive numbers and plentiful candidates for the priesthood, Irish dominated the American Catholic hierarchy in the mid-nineteenth century, but they were soon joined by other groups, starting with hundreds of thousands of Germans fleeing political revolution in 1848. The Germans, about half of whom were Catholic, had more money and education than the Irish who had arrived just before them, spoke a different language, and were less deferential to priests.

11. John Hughes, "The Decline of Protestantism, and Its Causes," in *The Complete Works of the Most Rev. John Hughes, D.D.*, ed. Lawrence Kehoe, 2 vols. (New York: Catholic Publication House, 1864), 2:101.

German Catholics did not see eye-to-eye with Irish leaders. Neither, in many cases, did the Italians, Slovaks, Poles, and others who immigrated in increasing numbers over the course of the century—or the Latino Catholics of Florida and the American Southwest, who did not migrate but found themselves enclosed by the expanding boundaries of the United States.

Immigration and its attendant tensions gave rise to the ethnic parish, a system in which Catholics who lived near one another but hailed from different cultures worshiped separately. Historians have illustrated this development with a look at the Bridgeport neighborhood of Chicago. Saint Bridget's Church, with a mostly Irish congregation, opened in 1850. To accommodate growth, another mostly Irish church, Nativity of Our Lord, opened in 1868, but there were already many Catholics in the neighborhood who could not understand English-language sermons or confess to an English-speaking priest. A church for Bohemians, Saint John Nepomucene, opened in 1871, and one for Germans, Saint Anthony of Padua, opened in 1873. Additional parishes for Irish, Germans, Poles, and Lithuanians were added until, by 1910, eleven Catholic churches stood within one square mile.[12]

Parenthetically, ethnic fragmentation also marked the American Orthodox experience in the nineteenth century. Unlike Roman Catholicism, which upholds the ideal of one global church under the leadership of the pope, Orthodoxy (also known collectively as Eastern Christianity or Eastern Orthodoxy) upholds the ideal of one church for each nation or people group, united by common liturgy and mutual recognition. Because Russian Orthodox missionaries were the first to arrive in territory that later became part of the United States (Alaska), in 1784, according to tradition America's Orthodox believers should all have recognized Russian jurisdiction until the American church was ready for its own hierarchy. But by the 1860s, when the Russian mission had spread south to California, Greek Orthodox had begun to cross the Atlantic and establish their own churches. Serbian Orthodox, Ukrainian Orthodox, and others followed. In cities with low concentrations of immigrants, multiethnic parishes formed, some of which later split when one nationality achieved a critical mass of parishioners. In the early twentieth century, Russian Orthodox oversight, never complete, collapsed as a result of the Russian Revolution, leaving the United States in the anomalous situation of having not one national Orthodox Church but several competing foreign jurisdictions. Today, Orthodox Christians make up about half of 1 percent of the American population, much smaller than the roughly 20 percent who

12. James M. O'Toole, *The Faithful: A History of Catholics in America* (Cambridge, MA: Belknap, 2008), 103; Ellen Skerrett, Edward R. Kantowicz, and Steven M. Avella, *Catholicism, Chicago Style* (Chicago: Loyola University Press, 1993), 8–11.

identify as Catholic or the roughly 40 percent who identify as some type of Protestant.

New Practices

Immigration had made Catholicism the single largest denomination in the United States by about 1850, but its institutional strength lagged behind its numerical growth. There were not enough priests, nuns, churches, and schools to serve all the immigrants, let alone to serve them all in their native languages. Catholics who lacked sufficient access to religious services and instruction were seen as being in danger of losing their faith or, worse, turning Protestant. To bolster religious commitment, the church developed a new outreach strategy, the parish mission, and encouraged an array of devotional practices.

Parish missions were a bit like the Protestant revivals so prominent in nineteenth-century America (see chap. 7), with traveling preachers and long, emotional services. Messages in either setting emphasized the torments of sin and hell, countered by the blessed relief available through confession. There were also significant differences. The Catholic prayers were different, the songs were sung by choirs rather than by the congregation until the 1880s, and success was measured not in sinners saved but in sacraments administered. Also, while Protestant revivals sometimes weakened church authority (see chap. 4), canon law—the rules for Catholic ministry—dictated that itinerant preachers work with local church leaders and hold meetings at only approved times and places.

Despite their similarities to Protestant revivals, parish missions were essentially European imports given an American twist. Mission preachers typically belonged to an outreach-oriented European religious order such as the Jesuits, Redemptorists, or Passionists. Their missions initially targeted ethnic populations (particularly Germans) and aimed to restore faltering Catholics rather than to convert Protestants to Catholicism. The latter task was taken up by an American-born convert to Catholicism, Isaac Hecker, who urged the creation of a new preaching order to evangelize Protestants. Hecker founded the Paulist Fathers in 1858 and pursued outreach through public lectures, modeled on the American Chautauqua adult education movement, rather than sacrament-centered, European-style missions. Another new order, the Josephites, was founded in 1871 to evangelize Black Americans.

The "devotional revolution" was another nineteenth-century European import with American variations. Whereas early American Catholicism had featured simple, home-based piety, in the 1850s Pope Pius IX encouraged standardized devotional practices for Catholics everywhere, many of them centered on the Blessed Sacrament. This is what some of the practices looked like, according to a French visitor describing laypeople's activities in any of New York's fifty Catholic churches in the later nineteenth century:

> Behold them, when the sanctuary bell announces the moment of consecration; they raise their hands, they extend their arms in the form of a cross, they pray and sigh aloud; at times some leave their pew and prostrate themselves in the aisle, in order to assume a more suppliant and adoring attitude. There, if you wait until the end of mass, you will be further edified. You will see them approach as near as possible to the high altar, before which they bow profoundly, making several genuflections, and frequently remain for a moment almost prostrate to the ground. From here they go to kneel at the altar of the Blessed Virgin, then before that of St. Joseph. Then follows a last and touching station before the body of the dead Christ which the Italians call the *pietá*; they pray here for a few moments, and respectfully press their lips to the five wounds of the Saviour. At the door of the church they take holy water, sign themselves with it repeatedly, and sprinkle their faces with it; then turning toward the tabernacle they make a last genuflection, as if to bid farewell to our Lord, and finally withdraw.[13]

In Catholic theology, when the priest consecrates the elements of the Eucharist, the bread and wine become, via transubstantiation, the body and blood of Christ. The outward appearance of the elements does not change, however, and Christ is not actually slain again, making the priest's act an "unbloody sacrifice." The people in this excerpt who bowed before the high altar, then, were bowing before the physical presence of Christ, as one might kneel before a king. And although they prayed, sighed, and lay down in the aisle during the church service, these behaviors were not considered disruptive. As a popular nineteenth-century prayer manual advised, the layperson could try to follow along with the Latin Mass, or meditate on the passion of Christ, or pray the Rosary, or "make use of any other devout exercise best suited to your own feelings of devotion, uniting all the while your intention to the intention of the sacrificing priest."[14]

These practices honoring the Blessed Sacrament, along with related practices that took place throughout the week or during special forty-hour vigils, had deep roots in Europe, as did the architecture that made them possible. Such devotionalism was renewed and expanded in the mid-nineteenth century for several reasons. In Europe, the devotions were one of the ways Pope Pius IX asserted church authority amid multiple revolutions and the founding

---

13. *Irish Faith in America: Recollections of a Missionary*, trans. Ella McMahon (New York: Benziger Brothers, 1881), 35–36.

14. Alphonsus Liguori, *The Mission Book of the Congregation of the Most Holy Redeemer* (Baltimore, 1862), quoted in Ann Taves, "Context and Meaning: Roman Catholic Devotion to the Blessed Sacrament in Mid-Nineteenth-Century America," *Church History* 54, no. 4 (December 1985): 484.

of modern Italy, during which the papacy faced the humbling loss of the Papal States. Put simply, Pius IX offset his declining political power with increasing spiritual power. This effort reached its apex at the First Vatican Council (1869–70), which decreed papal infallibility, the dogma that the pope cannot err "when in the exercise of his office as shepherd and teacher of all Christians, in virtue of his supreme apostolic authority, he defines a doctrine concerning faith or morals to be held by the whole Church." Though similar statements had been advanced in previous centuries, this uncompromising articulation of the doctrine was new; as late as 1800, Father John Cheverus, the first bishop of Boston, told a local newspaper that "to believe the Pope infallible is no part of our Creed, & no Roman Catholick ever pretended that he is."[15]

In the United States, the Catholic Church confronted different problems: its internal, ethnic divisions and the hostility of the surrounding Protestant culture. Here, the devotional revolution enabled Catholic laypeople to rally around symbols that bound them together while distinguishing them from Protestants. In the analysis of historian Ann Taves,

> With the separation of church and state, all denominations had been forced, as it were, onto the free market. Both Protestants and Catholics responded to these competitive demands by attempting to strengthen and intensify lay commitment, but they did so in different, though analogous, ways. Where Catholics held parish missions, mid-nineteenth-century evangelical Protestants held revivals; where Catholics promoted popular devotions, Protestants sang gospel hymns; where Catholics established confraternities and sodalities, Protestants established prayer groups and mission societies; and where Catholics emphasized the authority and infallibility of the pope, Protestants emphasized the authority and infallibility of the Bible.[16]

Protestant endeavors to influence America's religious marketplace and elevate the authority of the Bible will be examined in chapter 7.

American Countercurrents

Overall, US Catholicism in the nineteenth century became more European and hierarchical, but there were moves in the opposite direction as well. Ethnic minorities resisted efforts to standardize devotional practices, while bishops debated whether American democracy constituted a boon or a threat to the church.

15. Quoted in O'Toole, *The Faithful*, 46.
16. Taves, "Context and Meaning," 494.

Though backed by promised remission of sins (indulgences) and promoted at parish missions, devotions to the Blessed Sacrament did not entirely supplant older customs. Some immigrants retained passionate devotion to figures revered in their former homes, like the southern Italians in Harlem who celebrated the Madonna of Mount Carmel with an elaborate annual festival. Meanwhile, in the southwest, Latino Catholics built shrines testifying to the spiritual significance of their homeland. For example, El Santuario de Chimayo, built in New Mexico in 1816, recognized the site where a local friar miraculously discovered a crucifix with healing powers near the Santa Cruz River. The shrine became a pilgrimage destination and a source of holy dirt that is still used for healing. The French, Irish, and Spanish clergy sent to preside over this region met significant resistance to their efforts to Romanize religious practice.

A few high-profile American converts to Catholicism also argued for a locally grounded, unapologetically American faith. Writer and activist Orestes Brownson, who had been a Presbyterian, a Universalist, a Unitarian, and even

El Santuario de Chimayo in New Mexico is a major Catholic pilgrimage center. Pueblo peoples, who have lived near the site since the twelfth century, long believed that the dirt there has healing powers. Latino Catholics in the nineteenth century reinterpreted the site as a place of specifically Christian healing and miracles and built a church above "el pocito" (the little well). Pilgrims sometimes take vials of the dirt home with them.

Sister Blandina Segale Visits Billy the Kid in Jail

Although men set the direction for the American Catholic Church, nuns outnumbered priests four to one by the end of the nineteenth century and were, in many places, the public face of the church. One of the most colorful nineteenth-century nuns, Sister Blandina Segale, was born in Italy in 1850, joined the Sisters of Charity in 1868, and spent twenty-one years ministering in Santa Fe and Albuquerque. She recounted her many adventures on the frontier in letters to her younger sister. This one is dated May 16, 1881.

I have just returned from the jail. The two prisoners were chained hands and feet, but the "Kid," besides being cuffed hands and feet, was also fastened to the floor. You can imagine the extreme discomfort of the position. When I got into the prison-cell and "Billy" saw me, he said—as though we had met yesterday instead of four years ago—"I wish I could place a chair for you, Sister."

At a glance I saw the contents of the prison. Two empty nail kegs, one empty soap box, one backless chair, upon which sat the man who had shot our patient. After a few minutes' talk, the "Kid" said to me:

"Do what you can for Kelly," pointing to the chair, "this is his first offense, and he was not himself when he did it. I'll get out of this; you will see, Sister."

Think, dear Sister Justina, how many crimes might have been prevented, had someone had influence over "Billy" after his first murder. The plains are broad. His ascendancy was instantaneous over the minds of our free-lance cowboys, who are spurred on by a freedom that is not freedom. Finding himself captain and dictator, with no religious principles to check him, he became what he is—the greatest murderer of the Southwest.

Sister Blandina Segale, *At the End of the Santa Fe Trail* (Milwaukee: Bruce, 1948), 173.

founder of his own church before converting to Catholicism in 1844, argued in an 1856 essay that Catholics should "throw themselves fearlessly into the great current of American nation life" for their own benefit and that of the country as a whole. To help make America great, he wrote, Catholics "must identify ourselves with the country, accept loyally its institutions, confide in the grandeur of its mission, and be warmed and inspired by it. We must dismiss such of our old-world notions as have and can have no application here."[17] Isaac Hecker

17. Orestes A. Brownson, "Mission of America," in *The Works of Orestes A. Brownson: Collected and Arranged*, ed. Henry F. Brownson, vol. 11 (Detroit: Thorndike Nourse, 1884), 556, 577.

sounded similar notes, writing in 1887 that "Catholicity in religion sanctions republicanism in politics, and republicanism in politics favors Catholicity in religion."[18]

The most powerful clerics in the United States divided over the question of how *American* Catholicism could or should be. A New York theological society known as the Accademia became a hub for "Americanist" thinking, and its members advanced radical ideas, such as eliminating the requirement for priestly celibacy. A prominent group of Americanist bishops in the later nineteenth century, including Archbishop John Ireland of St. Paul, Minnesota, and Cardinal James Gibbons of Baltimore, also supported greater Catholic accommodation to American society and culture. These Americanists were opposed by Archbishop Michael Corrigan of New York and the bishops of Rochester, New York, and Cleveland, Ohio.

Pope Leo XIII weighed in on this debate in 1899 with the encyclical *Testem Benevolentiae Nostrae*, "Concerning New Opinions, Virtue, Nature and Grace, with Regard to Americanism." Framed as a response to a posthumous biography of Isaac Hecker and addressed to Cardinal Gibbons, the document declared "false" and "dangerous" the idea that "the Church should shape her teachings more in accord with the spirit of the age and relax some of her ancient severity and make some concessions to new opinions."[19] The liberal, modern, democratic direction taken by the Americanists would not make Catholicism attractive to outsiders, the pope warned, but it would cut Americans off from the rest of the Catholic Church, past and present. In a letter that remained unpublished until 1944, Cardinal Gibbons assured the pope that the errors he condemned in the encyclical bore no resemblance to the actual beliefs of any American Catholics.[20] Scholars still debate whether this climax of the "Americanist controversy" had a chilling effect on American Catholic intellectual life for decades or had relatively little effect at all.

Certainly, most American Catholics had other issues on their minds at the turn of the twentieth century. Another wave of immigration brought twenty million people to the United States between 1880 and 1920, with the majority arriving from Central, Eastern, and Southern Europe. Industrialization transformed work from a world of farms and small workshops into a world of factories and mines, ships and railroads, labor unions and robber barons.

---

18. Isaac Hecker, *The Church and the Age: An Exposition of the Catholic Church in View of the Needs and Aspirations of the Present Age* (New York: Office of the Catholic World, 1887), 87.

19. Pope Leo XIII, *Testem Benevolentiae Nostrae*, https://www.papalencyclicals.net/leo13 /l13teste.htm.

20. Gibbons's letter was published, in French, in *Catholic Historical Review* 30, no. 3 (October 1944): 347–48.

Technological advances in building construction—iron frames, electric lights, elevators—meant taller structures housing more people in America's teeming cities. As it had in the 1840s, the Catholic Church in the United States scrambled to recruit nuns and priests, open churches and schools, and fend off attacks—more often rhetorical and legal than violent, this time—from nativists.

Catholics met these needs with a new round of institutional innovations. Historian James O'Toole tells the story of Anna Hurban, an immigrant from Slovakia, and her pastor, Father Stephen Furdek, in Cleveland, Ohio. Father Furdek organized a Saint Joseph Society in 1889 to offer both devotional exercises and insurance plans in the days before workman's compensation. His group branched out into Slovak parishes across the Midwest. Hurban formed the First Catholic Slovak Ladies Union in 1892, which quickly expanded to dozens of affiliates with thousands of members. Her group opened an orphanage, published a newspaper, and ran schools dedicated to preserving Slovak language and culture.[21] Similar efforts sprang up in Catholic communities coast to coast as immigrants looked to their churches for help integrating into a new country while preserving cultural and religious distinctiveness. What it meant to be American and Catholic remained a vital question, one with as many answers as there were men and women finding ways to be faithful in a land very far from Rome.

The Third Plenary Council of Baltimore, held in 1884, ordered the production of an official prayer book, *A Manual of Prayers for the Use of the Catholic Laity*. The book included a list of saints' days and movable feasts, instruction on Christian doctrine and practice, and prayers and readings for all events that might occur in church or in daily life. The following prayer appeared in the section on Prime, the service of morning prayers traditionally held at the first hour of daylight.

> *O Lord God, King of heaven and earth, vouchsafe this day to direct and to sanctify, to rule and to govern, our souls and bodies, our senses, words, and actions, in Thy law, and in the works of Thy commandments; that both now and for ever we may deserve to be saved and delivered through Thy protection, O Saviour of the world, who livest and reignest, world without end. Amen.*[22]

21. O'Toole, *The Faithful*, 94–95.
22. *A Manual of Prayers for the Use of the Catholic Laity: The Official Prayer Book of the Catholic Church* (New York: Christian Press Association, 1886), 50.

————————————— FURTHER READING —————————————

Dolan, Jay P. *The American Catholic Experience: A History from Colonial Times to the Present*. New York: Doubleday, 1985.

————. *In Search of an American Catholicism: A History of Religion and Culture in Tension*. New York: Oxford University Press, 2002.

Massa, Mark, and Catherine Osborne, eds. *American Catholic History: A Documentary Reader*. 2nd ed. New York: New York University Press, 2017.

Matovina, Timothy M. *Latino Catholicism: Transformation in America's Largest Church*. Princeton: Princeton University Press, 2012.

McCartin, James P. *Prayers of the Faithful: The Shifting Spiritual Life of American Catholics*. Cambridge, MA: Harvard University Press, 2010.

McGreevy, John T. *Catholicism and American Freedom: A History*. New York: Norton, 2004.

Orsi, Robert. *The Madonna of 115th St.: Faith and Community in Italian Harlem, 1880–1950*. New Haven: Yale University Press, 1985.

O'Toole, James M. *The Faithful: A History of Catholics in America*. Cambridge, MA: Belknap, 2008.

Portier, William L. *Divided Friends: Portraits of the Roman Catholic Modernist Crisis in the United States*. Washington, DC: Catholic University of America Press, 2013.

Taves, Ann. *The Household of Faith: Roman Catholic Devotions in Mid-Nineteenth-Century America*. Notre Dame, IN: University of Notre Dame Press, 1986.

7

The Benevolent Empire

American Bible Society Founded, 1816

The revival at Cane Ridge, Kentucky, in August 1801 is often cited as the beginning of the Second Great Awakening, which lasted until roughly 1830. The Cane Ridge gathering was notable for its size—nearly twenty thousand people attended, at a time when the population of Kentucky's largest city, Lexington, numbered fewer than two thousand—and its ecumenism, with Presbyterian, Baptist, and Methodist preachers all participating. Doctrinally precise preaching (without benefit of a microphone) would not hold large, variegated crowds in such a setting, but congregational singing worked wonders to communicate a Christian message and inspire collective emotions. Songs by eighteenth-century revivalists like Charles Wesley remained popular in this era, but there were new songs too, such as "Brethren, We Have Met to Worship," written by Methodist minister George Atkins and first published in 1819. Set to an Appalachian folk tune, the song powerfully evokes the camp-meeting experience, linking spiritual conviction with a call to action.

> Brethren, we have met to worship,
> And adore the Lord our God;
> Will you pray with all your power,
> While we try to preach the word?

All is vain, unless the Spirit
Of the Holy One come down;
Brethren, pray, and holy manna
Will be showered all around.

Brethren, see poor sinners round you,
Trembling on the brink of woe;
Death is coming, hell is moving;
Can you bear to let them go?
See our fathers, see our mothers,
And our children sinking down;
Brethren, pray, and holy manna
Will be showered all around.[1]

Thanks to the voyage of Meriwether Lewis, William Clark, and the rest of the Corps of Discovery, the West captured Americans' imaginations at the opening of the nineteenth century. Newspapers carried scattered dispatches from the expedition as it proceeded, describing prairie dogs and cottonwoods, the Missouri River and the Pacific Ocean, helpful and hostile Native Americans. After the explorers returned, poets lauded them as heroes who had tamed the wilderness and mapped a path forward for the new nation. Some residents of the Eastern states became enchanted by visions of pristine land, towering timber, and abundant game. Others, though, worried about the new territories' spiritual condition. What if pioneers streamed into the churchless, lawless West, and the wilderness won?

These concerns animated the men who met at the Garden Street Dutch Reformed Church in New York on May 8, 1816, to discuss, as a history written one century later put it, "whether the new West could be led to learn God's ways in nation-building." More specifically, the assembled pastors, educators, and cultural leaders sought "some practicable method of carrying God's word westward to the thousands fast settling into content with irreligion."[2] If God's word was present on the frontier, the men believed, his ways would surely flourish.

The Garden Street assembly founded the American Bible Society (ABS), an organization dedicated to the efficient production and distribution of Bibles. An address announcing the new society assured potential supporters that "a contribution, saved from even a cheap indulgence, may send a Bible to a desolate family; may become a radiating point of 'grace and truth' to a neighbourhood of error and vice; and that a number of such contributions, made at really no

1. William Walker, *The Southern Harmony, and Musical Companion* (Philadelphia, 1835), 103.
2. Henry Otis Dwight, *The Centennial History of the American Bible Society*, 2 vols. (New York: Macmillan, 1916), 1:21.

expense, may illumine a large tract of country."[3] The cost of providing Bibles was tiny, the need great, and the rewards infinite.

The ABS represented a constellation of organizations, sometimes called the "Benevolent Empire," that shaped American life in the first half of the nineteenth century. These voluntary associations, fueled by revival and the freedoms of the First Amendment, touched all areas of society, spreading their founders' ideals of godly order. "Their efforts brought millions of Americans to take an active interest in public questions, public policy, and electoral politics, contributing mightily to the democratization of nineteenth-century American public life," wrote historian Kyle G. Volk.[4] Other historians, though, have seen in antebellum reform not free-wheeling democracy but the imposition of white, middle-class, Protestant, New England values on the rest of the nation. Both of these views contain significant truth. Many reformers did hope to make all of America more like New England, but the religious energies unleashed in the early republic could not be so easily channeled. Like the journey of the Corps of Discovery, reform efforts took twists and turns, never leading exactly where the reformers expected them to go.

Frontier Religion

The American settler population moved westward only slowly. Between 1790 and 1800, the mean center of the census-registered population (the point from which equal numbers of people lived in all directions) hopped from the east side of the Chesapeake Bay to the west side. By 1820 the center point stood at about the northern tip of Virginia, and it spent the next thirty years traversing what is now West Virginia before crossing into southern Ohio. Individual Americans traveled faster, however, and some aspects of their religion kept pace better than others.

Camp meetings, like the one at Cane Ridge in 1801, suited the shifting frontier perfectly. Whereas revivals during the First Great Awakening typically took place in churches or city squares, camp meetings were held in open spaces that could accommodate visitors from miles around. Itinerant preachers publicized the meetings on their circuits (the routes they took to serve fledgling congregations in multiple towns) and frequently joined forces for the events, across denominational lines. In addition to spiritual uplift, the camp meetings provided entertainment and opportunities to socialize. Business deals were struck and romances kindled as the sermons and songs rolled on for days.

3. Dwight, *Centennial History of the American Bible Society*, 1:28.
4. Kyle G. Volk, *Moral Minorities and the Making of American Democracy* (New York: Oxford University Press, 2014), 12.

Presbyterians (shown in this 1854 lithograph)—as well as Baptists, Methodists, and other Protestant groups—frequently held large outdoor worship services during the period later known as the Second Great Awakening.

Peter Cartwright's career demonstrates the interrelation of camp meetings, preaching circuits, and the westward movement of Protestant Christianity. As a young man in 1801, he attended a revival that had spun off from Cane Ridge. "On the Saturday evening of said meeting," he wrote in his autobiography, "I went, with weeping multitudes, and bowed before the stand, and earnestly prayed for mercy. In the midst of a solemn struggle of soul, an impression was made on my mind, as though a voice said to me, 'Thy sins are all forgiven thee.' Divine light flashed all round me, unspeakable joy sprung up in my soul. I rose to my feet, opened my eyes, and it really seemed as if I was in heaven; the trees, the leaves on them, and everything seemed, and I really thought were, praising God."[5]

The next year, at the age of sixteen, Cartwright became a Methodist exhorter. Education was not necessary, for, he wrote, "A Methodist preacher in those days, when he felt that God had called him to preach, instead of hunting up a college or biblical institute, hunted up a hardy pony of a horse, and some traveling apparatus, and with his library always at hand, namely, Bible, Hymn Book, and Discipline, he started, and with a text that never wore out nor grew stale, he cried, 'Behold the Lamb of God, that taketh away the sin of the world.'"[6] A

5. Peter Cartwright, *Autobiography of Peter Cartwright, the Backwoods Preacher*, ed. W. P. Strickland (New York: Carlton & Porter, 1857), 37.
6. Cartwright, *Autobiography of Peter Cartwright*, 243.

Library of Congress / from Joseph Smith, Old Redstone

decade after starting this ministry, he was appointed a presiding elder, a title analogous to a modern district superintendent. He preached widely, holding scores of meetings like the one at which he had been saved.

In 1823, Cartwright, by that time married and father to seven children, decided to sell his Kentucky farm and move to Illinois. He did not want his children growing up in an environment tainted by slavery. As a founder of the Illinois Annual Conference of the Methodist Episcopal Church, he oversaw a district that was four hundred miles long and encompassed two-thirds of the state. Adding a new facet to his authority, Cartwright was elected to the lower house of the Illinois General Assembly in 1828 and 1832. In the latter election, he defeated a fellow Kentucky transplant, Abraham Lincoln. Lincoln, in turn, defeated Cartwright for a seat in the US Congress in 1846.

Camp meetings and preaching circuits constituted a good start, but leaders back East feared that these developments could not tame the Western wilderness. The perceived threats—from Native American "savages," backwoods vices, irreligion, and burgeoning Roman Catholicism—were too great, the local resources too meager. Congregational minister Lyman Beecher, perhaps the most prominent Protestant cleric of his day, mingled enthusiasm and anxiety for the new territory in his famous 1835 tract *A Plea for the West*.

> The West is a young empire of mind, and power, and wealth, and free institutions, rushing up to a giant manhood, with a rapidity and a power never before witnessed below the sun. And if she carries with her the elements of her preservation, the experiment will be glorious—the joy of the nation—the joy of the whole earth, as she rises in the majesty of her intelligence and benevolence, and enterprise, for the emancipation of the world.
>
> It is equally clear, that the conflict which is to decide the destiny of the West, will be a conflict of institutions for the education of her sons, for purposes of superstition, or evangelical light; of despotism, or liberty. . . .
>
> But the population of the great West is . . . assembled from all the states of the Union, and from all the nations of Europe, and is rushing in like the waters of the flood, demanding for its preservation the immediate and universal action of those institutions which discipline the mind, and arm the conscience and the heart. And so various are the opinions and habits, and so recent and imperfect is the acquaintance, and so sparse are the settlements of the West, that no homogeneous public sentiment can be formed to legislate immediately into being the requisite institutions. And yet they are all needed immediately, in their utmost perfection and power. A nation is being "born in a day," and all the nurture of schools and literary institutions is needed, constantly and universally, to rear it up to a glorious and unperverted manhood.[7]

7. Lyman Beecher, *A Plea for the West* (Cincinnati: Truman & Smith, 1835), 11–12, 15–16.

Beecher delivered *A Plea for the West* as a speech in multiple Eastern seaboard cities while soliciting support for Lane Theological Seminary, which was founded in Cincinnati in 1832 to train Presbyterian clergy for Western ministry. Lane trustees lured Beecher from Boston to serve as the seminary's first president, then cringed when debates over revival methods and slavery split the school in 1834. The "Lane Rebels," who deemed Beecher insufficiently progressive, moved on to Oberlin College, the first school in the United States regularly to enroll women and Black Americans. Oberlin quickly became a center for antislavery activism.

A Plea for the West also articulated a foundation for the Benevolent Empire as a whole. The empire's interconnected organizations would advance Protestant "light" and "liberty" against Roman Catholic "superstition" and "despotism." (That argument was veiled in this excerpt, but it was clear enough elsewhere in the address to inspire a Protestant mob to burn an Ursuline convent outside Boston the day after Beecher spoke there in August 1834.) The empire would make the United States "the joy of the whole earth," fulfilling the destiny envisioned by John Winthrop in his "city on a hill" sermon (see chap. 2). To do this, the empire would cultivate the "homogeneous public sentiment" that its architects understood to be necessary for a great and godly society. In its softer forms, this effort meant bringing the fruits of civilization to people in need. In its harder-edged forms, it meant that anyone who deviated from the norms of civilization must be assimilated, subjugated, or exterminated.

The Benevolent Empire

Though the term "Benevolent Empire" was not applied to early nineteenth-century reform organizations until the 1930s, it aptly describes those organizations' motivations in terms that their founders would have understood. "Benevolent" meant then, as now, charitable and reflecting goodwill, but it also carried a special meaning derived from the theology of Samuel Hopkins (1721–1803), student of Jonathan Edwards and pastor of Sarah Osborn. Hopkins defined true Christian virtue as "disinterested benevolence," a desire to do good to all people without any regard for the self. At its extremity, the doctrine could be expressed as willingness to be "damned for the glory of God." More practically, it meant that no sacrifice was too great for a holy cause, and sacrifice for strangers was godlier than doing favors for friends. "When wired to the dynamite of revival," wrote historian David Kling, this belief "set off an explosion of vast human energy, both at home and abroad."[8]

8. David W. Kling, "The New Divinity and the Origins of the American Board of Commissioners for Foreign Missions," in *North American Foreign Missions, 1810–1914: Theology, Theory, and Policy*, ed. Wilbert R. Shenk (Grand Rapids: Eerdmans, 2004), 24.

The word "empire" encompassed a more complex set of meanings, because Americans in the early republic both loved and hated the idea. Americans had fought the Revolutionary War to sever themselves from the British Empire, and then they fought the War of 1812 to defend their fledgling independence. In light of this history, the word "empire" smacked of tyranny and foreign domination. At the same time, though, Americans envied the global reach of the British Empire and sought to emulate it, on a smaller scale, by pursuing a "manifest destiny" to extend the United States from the Atlantic to the Pacific Coast. American Protestants also admired the organizational capabilities of their British brethren and frequently copied British models as they founded their own charitable societies.

Combined, then, the terms "benevolent" and "empire" communicated a selfless attempt to do good to others that was, simultaneously, an attempt to bring others under control. The inherent contradictions of such efforts can be seen in an examination of three major areas of reform: religious publishing, antislavery activism, and temperance crusades.

Key Benevolent Empire Institutions (by founding year)

1806 American Board of Commissioners for Foreign Missions

1816 American Bible Society

1816 American Colonization Society

1824 American Sunday School Union

1825 American Tract Society

1826 American Home Missionary Society

1826 American Temperance Society

1833 American Anti-Slavery Society

1851 American and Foreign Sabbath Union

Religious Publishing

The American Bible Society (ABS) would not seem to be a likely source of controversy. Like the British and Foreign Bible Society, on which it was patterned, the organization specified that it would produce Scriptures "without note or comment"—just a standard English translation of the Bible, devoid of interpretative gloss that would privilege any denomination's theology. Lyman Beecher and Peter Cartwright, who differed in so many ways, commonly praised the work of the ABS. Beecher helped found the group and served as one of its secretaries. Cartwright noted the founding in his autobiography and claimed, "Nothing

The six-story Bible House in New York City served as the headquarters of the American Bible Society from 1853 to 1956.

but the principles of the Bible can save our happy nation or the world, and every friend of religion ought to spread the Bible to the utmost of his power and means."[9]

The ABS's Bible was, however, not a universally Christian book but instead a specifically Protestant one. It took the King James Version for its text rather than the Douay-Rheims translation favored by Roman Catholics. Furthermore, *sola scriptura*—"Scripture alone"— had been a rallying cry of Protestants since Martin Luther, contrasted with the Roman Catholic belief that Scripture must be read in the context of the church's historic wisdom about its meaning. Consequently, as stated in *The Catholic Encyclopedia* (1907), "The attitude of the [Catholic] Church toward the Bible societies is one of unmistakable opposition. Believing herself to be the divinely appointed custodian and interpreter of Holy Writ, she cannot without turning traitor to herself, approve the distribution of Scripture 'without note or comment.'"[10]

The conflict over ABS Bibles became most acute in the realm of education. In 1839, the ABS made it a priority to place Scriptures not only in every American household but also in every American classroom. "Education without religion, is education without virtue," warned Protestant theologian Horace Bushnell.[11] Catholic leaders agreed with this sentiment, but they disagreed about the use of ABS Bibles as a means of promoting religion and virtue. In 1843, Archbishop Francis Patrick Kenrick of Philadelphia asked the local school board to allow Catholic children to read a Catholic version of the Bible in school instead. His petition was granted, but many area citizens interpreted Kenrick's action as an attack on the Bible itself rather than a request for accommodation of religious diversity. A riot ensued, in which two Catholic churches were burned and thirteen people died.

Despite this opposition, Protestants continued to advance their style of Bible reading as a common good. In response to a different conflict over religion in

9. Cartwright, *Autobiography of Peter Cartwright*, 179.

10. James M. Gillis, "Bible Societies," in *The Catholic Encyclopedia*, vol. 2 (New York: Robert Appleton, 1907), 545.

11. Horace Bushnell, "Extracts from an Unpublished Discourse: Christianity and Common Schools," *Connecticut Common School Journal* 2, no. 7 (January 15, 1840): 102.

schools in Philadelphia, one that was ultimately decided by the US Supreme Court, Justice Joseph Story wrote in 1844, "Why may not the Bible, and especially the New Testament, without note or comment, be read and taught as a divine revelation in the [school]—its general precepts expounded, its evidences explained, and its glorious principles of morality inculcated? . . . Where are benevolence, the love of truth, sobriety, and industry, so powerfully and irresistibly inculcated as in the sacred volume?"[12] Many, many Americans concurred. By the 1860s, the ABS was regularly printing more than one million Bibles each year.[13]

The ABS pioneered developments in printing technology and distribution that spurred the growth of related religious publishing endeavors. The American Sunday School Union launched in Philadelphia in 1824 to foster Christian education, especially for poor children who lacked access to public schools, and to "publish and circulate moral and religious publications" for young readers. The next year, a merger of regional societies formed the American Tract Society, headquartered, like the ABS, in New York. This interdenominational, Protestant group aimed, in the words of its constitution, to "diffuse a knowledge of our Lord Jesus Christ as the Redeemer of sinners, and to promote the interests of vital godliness and sound morality."[14] Steam presses, traveling sales agents, and a network of affiliate societies all helped these organizations distribute religious literature on a massive scale. By 1850, the American Tract Society was producing five million tracts per year.

Religious publishing aided the westward push of the Benevolent Empire through the work of men like John Mason Peck. In 1817, Peck and a colleague formed the Western Baptist Mission Society in St. Louis, declaring, "We agree that our sole object on earth is to promote the religion of Christ in the western parts of America, both among the whites, Africans, and Native Americans; and that the means to be employed are, the preaching of the gospel, distributing the holy scriptures, religious tracts, &c. and establishing and promoting schools for the instruction of the youth."[15] Religious institutions were scarce in the Mississippi Valley, and Peck's support from the Baptists back East was a meager five dollars a week in 1822, so he also became an agent for the ABS and the American Tract Society. Devoted to print, he published *A Gazetteer of Illinois and Emigrant's Guide* to boost the state's population, as well as a Baptist paper,

12. *Vidal v. Girard's Executors*, 43 U.S. 127 (1844), https://supreme.justia.com/cases/federal/us/43/127/.

13. Paul C. Gutjahr, *An American Bible: A History of the Good Book in the United States, 1777–1880* (Stanford, CA: Stanford University Press, 1999), 35.

14. American Tract Society, https://curiosmith.com/pages/american-tract-society.

15. J. M. Peck and J. E. Welch, in the Baptist Board of Foreign Missions for the United States, "Mission to the Westward of the Mississippi River," *Latter Day Luminary* 1, no. 3 (May 1818): 150.

The Pioneer, to edify settlers once they arrived. In hopes of writing a definitive book on "Moral Progress of the Great Central Valley of the Western World," he collected thousands of records, but his library was lost in a fire in 1852, and his book remained unwritten.[16]

The flood of Bibles and other religious texts distributed in the antebellum period undoubtedly influenced American sensibilities. Nineteenth-century letters attest to a very high level of biblical literacy. But the work of the ABS also, quite unintentionally, undermined the pious Scripture reading that its founders sought to promote. As recounted by Paul C. Gutjahr in his book *An American Bible*, no other publishers could compete with the ABS on cost, so they packaged their more expensive Bibles with elaborate bindings and illustrations. Some of these fancy Bibles became family heirlooms, revered rather than read. Meanwhile, some purchasers of these Bibles looked at the pictures for entertainment instead of reading the text.

An effort by ABS board members to correct and standardize the King James text provoked another crisis. The revised text issued in 1851 featured only minor changes, but critics denounced them as an attack on God's holy word, forcing the ABS to revert to the older version in 1858. Seeds of doubt about the reliability of the text had been sown, though, and they were watered by advances in scholarship on ancient languages and literature in the later decades of the nineteenth century. The first real challenger to the King James, the Revised Version, appeared in 1881 and 1885 installments (New and Old Testaments), but by then Americans had already created or edited more than thirty new versions of the Bible. More radical revisions, such as Elizabeth Cady Stanton's 1895/98 *Woman's Bible*, were yet to come. The King James might have been a flawed text, but for nearly 250 years it unequivocally told English-speaking Protestants what the Bible said. As translations proliferated, readers could never again be quite so sure.

Antislavery Activism

The same year that the ABS was founded, a different group of well-connected men met in Washington, DC, to consider the plight of Black Americans. As recounted in chapter 5, most Black Americans were still enslaved in 1816, but the free Black population was growing as a result of escapes, individual emancipation, and the phasing out of slavery in Northern states. Free Blacks faced new challenges: violence, political disfranchisement, poverty, lack of

---

16. Matthew Lawrence, "John Mason Peck: A Biographical Sketch" (MA thesis, University of Illinois, 1914).

education and jobs, and the constant threat of re-enslavement. Moreover, even white Americans who opposed slavery shuddered at the idea of living as equal neighbors with Black citizens. The Washington gathering determined that the best way to alleviate white discomfort in a multiracial republic was to send the free Blacks to Africa. This became the mission of the American Colonization Society (ACS).

Colonization attracted a variety of supporters for a variety of reasons. One of the first proponents of the effort was Paul Cuffe, a Quaker shipping magnate of African American and Wampanoag heritage. He wanted to see the failing British colony of Sierra Leone become a haven of freedom and industry for Blacks, but neither the economics nor the politics of this idea panned out. Cuffe consulted with the founders of the ACS but withheld his own support because of the racism of members such as Henry Clay, a Kentucky politician who favored any halfway measures that would protect the institution of slavery. (Clay helped formulate the Missouri Compromise and, thirty years later, the Compromise of 1850.) Presbyterian minister and educator Rev. Robert Finley believed that a return to the "land of their fathers" would offer free Blacks an improvement on their "degraded situation" in the United States.[17] Missionary Samuel J. Mills, who helped organize the ACS, the ABS, and the American Board of Commissioners for Foreign Missions, saw colonization as part of a broad strategy of shining gospel light in every corner of the world. Scholar Ibram Kendi notes that, by 1832, legislators in every Northern state had passed resolutions endorsing colonization.[18]

With assistance from the US government, the ACS helped some twelve thousand African Americans settle in a new colony, Liberia. This "Land of the Free" declared its independence in 1847 (though the United States did not recognize the declaration until 1862), becoming the second-oldest Black republic in the world, after Haiti. But most Black Americans saw colonization as an attempt by white Americans to "purify" their own society of an undesirable element. Excerpts from an 1820 petition from the ACS to the US Congress illustrated this unsubtle racism:

> The last census shows the number of free people of color of the United States, and their rapid increase. Supposing them to increase in the same ratio, it will appear how large a proportion of our population will, in the course of even a few years, consist of persons of that description.

17. Memorial and petition of Robert Finley to the New Jersey Legislature, 1817.
18. Ibram X. Kendi, *Stamped from the Beginning: The Definitive History of Racist Ideas in America* (New York: Nation Books, 2016), 154.

No argument is necessary to show that this is very far indeed from constituting an increase of our physical strength; nor can there be a population, in any country, neutral as to its effects upon society. The least observation shews that this description of persons are not, and cannot be, either useful or happy among us; and many considerations, which need not be mentioned, prove, beyond dispute, that it is best, for all the parties interested, that there should be a separation; that those who are now free, and those who may become so hereafter, should be provided with the means of attaining to a state of respectability and happiness, which, it is certain, they have never yet reached, and, therefore, can never be likely to reach, in this country.[19]

Instances of such rhetoric directed at minority groups in American history are too numerous to count. Black Americans, Native Americans, Mexicans, and Irish immigrants bore the brunt of it in the first half of the nineteenth century. The argument in each case was basically the same: "they" are not like "us," and they never will be. Benevolent Empire organizations both consciously and unconsciously reinforced this us-versus-them mentality. When the organizations sought to galvanize supporters for action, they painted a rosy picture of well-meaning "us"; when the organizations emphasized the urgency of action, they painted a gloomy picture of needy "them." Rhetorical choices reinforced racial boundaries.[20]

The racism of the ACS was challenged in its own day by other benevolent organizations. As discussed in chapter 5, Black churches and voluntary societies provided leadership for their communities and a witness to white society. Within the world of majority-white philanthropy, a desire to help Black Americans gain freedom in the United States prompted the 1833 formation of the American Anti-Slavery Society. This group opposed the efforts of the ACS, stating in its founding Declaration of Sentiments, "We regard as delusive, cruel and dangerous, any scheme of expatriation which pretends to aid, either directly or indirectly, in the emancipation of the slaves, or to be a substitute for the immediate and total abolition of slavery."[21] The author of that statement, journalist William Lloyd Garrison, had briefly belonged to the ACS before rejecting its aims with a vengeance.

While the ACS and its founders were largely forgotten by later history, the Anti-Slavery Society and its principals achieved heroic status. Garrison spread

19. *Memorial of the President and Board of Managers of the American Colonization Society* (Washington, DC: Gales & Seaton, 1820), 3.

20. Susan M. Ryan, *The Grammar of Good Intentions: Race and the Antebellum Culture of Benevolence* (Ithaca, NY: Cornell University Press, 2003).

21. William Lloyd Garrison, "Declaration of Sentiments of the American Anti-Slavery Convention," Philadelphia, December 6, 1833, in *Selections from the Writings and Speeches of William Lloyd Garrison* (Boston: R. F. Wallcut, 1852), 69–70.

The masthead of the abolitionist paper *The Liberator* moved visually from a slave market at left to the gateway of emancipation at right, with Christ declaring in the middle, "I come to break the bonds of the oppressor."

the group's message in his newspaper, *The Liberator*, with financial support from society cofounder Arthur Tappan. Frederick Douglass, who had escaped from slavery, electrified the group's meetings with his eloquence. Another Black man who escaped from slavery, William Wells Brown, was not as gifted a speaker as Douglass but made a literary name for himself with an autobiography and the first novel written by an African American, *Clotel* (1853). Theodore Dwight Weld, with his wife, Angelina Grimké, and her sister, Sarah Grimké, produced the devastating 1839 book *American Slavery as It Is: Testimony of a Thousand Witnesses*. The Grimké sisters, along with Anti-Slavery Society members including Susan B. Anthony, Lucretia Mott, and Elizabeth Cady Stanton, went on to become noted advocates for women's rights.

The Anti-Slavery Society's cause was nobler than that of the Colonization Society, but its heroes had flaws too. In response to anti-abolitionist riots in New York in 1834, Tappan circulated a disclaimer stating that the society had no desire "to promote or encourage intermarriages between white and colored persons."[22] Tappan sought to maintain a decorous distance between men and women as well. When women, with Garrison's vocal support, moved into leadership positions in the society and linked women's liberation with the liberation of enslaved people, Tappan left to found a men's-only antislavery society. Garrison, for his part, grew increasingly strident in his attacks on not just slavery but the legal and religious underpinnings of the nation. In 1854, he publicly burned a copy of the Constitution and, separately, told a women's rights convention, "All reforms are anti-Bible."[23] (Garrison meant this as a compliment to reform and a

22. "American Anti-Slavery Society: Disclaimer," *The Times*, August 8, 1834, 2.

23. Elizabeth Cady Stanton, Susan B. Anthony, and Matilda Joslyn Gage, eds., *History of Woman Suffrage*, vol. 1 (Rochester, NY: Charles Mann, 1889), 383.

Change Comes Slowly

In this 1838 letter, abolitionist and author Lydia Maria Child cast social reform as a long process marked by false starts and opposition. She encouraged a friend to keep up the good work.

> When I remember what a remarkable testimony the early Friends [Quakers] bore (a testimony which seems to me more and more miraculous, the more I compare it with the spirit of the age in which they lived), I could almost find it in my heart to weep at the too palpable proofs that little now remains of that which was full of life. I was saying this, last winter, to George Ripley, a Unitarian minister of Boston. He replied beautifully, "Mourn not over their lifelessness. Truly the dead form alone remains; but the *spirit* that emanated from it is not dead, the *word* which they spake has gone out silently into everlasting time. What are these Temperance, and Peace, and Anti-Slavery Conventions, but a resuscitation of their principles? To me it is a beautiful illustration of the doctrine of the resurrection, when I thus see the spirit leaving the dead form and embodying itself anew."
>
> I feel for your trials, for I know by similar experience that at times they *will* press heavily on the overtaxed and discouraged soul. But we know what awaits those "who endure unto the end." I cannot say I pity you; for is it not a glorious privilege thus to struggle with the errors and sins of the time? Be not discouraged because the sphere of action seems narrow, and the influence limited; for every word and act that a human being sends forth lives forever. It is a spiritual seed cast into the wide field of opinion. Its results are too infinite for human calculation. It will appear and reappear through all time, always influencing the destiny of the human race for good or for evil.

> Lydia Maria Child to E. Carpenter, September 6, 1838, in *Letters of Lydia Maria Child* (Boston: Houghton, Mifflin, 1883), 22–23.

criticism of the Bible.) By that point, Garrison and Douglass, who had clashed repeatedly over politics and publishing agendas, could not stand each other.

The limits of white advocacy on behalf of Black Americans were evident, at least to many Black Americans. The published proceedings of the National Emigration Convention of Colored People, held in Cleveland, Ohio, in 1854 stated, "We are frequently asked by the impatient white American enquirer: 'What is it you black people want? What would the negro race desire at our hands more than we have done?' Our reply is, that *we ask nothing at your hands,* nor desire anything of *your giving*."[24] Rather than return to Africa or await the end of slavery in the United States, this group recommended that free Blacks emigrate to Canada, because no amount of white benevolence could make the United States a comfortable home any time in the foreseeable future.

Temperance Crusades

The eminent Lyman Beecher did not choose a side between colonization and abolition, declaring activists in both groups to be brethren in "one broad stream of benevolence."[25] He was convinced, however, that alcohol would doom the American empire. "Intemperance is the sin of our land," he preached in 1827, "and, with our boundless prosperity, is coming in upon us like a flood; and if anything shall defeat the hopes of the world, which hang upon our experiment of civil liberty, it is that river of fire, which is rolling through the land, destroying the vital air, and extending around an atmosphere of death."[26] And so, between his work with the American Bible Society and his move to Cincinnati, he cofounded the American Temperance Society (ATS), a national organization dedicated to solving the country's drinking problem.

Alcohol consumption was a genuine concern in the early 1800s. Scholars have estimated that, in 1825, the average American over the age of fifteen drank seven gallons of pure alcohol per year, which would translate into nearly forty gallons of alcohol-containing beverages. By contrast, average intake of alcohol at the beginning of the twenty-first century stood at just over two gallons per American.[27] In other words, Americans in the early republic drank more than three times as much as Americans two hundred years later.

Several factors contributed to the high level of alcohol consumption. One, ironically, was public health. Many Americans lacked access to clean drinking water in the early nineteenth century, so it was actually safer for them to drink alcoholic beverages with natural antiseptic properties. A second factor was economic. Whiskey, the most-consumed spirit in the early republic, efficiently turned the abundant grain grown on the frontier into a profitable, transportable product.

24. Cited in Ryan, *Grammar of Good Intentions*, 172.

25. Lyman Beecher, address to a Cincinnati colonization meeting, *African Repository and Colonial Journal* 10, no. 9 (November 1834): 280. The address originally was printed in the *Cincinnati Journal*.

26. Lyman Beecher, "The Nature and Occasions of Intemperance," in *Six Sermons on the Nature, Occasions, Signs, Evils, and Remedy of Intemperance*, 6th ed. (Boston: T. R. Marvin, 1828), 7.

27. Alice W. Campbell, "Temperance Movement," Social Welfare History Project, Virginia Commonwealth University, October 2017, https://socialwelfare.library.vcu.edu/religious/the-temperance-movement/.

TREE of TEMPERANCE
BY A.D. FILLMORE.

Nineteenth-century Tree of Temperance images made the moral, didactic argument that abstaining from alcohol would yield all manner of virtues, both Christian (such as peace, piety, and faith) and secular (such as industry, frugality, and patriotism).

Third, alcohol fueled social life. No wedding, funeral, harvest, political campaign, or even (according to the recollections of one late-nineteenth-century cleric) gathering of ministers was complete without libations.

In the rhetoric of temperance crusaders, though, alcohol consumption plainly reflected immorality. Tales of reformed drunkards became staples at revival meetings, while novels and tracts warned that the road to degradation started with a drink. "Wine is a mocker, strong drink is raging, and whosoever is deceived thereby is not wise," proclaimed a nineteenth-century Family Temperance Pledge, quoting Proverbs 20:1. The pledge also admonished, "Temperance leads to virtue and happiness. Intemperance leads to poverty and ruin."

"Temperance" was a bit of a misnomer for this movement. The word means "moderation" or "self-restraint," but the American Temperance Society promoted total abstinence from "ardent spirits."[28] Initially, the ATS spread its message through local chapters that urged people to take a no-drinking pledge. Within three years of its founding, the ATS boasted more than a thousand of these chapters, and some one hundred thousand people had signed the pledge. But voluntary abstinence could go only so far to combat the scourge of drunkenness. In the 1830s and 1840s, temperance groups sought legislation to prohibit or severely limit the sale of alcohol. If citizens would not restrain themselves from drinking, then the government would do it for them.

After an effort to outlaw most alcohol sales in the entire state of Massachusetts provoked a strong backlash, the temperance movement shifted its strategy to "local option" elections, in which the residents of a city or county could vote to go "dry." This strategy tied temperance to the exercise of democracy in an era when white Americans exulted in the right of self-determination,

28. See the virtual exhibit at https://www.librarycompany.org/ArdentSpirits/index.htm.

inspired by the common-man politics of President Andrew Jackson. Conceptually, then, the local option meant that Americans were not being forced to abstain from alcohol; they were being allowed to choose abstinence for their communities.

Not everyone affirmed this logic or the push to curb drinking. Locations that opted to go dry were clustered in the Northeast and upper Midwest, and the move appealed more to residents of small towns than to residents of large cities. Southern drinking cultures proved resistant to temperance, as did the drinking cultures of recent European immigrants—particularly Catholics, who felt (and were) targeted by Protestant reformers. Meanwhile, brewers and tavern owners formed trade groups to lobby for their business interests.

Local option campaigns also had a curious effect on women. Many women were stalwart temperance advocates, because women were viewed in the nineteenth century as moral guardians and also because women were likely to suffer from poverty and abuse if the men in their lives drank heavily. But women did not yet have the right to vote. Women who had been content to stay out of the grubby, masculine world of politics grew frustrated when they saw that ballots could be used to foster social virtue. Temperance crusades thus became, for many women, a political awakening, opening their eyes to moral work that could be accomplished outside women's designated "spheres" of home and church.

In 1874, politically activated women formed the Woman's Christian Temperance Union (WCTU), which became the largest women's organization in the country. Frances Willard, WCTU president from 1879 to her death in 1898, adopted the motto "Do Everything" to engage members in campaigns not only to combat drunkenness but also to cut tobacco use, fund schools and school lunches, end lynching, improve working conditions and sanitation, protect victims of rape, and stop child abuse. A push for women's right to vote linked all of these concerns, because without that leverage women could not compel legislators to pass what they viewed as socially redemptive laws. Of course, when the WCTU got what it wanted—the Eighteenth Amendment, which began Prohibition in 1920—social redemption was not exactly what followed, as drinking lessened but crime spiked. The Nineteenth Amendment, another Willard goal, was ratified later the same year, granting women the right to vote. The Nineteenth Amendment caused far fewer problems than the Eighteenth but also failed to initiate the transformation of politics for which suffrage supporters had hoped. Not that many women voted, initially, and those who did typically voted for the same candidates their husbands chose.

"For God and Home and Native Land"

This popular 1880s temperance song, written by Mrs. E. P. Moffitt of the Illinois WCTU, echoed the aim of godly nation-building expressed by older Benevolent Empire societies.

> We are coming in our might, To boldly battle for the Right,
> Against King Alcohol and band;
> Our flag we'll ne'er forsake, But our stand we'll bravely take,
> For God and Home and Native Land.
>
> [*refrain*] Old King Alcohol, We'll let you surely know
> We're coming with our ballots white as snow;
> You cannot flourish long in a cause so sadly wrong,
> For we're coming, coming, thirty million strong.
>
> For the offices of state, Our boys and girls we'll educate,
> Then all our homes we shall protect;
> Then sober men and true, Who will put our measures through,
> To ev'ry office we'll elect. [*refrain*]
>
> Then will be no bleeding hearts, Caused by Rum's destroying darts,
> When come these glorious temperance days;
> Oh, speed the happy time, In ev'ry land and clime,
> And we to God will give the praise! [*refrain*]

> Library of Congress, Music Division, https://www.loc.gov
> /item/sm1880.19870/.

Creativity or Control?

It is possible to understand the early nineteenth century as a period marked by religious ferment and experimentation, with new enthusiasms taking a wide range of forms.[29] Jacksonian democracy brought poor white men into the political process, while benevolent societies gave disfranchised Black Americans and women a taste of empowerment. Upstart revivalistic denominations, most notably Baptists and Methodists, moved nimbly on the frontier, rapidly overtaking the main colonial churches (Presbyterian, Congregational, and Episcopalian) in membership. New churches, such as the Disciples of Christ and Millerites

---

29. This is essentially Nathan O. Hatch's argument in his widely cited book *The Democratization of American Christianity* (New Haven: Yale University Press, 1989).

(ancestors of Seventh-day Adventists), formed, as did new religious movements, none more successful than the Church of Jesus Christ of Latter-day Saints, or Mormons. Men, and a few women, without formal credentials could be preachers, organizers, or founders of churches and colleges. Geographic mobility fostered social mobility, as a washed-out farmer or busted merchant could pull up stakes and reinvent himself farther west.

It is also possible to understand the early nineteenth century as a period during which religious and cultural elites, fearing both the wild frontier and growing demands for equality, turned the screws of social control. In his wryly titled book *A Shopkeeper's Millennium*, historian Paul E. Johnson argued, "The temperance, moral reform, and missionary societies of the 1820s had been organizations of gentlemen who wished to slow the course of social and political change and reinforce their domination over a hopelessly godless multitude."[30] In Johnson's estimation, the somewhat less genteel evangelicals who became leaders in these organizations from the 1830s onward continued the project of social control, only with more overtly religious goals and coarser methods: "Through individual conversion and public example, and increasingly through mass politics and outright coercion, they promised to eliminate sin from society and pave the way for the Second Coming."[31] Religion constrained rather than empowered, Johnson claimed, as "reformers" pushed whatever message seemed likely to keep their factory workers docile and sober.

Historians can debate these divergent readings of the period because evidence exists for both. The Benevolent Empire was benevolent; illiteracy, slavery, and alcoholism caused real suffering, which Christians could not in good conscience ignore. Benevolent organizations improved the lives of prisoners, orphans, and persons with disabilities and mental illnesses. Yet, the Benevolent Empire was also imperialistic, imposing some Americans' solutions on other Americans' problems. It is easy to understand why an exasperated nineteenth-century New York shirtmaker resisted another woman, renowned in the educational world, who was lecturing workers about good behavior. The shirtmaker retorted, "What rights have you that we haven't got? You are better dressed, have more learning and more money than we have. But these things give you no more right to come down here and tell us what we shall wear, and how we shall spend our money, than we have to go uptown and tell you how you shall spend your money and what you shall put on."[32] Bundling Protestant Christianity and

---

30. Paul E. Johnson, *A Shopkeeper's Millennium: Society and Revivals in Rochester, New York, 1815–1837* (New York: Hill & Wang, 1978), 5–6.

31. Johnson, *Shopkeeper's Millennium*, 6.

32. Mary Gay Humphreys, "The New York Working-Girl," *Scribner's Magazine* 20, no. 4 (October 1896): 505.

middle-class morality helped spread these interlocking ideas, but it provoked resistance to the package as well. Some Americans just wanted to be heard and respected, not lectured on respectability.

———————▼———————

The American Sunday School Union published many tales of pious children who died young. Their stories were meant to be inspiring as well as comforting to parents who lost children, and to children who lost siblings or friends—a nearly universal experience in the early nineteenth century. One poem, however, "For a Very Little Child in Sickness," in the collection *Hymns for Infant Minds*, held out hope that a child's prayer for healing might be answered.

> Almighty God, I'm very ill,
> But cure me, if it be thy will;
> For thou canst take away my pain,
> And make me strong and well again.
>
> Let me be patient every day,
> And mind what those who nurse me say;
> And grant that all I have to take
> May do me good, for Jesus' sake.[33]

FURTHER READING

Abzug, Robert H. *Cosmos Crumbling: American Reform and the Religious Imagination.* New York: Oxford University Press, 1994.

Conroy-Krutz, Emily. *Christian Imperialism: Converting the World in the Early American Republic.* Ithaca, NY: Cornell University Press, 2015.

Fea, John. *The Bible Cause: A History of the American Bible Society.* New York: Oxford University Press, 2016.

Graham, Stephen R. *Cosmos in the Chaos: Philip Schaff's Interpretation of Nineteenth-Century American Religion.* Grand Rapids: Eerdmans, 1995.

Gutjahr, Paul C. *An American Bible: A History of the Good Book in the United States, 1777–1880.* Stanford, CA: Stanford University Press, 1999.

Hewitt, Nancy A. *Women's Activism and Social Change: Rochester, New York, 1822–1872.* Ithaca, NY: Cornell University Press, 1984.

McCarthy, Kathleen D. *American Creed: Philanthropy and the Rise of Civil Society, 1700–1865.* Chicago: University of Chicago Press, 2005.

33. Ann Taylor, *Hymns for Infant Minds* (Philadelphia: American Sunday School Union, 1828), 53.

Ryan, Susan M. *The Grammar of Good Intentions: Race and the Antebellum Culture of Benevolence*. Ithaca, NY: Cornell University Press, 2003.

Thuesen, Peter J. *In Discordance with the Scriptures: American Protestant Battles over Translating the Bible*. New York: Oxford University Press, 1999.

Tyrrell, Ian. *Woman's World/Woman's Empire: The Woman's Christian Temperance Union in International Perspective, 1880–1930*. Chapel Hill: University of North Carolina Press, 2010.

Volk, Kyle G. *Moral Minorities and the Making of American Democracy*. New York: Oxford University Press, 2014.

8

Houses Divided

Methodist Church Splits over Slavery, 1844

Long before slavery fractured the Methodist Church in the United States, church leaders found small ways to communicate their position on the increasingly fraught topic. One skirmish concerned the hymn "O'er the Gloomy Hills of Darkness." The author, Welsh hymnist William Williams Pantycelyn, penned the lyrics in 1772 with an eye toward raising enthusiasm for missionary activity. The second verse bothered American enslavers, though, so they changed the words. As abolitionist Ebenezer Davies asserted in his book *American Scenes and Christian Slavery* (1849), "Slave-holders, and the abettors of that horrid system which makes it a crime to teach a negro to read the Word of God, felt perhaps that they could not devoutly and consistently sing 'Let the Indian, let the negro,' &c." Later hymnals dropped the verse, and the entire song fell out of favor with hymnal editors in the 1960s, as Christians grew uncomfortable with its rhetoric of colonization. Here are the first two verses of the 1772 text, adapted for readability.

> O'er the gloomy Hills of Darkness
> Look my Soul, be still and gaze,
> All the Promises do travel
> On a glorious Day of Grace,
> Blessed Jubilee,
> Let thy glorious Morning dawn.

> Let the Indian, let the Negro,[1]
> Let the rude Barbarian see
> That divine and glorious Conquest
> Once obtain'd on Calvary;
> Let the Gospel
> Word resound from Pole to Pole.[2]

As with every church conflict, there was an issue at hand and an issue at large. The issue at hand concerned James Osgood Andrew, a bishop in the Methodist Episcopal Church. Andrew was well-liked and pedigreed, son of the first Georgia native to minister as a Methodist. He had been licensed to preach in 1812 and had worked his way up through the church hierarchy to election as bishop over a Georgia district in 1832. He was also the first president of the board of trustees of Emory College, which evolved into Emory University. But Andrew owned slaves. This fact should have been a problem long before 1844, but that was the year matters finally came to a head.

The founder of Methodism, John Wesley, adamantly opposed slavery. He inscribed his opposition in the General Rules for the church in 1743, which forbade the buying or selling of human beings. In the 1774 tract *Thoughts upon Slavery*, after expounding the horrors of the slave trade, he wrote, "Where is the justice of inflicting the severest evils, on those who have done us no wrong? Of depriving those that never injured us in word or deed, of every comfort of life? Of tearing them from their native country, and depriving them of liberty itself?"[3] Anticipating his readers' protestations that slavery was both legal and necessary for building up wealth in the British Empire, he replied, "I deny that villany [sic] is ever necessary. It is impossible that it should ever be necessary, for any reasonable creature to violate all the laws of justice, mercy, and truth."[4] When Methodism was formally established in the United States as a denomination separate from Anglicanism in 1784, its preachers were not permitted to own slaves, and any slave-owning laypeople were supposed to be denied Communion and expelled from fellowship. In Maryland, the Southern state initially most receptive to Methodist preaching, more than eighteen hundred enslaved persons were freed in predominantly Methodist areas between 1783 and 1799.[5]

---

1. Many, though not all, American hymnals substituted for this line, "Let the dark benighted pagan."

2. Daniel Protheroe, ed., *Cân a Mawl, Song and Praise: The Hymnal of the Calvinistic Methodist Church of the United States of America* (Chicago: The General Assembly, 1918), no. 164.

3. John Wesley, "Thoughts upon Slavery," in *A Collection of Religious Tracts* (Philadelphia: Joseph Crukshank, 1774), 34.

4. Wesley, "Thoughts upon Slavery," 38.

5. Donald G. Mathews, *Slavery and Methodism: A Chapter in American Morality, 1780–1845* (Princeton: Princeton University Press, 1965), 18.

The Methodists' antislavery policy, among the boldest in the United States at the time, lasted about six months. Amid vociferous opposition from clergy and laity in Virginia and North Carolina, where more than half of all American Methodists lived, the church repealed its strict rules in 1785 while still vowing to combat slavery "by all wise and prudent means."[6] What this meant in practice was that some Methodists persisted in writing and preaching against slavery, while others kept slaves, allowed their parishioners to keep slaves, and started making the arguments that Wesley knew they would: slavery was permitted by law, emancipating enslaved persons was in some places *not* permitted by law, and it would be unreasonable to force enslavers to surrender their greatest assets. White Southerners would not convert to Methodism at that price.

In this way, an issue that some people within the church deemed crystal clear and morally imperative struck others as divisive, distracting, a threat to evangelism and church growth. Historian Donald G. Mathews observed, "The Methodist clergy would have to make the choice between purity and popularity."[7] Although both positions had forceful adherents, the popularity side drew the antislavery purists deeper and deeper into compromise in the early decades of the nineteenth century. The United States as a whole followed a similar path, with the "Three-Fifths Compromise" in the Constitution (1787), the Missouri Compromise (1820), and the Congressional "gag rule" forestalling any discussion of antislavery legislation (1836–44), all serving to entrench slavery and extend its reach across the expanding nation.

Defections from Methodism shifted the balance within the church and ultimately pushed it off the fence of indecision. As recounted in chapter 5, some free Black Methodists in the North, unwilling to accept segregation in the sanctuary, broke off to form the African Methodist Episcopal Church in 1816. Another Black denomination formed five years later, the African Methodist Episcopal Zion Church. These departures had minimal impact on the white church because Black ministers had never been allowed much of a voice in denominational proceedings anyway. By 1840, as recounted by historian Frederick A. Norwood, internal Methodist politics were dominated by "the power of the South, aided by

6. Abel Stevens, *A Compendious History of American Methodism* (New York: Carlton & Porter, 1867), 263.

7. Mathews, *Slavery and Methodism*, 18. The Three-Fifths Compromise counted enslaved persons as three-fifths of a person for the purpose of Congressional representation. States with large enslaved populations got to send more members to the House of Representatives this way, even though the enslaved persons could not vote. The Missouri Compromise admitted Missouri to the Union as a slave state and Maine as a free state, maintaining parity in the number of senators representing slave and free states. It also drew a line across the western territories, prohibiting slavery north of the line and permitting it south of the line.

those who wished to prevent schism at all costs."[8] Exasperated white antislavery Methodists, led by Orange Scott and La Roy Sunderland, withdrew to form their own church body, the Wesleyan Methodist Connection, in 1843. Because it involved several thousand church members and was led by men who had been prominent in the Methodist hierarchy, this defection actually strengthened antislavery arguments within the church. Church leaders had worried primarily about losing support among enslavers, but the Wesleyan Methodist schism demonstrated that capitulation on slavery could drive away antislavery Methodists instead. Compromise had limits, and a choice had to be made.

Against this backdrop, the case of Bishop Andrew came before the Methodist governing body, the General Conference, in 1844. Andrew had not owned enslaved persons when he was elected bishop in 1832, but by 1844 he had acquired about a dozen. All but one of them came into his possession when he married a woman who already counted them among her property. In the version of his story recounted in most published histories, and in interpretations given by later tour guides at his homesite in Oxford, Georgia, Andrew was an "accidental slaveowner" who had not, intentionally, violated John Wesley's prohibitions on buying or selling human beings. He had, rather, conducted himself as well as a Southern white man of his era could have, and his life became controversial only when the Northern abolitionists attacked him.

The different version of the story, although not a major factor in the General Conference debate, presents him much less favorably. Andrew claimed, in an 1844 letter to his fellow Methodist bishops, that around 1836 a female parishioner had bequeathed to him a young mulatto girl, Kitty, with the stipulation that she would be freed and sent to Liberia when she turned nineteen. But the state of Georgia would not permit him to free her, Andrew wrote, and at any rate, she preferred to stay with him, for he treated her as well as a member of the family. When anthropologist Mark Auslander investigated this history at length, he could find no evidence of the "Mrs. Powers" who had allegedly bequeathed Kitty to Andrew, nor was it plausible that Kitty freely chose to stay with the bishop's family because she was happy in their service. Rather, what evidence Auslander could find suggested that Kitty, like so many beautiful, mixed-race enslaved women, had been coerced into a sexual relationship with Andrew, and the minister did not want to be parted from her, even though both he and she married other people. The Black community in Oxford had always told this version of the story, while white residents preferred a "myth of Kitty" that cast race relations, past and present, as harmonious and proper. Bishop Andrew had potent reasons to tell the myth rather than the truth, and his white

8. Frederick A. Norwood, *The Story of American Methodism* (Nashville: Abingdon, 1974), 194.

peers had potent reasons to believe him.[9]

The 1844 General Conference confined itself to a narrower question: Could Andrew, an enslaver, continue to serve as a bishop in the Methodist Episcopal Church? By a vote of 110 to 69, the answer was no, Andrew could be an enslaver or a bishop, but not both. Southern church leaders who had voted in the minority immediately protested, and a week later they issued a "Plan of Separation" outlining a procedure to split the church along sectional lines. The pro-slavery faction blamed the schism on the anti-

Whether James Osgood Andrew could be both an enslaver and a Methodist bishop was the question that split his denomination.

slavery Northerners, who were, in their view, sinfully unwilling to compromise. Thus the logic of secession took root in the country's largest, most geographically dispersed Protestant denomination. Baptists split in much the same way in 1845, followed by Presbyterians in 1858. Specific issues related to doctrine and polity affected how these splits occurred, but in each case the why—slavery—mattered more than the who or the how. Calvinist or Arminian in theology, episcopal or congregational or presbyterian in governance, these churches faced the same impasse and were equally unable to navigate it.

There are at least three ways in which these slavery schisms acted as turning points in American church history. Denominational histories emphasize the institutional effects, which were significant and long-lasting. Northern and Southern Methodists, Baptists, and Presbyterians developed competing hierarchies, missionary efforts, and networks of conferences, colleges, and publishing houses. This vast bureaucracy constituted one reason why the churches took decades to reunify—or, in the case of the Baptists, never did—but the institutional details are mostly of interest to denominational insiders and therefore will not be discussed here. This chapter will instead focus on two other areas in which the slavery-related church splits played a major role: American politics and biblical interpretation. The ruptures of the mid-nineteenth century permanently disfigured both the nation and Protestant theology.

9. Mark Auslander, *The Accidental Slaveowner: Revisiting a Myth of Race and Finding an American Family* (Athens: University of Georgia Press, 2011).

From Ecclesial Conflict to Civil War

Many Americans in the 1840s and 1850s anticipated that church splits would exacerbate political division. Kentucky senator Henry Clay, for example, was nicknamed the "Great Compromiser" for his brokering of numerous deals to postpone a showdown over slavery. His efforts culminated in the Compromise of 1850, which admitted California to the Union as a free state, remapped the territory that had been ceded to the United States after the Mexican-American War, and ordered residents of free states to return "fugitive" slaves to their masters. (Even though slavery was concentrated in the Southeast, its impact stretched from coast to coast.) Near the end of his life in 1852, Clay feared that the spirit of conflict erupting in the nation's churches would spoil all his deal-making. In an interview with the editor of the *Presbyterian Herald*, he said, "I tell you this sundering of religious ties which have hitherto bound our people together, I consider the greatest source of danger to our country. If our religious men cannot live together in peace, what can be expected of our politicians, very few of whom profess to be governed by the great principles of love?"[10] Leading secessionist thinker John Calhoun of South Carolina agreed that if the denominational ties linking Americans across sectional lines snapped, "nothing will be left to hold the States together except force."[11]

It is doubtful that unified Protestant denominations could have prevented the Civil War, because political and economic factors had set the slaveholding and free states on a collision course. By 1860, slavery had already been abolished in nineteen states and most of the Western Hemisphere, leaving enslavers in the remaining fifteen slave states defiant and defensive. They were unwilling to give up the four million bodies they owned, which Abraham Lincoln estimated to be worth $2 billion altogether.[12] The two billion pounds of cotton these enslaved persons produced annually represented 60 percent of all American exports and brought in nearly $200 million dollars per year.[13] There was no viable path for slavery merely to wither away, or for Northerners fired up by abolitionist activism to drop their crusade against it. No amount of sermonizing could make slavery more palatable or less profitable. Bonds of Christian fellowship were not stronger than the bonds of slavery.

10. Quoted in C. C. Goen, *Broken Churches, Broken Nation: Denominational Schisms and the Coming of the Civil War* (Macon, GA: Mercer University Press, 1985), 106.
11. John C. Calhoun, "Speech on the Slavery Question," March 4, 1850, in Goen, *Broken Churches, Broken Nation*, 105.
12. Abraham Lincoln, speech given at Hartford, Connecticut, March 5, 1860. A transcript of this speech is available at https://founding.com/founders-library/american-political-figures/abraham-lincoln/speech-at-new-haven-connecticut-march-6-1860-2/.
13. On the importance of cotton in the American economy, see Sven Beckert, *Empire of Cotton: A Global History* (New York: Vintage Books, 2015).

While unified churches might have postponed or ameliorated the conflict that exploded in the Civil War, divided churches undoubtedly made it worse, removing any motive or mechanism for preserving vestiges of goodwill. As Southern states moved toward secession, President James Buchanan called for a national day of fasting, humiliation, and prayer, a type of observance that had been used by civil authorities since early English colonization to bring people together to pray for divine favor. Some preachers did exhort their flocks to remain calm on that day, January 4, 1861, though rarely without making their preference for the Union or the Confederacy known. Others fired their rhetorical cannons. In Coldwater, Michigan, Presbyterian minister Horace C. Hovey complained about Buchanan's conciliatory request: "We see an imbecile old man wringing his hands, in the halls of the White House, instead of a hero, wielding his sword on the plains of South Carolina, where traitors are preparing the munitions of war." Hovey refused to "assume a timid air, and cower behind a 'wholesome dread of preaching politics,'" claiming instead that the trumpet of the Lord was at his lips.[14] Meanwhile, at St. Peter's Church in Baltimore, Episcopal minister George D. Cummins assured his congregation that slavery was a God-ordained, generally well-run institution, and "there is power enough in the Christianity of the South to grapple with and solve all the difficulties of this great question, if left unhindered by interference from without."[15] His sermon was titled "The African a Trust from God to the American."

Polarized churches during the Civil War functioned somewhat like polarized news outlets in the twenty-first century. The Civil War was a boon to journalism, with new technologies such as the telegraph and photography, along with recently formed wire services such as the Associated Press, carrying more information farther and faster than ever before. Nonetheless, spoken and printed sermons remained a major source of information and, more importantly, interpretation of increasingly alarming developments. On April 12, 1861, Southern forces fired on Fort Sumter in South Carolina, officially beginning the war. Three days later, the recently inaugurated President Abraham Lincoln declared the Southern action an insurrection and called for a militia of seventy-five thousand to stop it. Heavy fighting at the First Battle of Bull Run, in July 1861, dashed hopes for a swift resolution to the conflict, but its toll of 4,700 killed, wounded, or captured would soon seem paltry. In the Second Battle of Bull Run, in August 1862, casualties soared to 21,700 killed, wounded, captured, or missing, twice as many on the Union side as on the Confederate. Americans might read these numbers in their partisan newspapers (the ideal of unbiased news did not arise

14. Rev. Horace C. Hovey, "The National Fast: A Sermon, Preached at Coldwater, Mich., January 4, 1861" (Coldwater, MI: Republican Print, 1861), 3–4.
15. Rev. George D. Cummins, "The African a Trust from God to the American: A Sermon Delivered on the Day National Humiliation, Fasting and Prayer" (Baltimore: John D. Toy, 1861), 26.

Slavery, Religion, and Secession

Excerpts from state declarations of secession demonstrate the centrality of slavery, often described using Christian language, to the Confederacy.

South Carolina (Dec. 20, 1860)

We affirm that these ends for which this [Federal] Government was instituted have been defeated, and the Government itself has been made destructive of them by the action of the non-slaveholding States. Those States have assume [sic] the right of deciding upon the propriety of our domestic institutions; and have denied the rights of property established in fifteen of the States and recognized by the Constitution; they have denounced as sinful the institution of slavery; they have permitted open establishment among them of societies, whose avowed object is to disturb the peace and to eloign the property of the citizens of other States. They have encouraged and assisted thousands of our slaves to leave their homes; and those who remain, have been incited by emissaries, books and pictures to servile insurrection.

Mississippi (Jan. 9, 1861)

Our position is thoroughly identified with the institution of slavery—the greatest material interest of the world. Its labor supplies the product which constitutes by far the largest and most important portions of commerce of the earth. These products are peculiar to the climate verging on the tropical regions, and by an imperious law of nature, none but the black race can bear exposure to the tropical sun. These products have become necessities ▶

until the mid-twentieth century), but they looked to their pastors for help in processing them, and what they heard depended entirely on where their church and its pastor stood. In his sweeping moral history of the war, *Upon the Altar of the Nation*, Harry S. Stout noted that "the clergy were virtually cheerleaders all," less inclined to sober, balanced reflection than to rabid partisanship.[16]

Pastors were not more biased than politicians or the press, but partisanship in churches affected minds, bodies, and souls in unique ways. The preaching of holy war, widespread in both North and South, combined numerous concepts related to divine providence, peoplehood, good and evil, patriarchy, sacrifice, and violence. Once fused into what scholars now call "Christian nationalism,"

16. Harry S. Stout, *Upon the Altar of the Nation: A Moral History of the Civil War* (New York: Viking, 2006), xvii.

of the world, and a blow at slavery is a blow at commerce and civilization. That blow has been long aimed at the institution, and was at the point of reaching its consummation. There was no choice left us but submission to the mandates of abolition, or a dissolution of the Union, whose principles had been subverted to work out our ruin.

Texas (Feb. 1, 1861)

We hold, as undeniable truths, that the governments of the various States, and of the Confederacy itself, were established exclusively by the white race, for themselves and their posterity; that the African race had no agency in their establishment; that they were rightfully held and regarded as an inferior and dependent race, and in that condition only could their existence in this country be rendered beneficial or tolerable.

That, in this free government, *all white men are, and of right ought to be, entitled to equal civil and political rights*; that the servitude of the African race, as existing in these States, is mutually beneficial to both bond and free, and is abundantly authorized and justified by the experience of mankind, and the revealed will of the Almighty Creator, as recognized by all Christian nations; while the destruction of the existing relations between the two races, as advocated by our sectional enemies, would bring inevitable calamities upon both and desolation upon the fifteen slave-holding States.

Full secession statements are available at "The Declaration of Causes of Seceding States," American Battlefield Trust, https://www.battlefields.org/learn/primary-sources/declaration-causes-seceding-states (emphasis original).

these ideas were incredibly difficult to tease apart or examine critically. Singing these ideas in such hymns as "The Battle Hymn of the Republic" and "God Save the South" lodged them even more deeply in memory, while active verbs in the lyrics and the communal act of singing roused bodies to action.

And then there were the funerals. So many funerals. An estimated 620,000 soldiers died between 1861 and 1865, plus an estimated 50,000 civilians killed by bullets, starvation, riots, or disease. The sheer, unprecedented scale of death—peaking at more than 3,600 killed in one day at Antietam—meant that many soldiers were not given full burial rites, though they might have been memorialized en masse in a civil ceremony. Even so, churchly rituals of death dominated congregational life. Mary Chesnut, a diarist in South Carolina, wrote that the sound of a funeral march was nearly constant in her community. Ministers drew on Scriptures and the details of military condolence letters to craft myriad

Selected Verses from the Unofficial Anthems of North and South

"Battle Hymn of the Republic"

1. Mine eyes have seen the glory of the coming of the Lord;
He is trampling out the vintage where the grapes of wrath are stored;
He hath loosed the fateful lightning of His terrible swift sword:
His truth is marching on.

[*refrain*] Glory, glory hallelujah!
Glory, glory hallelujah!
Glory, glory hallelujah!
His truth is marching on.

3. I have read a fiery gospel writ in burnished rows of steel:
"As ye deal with my contemners, so with you my grace shall deal";
Let the Hero, born of woman, crush the serpent with his heel,
Since God is marching on. [*refrain*]

5. In the beauty of the lilies Christ was born across the sea,
With a glory in His bosom that transfigures you and me.
As He died to make men holy, let us die to make men free,
While God is marching on. [*refrain*]

Originally published in *Atlantic Monthly* 9, no. 52 (February 1862). ▶

eulogies, attempting to cast every loss as a good death in service of a noble cause. Historian Drew Gilpin Faust, in her book *This Republic of Suffering*, wrote, "The funeral sermon, like the ritual that surrounded it, was a memorial, not in granite, but in words; it sought, like the Good Death itself, to ensure that dying was not an end, not an isolated act, itself undertaken in isolation, but a foundation for both spiritual and social immortality—for eternal life and lasting memory."[17] Each death made the war at once more personal and more cosmically significant.

Ironically, rather than cause either side to tire of brutality, the staggering casualties amplified calls for ever greater sacrifice. Surrender would mean that one's father, brother, or son died in vain. Christian theology accelerated the death spiral by offering Jesus Christ and the martyrs of church history as exemplars. According to historian Mark Schantz, "Americans had been well schooled to

17. Drew Gilpin Faust, *This Republic of Suffering: Death and the American Civil War* (New York: Knopf, 2008), 163.

"God Save the South"

1. God save the South, God save the South,
Her altars and firesides, God save the South!
Now that the war is nigh, now that we arm to die,
Chanting our battle cry, "Freedom or death!"
Chanting our battle cry, "Freedom or death!"

3. God made the right stronger than might,
Millions would trample us down in their pride.
Lay Thou their legions low, roll back the ruthless foe,
Let the proud spoiler know God's on our side.
Let the proud spoiler know God's on our side.

6. War to the hilt, theirs be the guilt,
Who fetter the free man to ransom the slave.
Up then, and undismay'd, sheathe not the battle blade,
Till the last foe is laid low in the grave!
Till the last foe is laid low in the grave!

Lyrics by Ernest Halpin, music by Charles W. A. Ellerbrock,
1861.

see the beauty inherent in death, to see the world that waited on a distant shore beyond this one and to celebrate the deaths of those who had fallen in a noble cause."[18] Within such a framework, there was no logical, necessary limit to the bloodshed. Holy war consumed all. Harry Stout observed, "For the Civil War to achieve its messianic destiny and inculcate an ongoing civil religion, it required a blood sacrifice that appeared total."[19] The desperate search for meaning amid such prodigious trauma entrenched each faction so firmly in its own ideology that it could no longer comprehend the humanity of the other side. Churches became ideological bunkers, surrounded by graves.

Battles for the Bible

The dueling modes of biblical interpretation undergirding the Northern and Southern causes might have lacked the visceral punch of battle hymns and

18. Mark S. Schantz, *Awaiting the Heavenly Country: The Civil War and America's Culture of Death* (Ithaca, NY: Cornell University Press, 2008), 125.
19. Stout, *Upon the Altar of the Nation*, 459.

Events organized around mourning President Abraham Lincoln's assassination in April 1865 spanned three weeks and seven states, including the public viewing in New York City pictured in this magazine illustration. It was the most elaborate memorial related to the Civil War—although far from the only one—in a conflict that caused as many as thirty-six hundred deaths per day.

funerals, but their effects were perhaps more durable, persisting beyond the ebb of high emotion. Historian Mark Noll persuasively frames the war as a theological crisis, one from which American Protestant churches never fully recovered.[20]

Since the Reformation, Protestants had relied on the principle of *sola scriptura*, "Scripture alone," as their source of definitive truth. In early America, this principle was combined with a philosophy known as Scottish commonsense realism, which held that the external world could be perceived accurately by everyone using their senses and their brains. The famous line in the Declaration of Independence, "We hold these truths to be self-evident," encapsulated the confidence conferred by this philosophical approach. *Sola scriptura* plus commonsense realism added up to the deceptively simple assertion that the Bible meant what it said and said what it meant.

But what did the Bible say, or mean, about slavery? Southerners used passages like the so-called curse of Ham (Gen. 9:20–27); "Slaves, obey your earthly masters" (Eph. 6:5); and the letter to Philemon to argue that the Bible sanc-

20. Mark A. Noll, *The Civil War as a Theological Crisis* (Chapel Hill: University of North Carolina Press, 2006).

tioned or even mandated white ownership of Black slaves. Northern abolitionists pointed instead to passages like "there is neither bond nor free . . . for ye
are all one in Christ Jesus" (Gal. 3:28); Paul's condemnation of the slave trade
(1 Tim. 1:10); and an alternate reading of the letter to Philemon to argue that
slavery was wholly contrary to God's will. The Bible did not speak clearly with
one voice on this issue, but there were more verses that, if read literally, supported slavery than supported abolition. The text nowhere proclaims, "Masters,
free your slaves."

Consequently, abolitionists had to make more complicated biblical arguments. They appealed to historical context, asserting that slavery as practiced
in the Bible was categorically different from the chattel slavery of the American
South, which treated human beings and their children as property in perpetuity.
They examined linguistics, contending that Hebrew and Greek terms translated
in English Bibles as "slave" would be better rendered "servant" or "hired hand,"
indicating time-limited contract labor rather than an immutable, heritable status.
They also looked past specific verses to their sense of God's nature and overall
plan for humanity. Surely, abolitionists reasoned, a loving God who created the
whole human race, led his chosen people out of enslavement in Egypt, and sent
his Son to free members of every nation from bondage to sin, would not condone
slavery. Instead, "where the Spirit of the Lord is, there is liberty" (2 Cor. 3:17).

None of these approaches—history, linguistics, or looking past specific verses
to larger biblical themes—impressed Southern enslavers. Rather, enslavers became convinced that the South alone remained faithful to the Bible, and their
defense of the "peculiar institution" of slavery was simultaneously a defense
of true Christianity. As pro-slavery Disciples of Christ minister and college
president James P. Shannon put it, "I hardly know which is most unaccount-
able, the profound ignorance of the Bible, or the sublimity of cool impudence
and infidelity manifested by those who profess to be Christians, and yet dare
affirm that the Book of God gives no sanction to slaveholding."[21] Protestants
recognized no higher authority, such as a pope or ecumenical council, that could
adjudicate between abolitionist claims that enslavers read the Bible wrong, and
enslavers' claims that abolitionists had no respect for the Bible at all. When civil
authorities could not settle the dispute either, the only option was violence.

Understanding the Civil War as a theological crisis connects it to earlier wars
of religion in Europe and to developments later in American church history.
Some Catholic observers saw the war as evidence that Protestantism was fundamentally unsound. A New York Catholic newspaper said of Protestantism in

---

21. Quoted in Isaac Allen, *Is Slavery Sanctioned by the Bible?* (Boston: American Tract Society,
1860), 1.

Excerpt from Abraham Lincoln's Second Inaugural Address, 1864

Although President Lincoln was a member of no church and rejected many tenets of Christianity, his second inaugural address plumbed theological depths that the trained ministers in the era failed to reach. A section from the central paragraph reads as follows:

> Neither party expected for the war the magnitude or the duration which it has already attained. Neither anticipated that the cause of the conflict might cease with or even before the conflict itself should cease. Each looked for an easier triumph, and a result less fundamental and astounding. Both read the same Bible and pray to the same God, and each invokes His aid against the other. It may seem strange that any men should dare to ask a just God's assistance in wringing their bread from the sweat of other men's faces, but let us judge not, that we be not judged. The prayers of both could not be answered. That of neither has been answered fully. The Almighty has His own purposes. "Woe unto the world because of offenses; for it must needs be that offenses come, but woe to that man by whom the offense cometh." . . . Fondly do we hope, fervently do we pray, that this mighty scourge of war may speedily pass away. Yet, if God wills that it continue until all the wealth piled by the bondsman's two hundred and fifty years of unrequited toil shall be sunk, and until every drop of blood drawn with the lash shall be paid by another drawn with the sword, as was said three thousand years ago, so still it must be said, "the judgments of the Lord are true and righteous altogether."
>
> The American Presidency Project, https://www.presidency.ucsb.edu /documents/inaugural-address-35.

1865 that "its origin is the spirit of secession and revolt, . . . its history is but a chronicle of insurrection."[22] Other observers, following the Enlightenment turn of the eighteenth century, decided that a secular social order based on reason and toleration had to be better than one grounded on faith, considering how much violence the allegedly faithful committed. Looking forward in American history, the two-party, conservative/liberal alignment of American Christianity that is often dated to the period after World War II was already sketched out by the middle of the nineteenth century. According to Mark Noll, "Considered as an episode in the history of theology, the Civil War occurred during a critical

22. Noll, *Civil War as a Theological Crisis*, 127.

transition from theological certainties that had prevailed since the early six-teenth century and toward new paths characteristic of the recent past. Some of the new paths would still be seriously Christian—though in contradictory liberal, modernist, fundamentalist, pietist, primitivist, and traditionalist variet-ies. But more and more intellectual leaders would be secular, agnostic, or simply uninterested in religion."[23] *Sola scriptura* and commonsense realism were sorely tested by the war, and they did not hold.

From Civil War to Civil Religions

Civil religion is hard to define but easy to spot. It is found in patriotic hymns, in prayers at civic ceremonies, on currency ("In God We Trust"), and wherever the Christian flag and the American flag stand side by side. Christian historian Robert Linder wrote that civil religion "mixes piety with patriotism and tra-ditional religion with national life until it is impossible to distinguish between them."[24] The United States is just one of many nations past and present to use civil religion as a social glue, but Americans have laid it on especially thick in an effort to cover a large geographic area, a diverse population, and a history rife with conflict. As with everything else discussed in this chapter, civil religion developed quite differently in the North and South.

Combat finally ground to a halt with General Robert E. Lee's surrender to General Ulysses S. Grant at Appomattox on April 9, 1865, but the most mo-mentous death of the war was yet to come. Lee surrendered on Palm Sunday. Later that week, on Good Friday, President Lincoln was mortally wounded by embittered Southerner John Wilkes Booth. The symbolism could not have been clearer to Union partisans, who had for years sung the words "As He died to make men holy, let us die to make men free." (This glorification of sacrifice struck later hymnal editors as extreme, so the line was changed to "let us live to make men free.") In the North, Lincoln ascended to the pantheon of civil religion alongside George Washington, the savior and father of the nation respectively.

The elevation of a political god alongside the God of the Bible should have been problematic for Christians, but in the charged atmosphere of that week, circumspection was in short supply. "Let them [the South] perish!" roared Rev. Robert Russell Booth at Mercer Street Presbyterian Church in New York City, representing widespread sentiment in the North. "In the grave of our martyred President, let the last vestige of them be buried, and let their memory rot, never

23. Noll, *Civil War as a Theological Crisis*, 92.

24. Robert D. Linder, "Reagan at Kansas State: Civil Religion in the Service of the New Right," *Reformed Journal* 32, no. 12 (December 1982): 13–14.

Philadelphia Photographic Co. / Library of Congress

WASHINGTON & LINCOLN. (APOTHEOSIS.)

In an image produced in Philadelphia soon after Lincoln's death, President George Washington welcomes Lincoln to heaven with a laurel crown. Labeled "Apotheosis," the image reflected both men's status as gods in American civil religion.

to be spoken of with approval hereafter by a true patriot or Christian man!"[25] Famed Black orator Frederick Douglass was more shaken than outraged, writing that at the news of Lincoln's death, "A hush fell upon the land, as though each man in it heard a voice from heaven, an uninterpreted sound from the sky and had paused to learn its meaning."[26] Perhaps Douglass sensed immediately that Lincoln's assassination would impede progress toward full recognition of Black rights and dignity, a cause that Lincoln had belatedly embraced. In a speech on the Tuesday of that fateful week, Lincoln had advocated equality in public education and called for Black veterans to gain the right to vote. His assassin, Booth, reportedly had responded, "That means n— citizenship. That is the last speech he will ever make."[27] It was, and Booth's bullet had its desired effect. Lincoln's successor, Andrew Johnson, was a former enslaver and notorious racist.

Owing in part to this transition in the White House, civil rights that seemed within reach in 1865 would instead be hard-fought for another century and beyond.

However problematic was the North's hero worship of Lincoln, the postwar civil religion that took hold in the South, known as the Lost Cause, was far more insidious. The vanquished South faced greater challenges: economy wrecked, landscape destroyed, political autonomy taken away during the period of Reconstruction (1865–77). One in three Southern households had lost a family member in the war. To make matters worse, the rhetoric of holy war had implicated God's providence and Scriptures in the outcome of battle. When it all came crashing down, Southerners could either rethink everything they had

25. Quoted in Stout, *Upon the Altar of the Nation*, 449.
26. Quoted in David W. Blight, *Frederick Douglass: Prophet of Freedom* (New York: Simon & Schuster, 2018), 460.
27. William H. Herndon, *Herndon's Lincoln: The True Story of a Great Life* (Chicago: Belford-Clarke, 1890), 3:579.

believed or find a way to frame their losses as a refining fire, preparing them for greater glory. They overwhelmingly chose the latter course, applying to themselves the words of Hebrews 12:6: "For whom the Lord loveth he chasteneth."

Although less taxing than humble soul-searching would have been, reframing defeat as a setback in a longer story of triumph took a lot of work. It required romanticizing the antebellum South as a land of contented slaves and godly households. Dead Confederates must be recalled as heroic men of God who experienced religious revival in the camps. Confederate symbols, especially the flag, must be invested with pride rather than shame. White children must be taught a usable past, not one in which their ancestors were the villains. This work needed statues, sermons, tracts, textbooks, public and secret societies (the United Daughters of the Confederacy, the Ku Klux Klan), evangelists, testimonies, and carefully curated historic preservation. Southern churches eagerly contributed to these efforts. Historian Charles Reagan Wilson noted that congregations collected funds for the Robert E. Lee monument in Richmond, Virginia; invited Confederate heroes to speak at revival meetings; and shared their denominational presses with publications such as *Confederate Veteran*, which was printed by the Southern Methodist publishing house in Nashville.[28] There were even Confederate catechisms, which children could memorize and recite to win prizes. A 1904 version included questions and answers such as these:

1. What causes led to the war between the States, from 1861 to 1865?

   The disregard, on the part of States of the North, for the rights of the Southern or slave-holding States.

13. How were the slaves treated?

   With great kindness and care in nearly all cases, a cruel master being rare, and lost the respect of his neighbors if he treated his slaves badly. Self interest would have prompted good treatment if a higher feeling of humanity had not.

14. What was the feeling of the slaves towards their masters?

   They were faithful and devoted and were always ready and willing to serve them.[29]

All of this painstaking labor bolstered, in Wilson's words, "a Southern religious-moral identity, an identity as a chosen people."[30] This identity long outlived the Confederate States of America.

28. Charles Reagan Wilson, *Baptized in Blood: The Religion of the Lost Cause, 1865–1920* (Athens: University of Georgia Press, 1980), 34.

29. Cornelia Branch Stone, *U. D. C. Catechism for Children* (Staunton, VA: J. E. B. Stuart Chapter No. 10, U. D. C., 1904).

30. Wilson, *Baptized in Blood*, 1.

Organizations such as the United Daughters of the Confederacy spread the religion of the Lost Cause through monuments, events, periodicals, and a catechism for children.

The differences exposed by the Civil War and its aftermath would seem irreconcilable. It is not possible to view slavery as both consonant with and contrary to God's will, nor to simultaneously revere and revile Confederate leaders. The image of insurrectionists carrying Confederate battle flags as they stormed the US Capitol on January 6, 2021, demonstrated that Lost Cause civil religion and mainstream American civil religion remain fundamentally at odds. Even so, white Americans North and South found many ways to work together in the decades after the Civil War, as long as they politely agreed not to reckon with racism.[31]

As the split in the Methodist Church presaged the war, the reunification of that church exemplified the incomplete peace that came afterward. Northern and Southern Methodists began extending hands of friendship as early as the 1870s, sending delegates to each other's General Conferences. By the 1890s, a joint commission on federation had formed, including representatives from the Methodist Episcopal Church (North); the Methodist Episcopal Church, South; and the Methodist Protestant Church, another white faction that had broken off back in 1828 because of governance issues. (The Black

31. See David W. Blight, *Race and Reunion: The Civil War in American Memory* (Cambridge, MA: Harvard University Press, 2001).

Methodist denominations, the AME Church and the AME Zion Church, did not participate.) In the 1920s, a formal plan of reunion failed to garner support among the required three-fourths majority of annual conferences in each of the participating denominations, but additional lobbying, adjustments to the plan, and cooperative efforts such as a shared hymnal moved the majority toward approval of the merger. A sticking point persisted, though: What should be done about the roughly three hundred thousand Black members of the three uniting churches, who were organized mostly into segregated annual conferences?

Competing views on race within American Methodism in the early twentieth century were not identical to those a century earlier, but there were echoes. One Northern faction, descendants of the abolitionists, pressed for full equality. Most white Southerners insisted on segregation and fiercely resented criticism from outsiders. Black Methodists, like Black Americans generally, knew that separate structures were never equal. When reunification was finally approved in 1939, the newly created Methodist Church was organized into five geographic jurisdictions for the white majority and a sixth, Central Jurisdiction, for Black members—with a white presiding bishop. A strong majority of white Northerners approved, considering this compromise the best deal they would get from their Southern counterparts. A majority of white Southerners approved the plan as well, although a splinter group took a legal challenge all the way to the Supreme Court and ultimately formed their own, tiny Southern Methodist Church. Seventeen of the nineteen Black annual conferences voted against the Plan of Union, but, as usual, their voices were not heeded. Judging the result a victory, Bishop Edwin H. Hughes, the senior chairman of the Methodist Unification Commission, wrote, "Our commission was not set to remake the Church, but to reunite the Church." Division came at a steep cost, but so did unity.[32]

Henry McNeal Turner (1834–1915), born a free Black man in South Carolina, was licensed to preach in the Methodist Episcopal Church, South, in 1853. In 1858, he moved to St. Louis and was ordained a minister in the African Methodist Episcopal Church. During the Civil War, he organized one of the first Black regiments and served as its chaplain. The Union victory filled him with enthusiasm for the party of Lincoln, so he helped found the Republican Party of Georgia and was elected to the state legislature. White Southerners soon robbed Black citizens of their newly gained rights, though, through political machinations and violence. By 1876, Turner's optimism had evaporated. Turner often wrote letters

32. Quoted in Norwood, *Story of American Methodism*, 407–8.

for publication, and he closed his December 14 letter to the *Christian Recorder* with a startling prayer:

> *May God slash this nation; may it writhe; may it groan and sigh; and may I bleed and die, or else learn wisdom; learn humanity black or white, brown or red.*[33]

———————————— **FURTHER READING** ————————————

Blum, Edward J. *Reforging the White Republic: Race, Religion, and American Nationalism, 1865–1898.* Baton Rouge: Louisiana State University Press, 2005.

Byrd, James P. *A Holy Baptism of Fire and Blood: The Bible and the American Civil War.* New York: Oxford University Press, 2021.

Carwardine, Richard J. *Evangelicals and Politics in Antebellum America.* New Haven: Yale University Press, 1993.

Faust, Drew Gilpin. *This Republic of Suffering: Death and the American Civil War.* New York: Knopf, 2008.

Heyrman, Christine Leigh. *Southern Cross: The Beginnings of the Bible Belt.* Chapel Hill: University of North Carolina Press, 1998.

Jemison, Elizabeth. *Christian Citizens: Reading the Bible in Black and White in the Post-emancipation South.* Chapel Hill: University of North Carolina Press, 2020.

Johnson, Andre E. *The Forgotten Prophet: Bishop Henry McNeal Turner and the African-American Prophetic Tradition.* Lanham, MD: Lexington Books, 2012.

Mathews, Donald G. *Slavery and Methodism: A Chapter in American Morality, 1780–1845.* Princeton: Princeton University Press, 1965.

Noll, Mark A. *The Civil War as a Theological Crisis.* Chapel Hill: University of North Carolina Press, 2006.

Snay, Mitchell. *Gospel of Disunion: Religion and Separatism in the Antebellum South.* Chapel Hill: University of North Carolina Press, 1997.

Stout, Harry S. *Upon the Altar of the Nation: A Moral History of the Civil War.* New York: Viking, 2006.

Stowell, Daniel W. *Rebuilding Zion: The Religious Reconstruction of the South, 1863–1877.* New York: Oxford University Press, 1998.

Wilson, Charles Reagan. *Baptized in Blood: The Religion of the Lost Cause, 1865–1920.* Athens: University of Georgia Press, 1980.

33. Henry McNeal Turner, letter to the editor of December 14, 1876, *Christian Recorder*, The #HMTProject, http://www.thehenrymcnealturnerproject.org/2017/10/untitled-december-14-1876.html.

9

Muscular Missions

Student Volunteer Movement Launched, 1886

The most famous evangelist of the late nineteenth century, Dwight L. Moody (1837–99), frequently appeared onstage with song leader Ira D. Sankey, but his circle included other musicians as well. His friend Daniel Webster Whittle wrote some two hundred hymns, including "I Know Whom I Have Believed" and "Showers of Blessing." Whittle's daughter, May, attended a school founded by Moody at Northfield, Massachusetts. She married Moody's son William and went on to co-lead the school with her husband for decades. May was also an accomplished musician who collaborated with her father on several hymns, including one that the pair finished just before Whittle's death in 1901. "The Story of Jesus Can Never Grow Old" illustrates the combination of gospel preaching and social consciousness that characterized evangelicals in the era.

> They tell me the story of Jesus is old,
> And they ask that we preach something new;
> They say that the Babe and the Man of the cross,
> For the wise of this world will not do.
>
> [*refrain*] It can never grow old,
> It can never grow old,
> Though a million times over the story is told;

While there is injustice and pain in the world,
The story of Jesus can never grow old.[1]

------------▼------------

Something was stirring at Mount Hermon, the school for boys that evangelist Dwight L. Moody had founded near Northfield, Massachusetts. Several
hundred college students who were affiliated with the Young Men's Christian
Association (YMCA) met there for a Bible conference in the summer of 1886,
and meetings took an unscheduled turn. Robert Wilder, a recent Princeton University graduate who had been reared by missionary parents in India, pressed
organizers for an evening devoted to foreign missions. Wilder was one of about
twenty conference participants who intended to become missionaries, and he
believed that many of his fellows could be called in the same direction. Might
he and a few other young men speak on the needs of the world to the assembly?
Moody agreed.

The resulting "Meeting of the Ten Nations" became a legend. Representatives
of ten mission fields spoke; some of them, including Wilder, were sons of missionaries who grew up overseas (in India, China, and Persia), while others spoke
for their native cultures (Sioux, Japanese, Thai, Armenian, Danish, Norwegian,
and German). Each three-minute presentation ended with the words "God is
love" in the foreign language. Audience members were enrapt, and many went
directly from the meeting to their room or to sit under a nearby tree, praying
to discern whether they too should become missionaries. A local newspaper
reported the next day, "The missionary spirit is rampant among the students
now. The interest is strong, vigorous and healthful. Rousing meetings have been
the result, and these are taken up and carried on in an energetic business-like
way that is refreshing to the men who happen to be fresh from lukewarm communities and churches and lifeless meetings."[2] By the end of the conference,
one hundred men—the "Mount Hermon 100"—had signed a document called
the Princeton Declaration, committing themselves to missionary service. The
Student Volunteer Movement (SVM) was born.

Within the movement, this event was celebrated as an outpouring of the Holy
Spirit, "a sort of Pentecost," as one speaker at the meeting put it.[3] That interpretation cannot be waved away with a skeptical hand. There were, however,
other forces in play as well, as the newspaper account indicates. The writer's
emphasis on strength, vigor, and health alludes to muscular Christianity, an ide-

1. This version is from Charles McCallon Alexander, ed., *Victorious Life Hymns* (Philadelphia:
The Sunday School Times Company, 1919), no. 31.
2. Quoted in Ruth Wilder Braisted, *In This Generation: The Story of Robert P. Wilder* (New
York: Friendship Press, 1941), 26.
3. Braisted, *In This Generation*, 26.

One hundred young men from this YMCA Bible conference volunteered to become foreign missionaries, launching a new phase of American Protestant missions activity.

ology surging through the English-speaking world at the time. The business-like energy of the meeting reflects prominent businessmen's investment in Protestant missionary endeavors as well as a broader fascination with business during the Gilded Age (1870–1900). The contrast between the rousing Mount Hermon conference and the students' allegedly lukewarm, lifeless home churches hints at the drama associated with missionary service, a drama frequently heightened with military language. Recalling a speech by Baptist missionary William Ashmore at the Mount Hermon conference, John R. Mott, a Princeton Declaration signatory and first chairman of the SVM, wrote, "He knew how to get hold of college men. I will tell you the way to do it, and that is to place something before them which is tremendously difficult. He presented missions as a war of conquest and not as a mere wrecking expedition."[4] It was no accident that American Protestant foreign missions ramped up at the same time the United States began to assert itself as a global power. More strength and larger scale made it even more important for Americans to think carefully about the impact

4. John R. Mott, "The Beginnings of the Student Volunteer Movement," in *The Student Volunteer Movement after Twenty-Five Years* (New York: Student Volunteer Movement for Foreign Missions, 1911), 12–13.

they would have on the world. Would they engage in a "war of conquest," or would they learn to tread more lightly?

Shifting Frontiers

Missionary activity began as soon as Europeans arrived in the Americas, taking different forms depending on the theology of the Europeans involved, the response of the missionized, and the political and economic context for the encounter. Missionary outreach by English-speaking Protestants, the lineage of the young men gathered at Mount Hermon in 1886, got off to a slow start. Although the idea of sharing Christianity with Native Americans was present in the English colonies—the Great Seal of Massachusetts, for example, drawing on Acts 16:9, pictured a Native man pleading, "Come over and help us"—cross-cultural missions did not rank high on colonists' list of priorities. Mostly, white colonists saw the Native populations as dangerous savages who occupied land that colonists wanted for farming and hunting. Even the colonists who were inspired by early missionaries such as David Brainerd spent so much energy building their own society that there was little left over for domestic missions, let alone for sending missionaries to distant lands. Expansion of Christian civilization took precedence over ministry to members of other cultures.

This attitude spread as the nation swelled following independence. The westward growth of the United States through the nineteenth century is romanticized as a period of cowboys and pioneers and "manifest destiny," but it is better characterized as a phase of imperial expansion during which much of the land that now lies within US borders was foreign territory. The history of Protestant missions helps bring this more accurate picture into focus. In 1810, an interdenominational (but predominantly Presbyterian and Congregational) missions agency, the American Board of Commissioners for Foreign Missions (ABCFM), was launched to raise money for and coordinate missionary activity. It sent its first missionaries to India in 1812: Adoniram and Ann Haseltine Judson, Samuel and Roxana Peck Nott, Samuel and Harriett Newell, Gordon Hall, and Luther Rice. However, the ABCFM governing board admitted in 1816 that "many friends of missions, not only in this country, but also in Europe, have thought it strange, that while so much has been doing for the distant heathen of India, so little should have been done for the not less destitute tribes on our continent, and within our own borders."[5] The British, who ruled India, did not want American meddlers to upset the structures they had built to scaffold their

---

5. American Board of Commissioners for Foreign Missions, "Report of the Prudential Committee," *Panoplist and Missionary Magazine* 12, no. 10 (October 1816): 451. Two of the first ABCFM

colonial project. In fact, the British East India Company denied entry to the first ABCFM missionaries, so the group split up. Some members sneaked into India with the help of a sympathetic governor, some relocated to Burma (now Myanmar) and Ceylon (now Sri Lanka), and one returned to the United States. Faced with opposition abroad and opportunities nearer home, the ABCFM spent half of its money in its first decade on outreach to Native Americans, principally Cherokees, Chickasaws, Choctaws, and Dakotas.

As it grew, the ABCFM continued to fund missions within US territories but increasingly shifted its focus abroad. Mission locations added in 1820 included the Middle East, with outreach both to Muslims and to Christian minorities within the Ottoman Empire; and the Sandwich Islands, known today as Hawaiʻi. Of these, the mission to Hawaiʻi was by far the most successful. In the 1830s, ABCFM missionaries began work in China, Southeast Asia, Africa, and the Oregon Country. By 1835, the ABCFM was probably the largest voluntary organization in the United States, having raised more than $1.4 million, printed and distributed 90 million pages of religious literature, opened 63 overseas mission stations with a total of 311 staff members, and begun 474 schools serving more than 80,000 students.[6]

Not all ABCFM efforts succeeded. Some stations closed within a few years or were transferred to other agencies. The first missionaries to Sumatra, for example, were killed by cannibals. The mission to Oregon, led by Presbyterians Marcus and Narcissa Whitman, also ended in tragedy. In 1847, Cayuse tribe members, ravaged by measles and resentful of the Whitmans' high-handed tactics, killed the Whitmans and about a dozen settlers whom they had, against the wishes of the ABCFM, brought with them. The ABCFM soon closed all its Northwest stations. Then the Civil War disrupted American missionary work in North America and abroad. After the war, President Ulysses S. Grant's "Peace Policy" gave Protestant denominations a leading role in managing Native American affairs (see chap. 3), but a decade of frustration and failure ended this experiment.

As the American West was increasingly militarized, American Protestants looked more and more to foreign fields. Between 1865 and 1885, the ABCFM expanded work in China while adding sites in Japan, Angola, Mexico, Spain, Italy, and among the Czech population of Austria-Hungary, the latter four targeting disaffected Roman Catholics. Additional mission societies formed, and hundreds more Americans set out as foreign missionaries. Unlike missionaries

---

missionaries, Ann and Adoniram Judson, converted to the Baptist faith en route to India, so by the time they took up work in Burma, they were affiliated with a Baptist denominational convention.

6. Robert Wuthnow, *Boundless Faith: The Global Outreach of American Churches* (Berkeley: University of California Press, 2010), 98.

The Last Stand of Hawai'i's Christian Queen

Lili'uokalani, a baptized, missionary-educated, devout Christian, became queen of Hawai'i upon the death of her brother in 1891. She spent her brief reign defending the rights of native Hawaiians against encroachment by white American business and military leaders. Her pleas failed, including this appeal to Christian conscience, from her 1898 book *Hawaii's Story by Hawaii's Queen*:

> I shall not claim that in the days of Captain Cook our people were civilized. I shall not claim anything more for their progress in civilization and Christian morality than has been already attested by missionary writers. Perhaps I may safely claim even less, admitting the criticism of some intelligent visitors who were *not* missionaries,—that the habits and prejudices of New England Puritanism were not well adapted to the genius of a tropical people, nor capable of being thoroughly ingrafted upon them.
>
> But Christianity in substance they have accepted; and I know of no people who have developed a tenderer Christian conscience, or who have shown themselves more ready to obey its behests. Nor has any people known to history shown a greater reverence and love for their Christian teachers, or filled the measure of a grateful return more overflowingly. And where else in the world's history is it written that a savage people, pagan for ages, with fixed hereditary customs and beliefs, have made equal progress in civilization and Christianity in the same space of time? And what people has ever been subjected during such an evolution to such a flood of external demoralizing influences? . . .
>
> Perhaps there is a kind of right, depending upon the precedents of all ages, and known as the "Right of Conquest," under which robbers and ma-rauders may establish themselves in possession of whatsoever they are strong enough to ravish from their fellows. I will not pretend to decide how far civilization and Christian enlightenment have outlawed it. But we have known for many years that our Island monarchy has relied upon the protection always extended to us by the policy and the assured friendship of the great American republic.
>
> If we have nourished in our bosom those who have sought our ruin, it has been because they were of the people whom we believed to be our dearest friends and allies.

Lili'uokalani, *Hawaii's Story by Hawaii's Queen* (Boston: Lee & Shephard, 1898),
366–69.

from Great Britain and Europe, who outnumbered American missionaries throughout the nineteenth century, the Americans did not have much opportunity (or temptation) to cross over into political or diplomatic service, because the United States had little colonial presence outside its borders. For example, at the 1884 Berlin Conference that carved most of Africa into European colonies, American diplomats participated but claimed no land. Americans cast this political weakness as a spiritual strength. Historian William Hutchison observed that "where others were dispatching civil servants, American society was commissioning religious workers."[7]

In the very last decade of the nineteenth century, though, the United States rapidly expanded its global footprint. In a famous speech on the four hundredth anniversary of Columbus's voyage, historian Frederick Jackson Turner warned that the American frontier was closed, with white settlement stretching from sea to sea, and he worried that national vitality would ebb without new lands to conquer. Americans soon demonstrated eagerness to find new frontiers. First, the son of ABCFM missionaries to Hawai'i, Sanford B. Dole, engineered a coup, dethroning Queen Lili'uokalani and attempting to convince the US government to annex the islands. Some politicians hesitated to annex territory where residents adamantly did not want to be part of the United States, but Dole and his military allies kept pressing. Then, on February 15, 1898, the American naval cruiser *Maine* mysteriously exploded in Havana Harbor, drawing the United States into the Cuban war of independence from Spain. The Spanish Empire was very weak by this point, and the United States saw its chance to join the scramble for colonies. Following a ten-week war in the Caribbean and the Pacific, Spain signed a treaty granting the United States temporary control over Cuba and ceding possession of Puerto Rico, Guam, and the Philippines. The naval base at Pearl Harbor proved so valuable during the war that the United States finalized its takeover of the Hawaiian Islands as well. And so, about a century after fighting for its own independence, the United States became a colonial empire, modest by European standards but eager to extend its economic, military, and religious influence. Several key figures spearheaded the religious aspects of this project, and examining their lives highlights its complexities and tensions.

Recruiters: Robert and Grace Wilder

Having launched the event that prompted the "Mount Hermon 100" to enlist as missionaries, Robert Wilder immediately sought to recruit more volunteers.

---

7. William R. Hutchison, *Errand to the World: American Protestant Thought and Foreign Missions* (Chicago: University of Chicago Press, 1987), 93.

Robert Wilder made hundreds of college visits to recruit missionaries, while his sister, Grace, prayed and wrote for the cause.

He was inspired by the "Cambridge Seven," a small group of evangelical students who toured colleges in England and Scotland before beginning missionary endeavors in China in 1885. One member of that group, C. T. Studd, was a famous cricket player; a second had rowed for Cambridge in the annual race against its archrival, Oxford; a third was the son of a baronet; a fourth was a lieutenant in the Royal Artillery. All were paragons of muscular Christianity, and they stunned their compatriots by giving up promising secular careers for service with the China Inland Mission. Wilder hoped to tour American colleges with a similar team, but most of his potential teammates bowed out.

Fortunately, he still had one partner, Princeton classmate John N. Forman, who was also the son of missionary parents; and a funder, Daniel W. McWilliams, the secretary and treasurer of the Manhattan Elevated Railway Company. D. L. Moody had great success in cultivating wealthy donors for his ministries, and the next generation of mission organizers continued this pattern. With Forman's assistance and McWilliams's support, Wilder visited 162 colleges in the year after the Mount Hermon conference, enrolling more than 2,100 missionary volunteers, one-fourth of them women. Deeply impressed, Princeton University president James McCosh asked, "Has any such offering of living men and women been presented in this age—in this country—in any age, or any country, since Pentecost?"[8]

Robert was also inspired by his sister Grace, whose contributions to missionary recruitment were less public but still significant. The siblings had spent most of their childhood years in India and remained committed to the work their parents had begun there. Two years older than Robert, Grace attended Mount Holyoke, a women's college founded in 1837. The school's first president, Mary Lyon, saw foreign missions as "our nation's great feature of the morally

8. Quoted in Michael Parker, *The Kingdom of Character: The Student Volunteer Movement for Foreign Missions (1886–1926)* (Lanham, MD: American Society of Missiology; University Press of America, 1998), 11.

sublime" and deemed the biographies of missionaries "one of the richest fields of thought, of meditation, and of feeling."[9] Mount Holyoke sent a steady stream of alumnae abroad, initially as wives of male missionaries, because the early ABCFM would not commission unmarried women. By the later nineteenth century, more American women were pursuing higher education and applying for mission posts. Women's colleges were often called missionary factories in the press, and women within several Protestant denominations assembled their own mission boards to support female missionaries. Grace Wilder participated enthusiastically in this tradition, praying for the salvation of those she called the "heathen," leading a Bible study on campus for potential future missionaries, and writing a much-reprinted pamphlet, "Shall I Go? Thoughts for Girls, by One of Them." Additionally, when Robert hesitated to undertake the college tour because his father, former India missionary Royal Wilder, was dying, Grace offered to care for Royal and take over editing his monthly journal, the *Missionary Review*. Grace's behind-the-scenes work made Robert's more visible efforts possible.

For women, foreign mission service represented not so much the allure of conquest as the chance to live a fuller life than they could at home. American women's professional opportunities did not keep pace with their rising education levels. In some professions, doors that were once open swung shut in the nineteenth century. For example, midwives and female healers provided much of the medical care in the Colonial period and early republic, but male physicians, organized as the American Medical Association in 1847, redefined medicine as the domain of credentialed men only. Similarly, churches that had supported women evangelists during eras of revival subsequently built seminaries to formalize ministerial training and refused to enroll women. Women who felt called to tend bodies or souls had to become missionaries to do it. Teaching was one of the only professions that became predominantly female during the nineteenth century, but American teachers often chafed at the close scrutiny to which they were subjected by male administrators and opinionated community members. Teaching overseas, a very popular option for female missionaries, was in many ways harder but freer.

After his exhausting year of travel to colleges, Robert Wilder spent a year of study at Union Theological Seminary in New York. Volunteers continued to sign the pledge that he had promoted, promising, "We are willing and desirous, God permitting, to become foreign missionaries," but momentum was

9. Mary Lyon, *A Missionary Offering* (1843), quoted in Joseph Conforti, "Mary Lyon, the Founding of Mount Holyoke College, and the Cultural Revival of Jonathan Edwards," *Religion and American Culture* 3, no. 1 (Winter 1993): 80.

flagging, so Wilder hit the campus trail again in 1888.[10] By 1891, the year of the first SVM Quadrennial Convention, he had helped to recruit some six thousand volunteers. The next year he married and sailed to India to become a missionary himself. Grace got there before him. She and their widowed mother had returned to India in 1887. Both women died there (Grace in 1911, her mother in 1910) and are buried at Wilder Memorial Church, in Kolhapur, which had been founded by Royal in 1859 and remains a Protestant landmark.

Organizers: John R. Mott and Ruth Rouse

Pledging a willingness to become a missionary was just a first step. The thousands of student volunteers needed structure and direction to follow through on their pledges, and the movement could not continue to rely on Wilder's recruiting energy. That is where John R. Mott came in.

Unlike the Wilders, Mott grew up not on a mission field but in small-town Iowa. He became interested in missions while attending Cornell University, where he heard J. E. K. Studd—brother of "Cambridge Seven" cricketer C. T. Studd—preach on the text "Seek ye first the kingdom of God" (Matt. 6:33). Mott invested his organizational talents first in the Cornell chapter of the YMCA, through which he connected with Moody and Wilder at Mount Hermon. Upon graduating from Cornell, he accepted a one-year position as traveling secretary for the YMCA, which turned into a forty-year career. Despite signing the Princeton Pledge at Mount Hermon, he never became a foreign missionary himself. Instead, he built organizations that linked mission-minded Protestants around the globe, including the SVM and the World Student Christian Federation.

Mott constructed his network on the foundation of the YMCA, which featured vast resources and some intrinsic tensions. The YMCA was founded in London in 1844 to keep young, working-class men off the streets in the hours after their factory shifts. YMCA centers offered Bible studies, wholesome social activities, and exercise facilities to compete with the vices of the city. A parallel organization for women, the YWCA, was founded about a decade later, and both rapidly opened branches in other countries. During the Civil War, most American branches closed, and the YMCA focused instead on providing Bibles and spiritual guidance to soldiers. (This is how Moody spent the war.) In the later nineteenth century, the YMCA and YWCA

10. The full pledge pamphlet can be viewed online at https://digitalcollections.drew.edu/Special Collections/19thCenturyPamphlets/Student_Volunteer_Movement/19th_Student%20Volunteer %20Movement_The%20Volunteer%20Pledge.pdf.

had urban locations mostly providing social services for working-
class people and college branches
more focused on evangelism and
missions. Generally, these different emphases coexisted harmoniously, even though urban laborers
and evangelistic college students
did not have much in common.
Wilder recruited many missionaries through collegiate Y chapters.
Mott, in turn, determined that the
optimal structure for the emerging Student Volunteer Movement
was for it to serve as the foreign
missions department of the YMCA
and YWCA.

Building and funding the missionary movement
required the energies of many organizers, including John R. Mott (standing, right) and Ruth
Rouse (seated).

Mott had very big plans for the
fledgling SVM. In a 1939 retrospec-
tive, he outlined five major goals:

> To lead students to a thorough consideration of the claims of foreign missions
> upon them personally as a lifework; to foster this purpose by guiding students
> who become volunteers in their study and activity for missions until they come
> under the immediate direction of the Mission Boards; to unite all volunteers in
> a common, organized, aggressive movement; to secure a sufficient number of
> well-qualified volunteers to meet the demands of the various Mission Boards;
> and to create and maintain an intelligent sympathetic and active interest in foreign
> missions on the part of students who are to remain at home in order to ensure
> the strong backing of the missionary enterprise by their advocacy, their gifts and
> their prayers.[11]

Mott's goals, too, involved intrinsic tensions. He sought to unite all volunteers
in a common movement, but they would serve under separate mission boards,
some denominational and some interdenominational. These boards frequently
disagreed on matters of theology, polity (church governance), and what it meant
to be well-qualified for service. Mott's vision required both volunteers who
renounced secular careers to go abroad and sympathetic backers who stayed
home to provide funding. (Mott enjoyed significant financial support from

11. John R. Mott, *Five Decades and a Forward View* (New York: Harper & Brothers, 1939), 8.

Letter from Lottie Moon

Charlotte "Lottie" Digges Moon, the famous Southern Baptist missionary to China for whom the denomination's annual missions offering is named, sent an upbeat report to her mission board secretary in 1910. In it, she referred to a centuries-old practice of tightly wrapping girls' feet, which was thought to enhance beauty but in fact severely and permanently hindered their ability to walk. The practice was finally dying out in the early twentieth century, owing to activism by Chinese reformers and Christian missionaries.

> My two schools for girls are a joy to me. It is delightful to see the diligence in study, good deportment & constant attendance of these girls, nearly all of whom come from non-Christian families. There is a very remarkable movement in Tengchow now towards the education of girls & the unbinding or non-binding of their feet. Along with this, there is a kind of groping-in-the-dark among the women for something better than they have,—which something is Christianity. Two women, each past sixty, have confessed lately, one that she is secretly a Christian, & another, only yesterday, that she & her grandson learned hymns & prayers at night with closed window lest the neighbors should laugh at them. The grandson goes to school & teaches his grandmother orally from a book Mrs. King gave him. And so the leaven works. Did it not ▶

men like oil baron John D. Rockefeller and farm machinery magnate Cyrus McCormick, both of whom had previously funded Moody's work.) What missionaries decided needed to be done in the field did not always match what donors wanted. And while, on the far side of one world war and the cusp of another, Mott did not use "war of conquest" language, he retained a predilection for aggressive action. His watchwords, and those of the SVM, were "The evangelization of the world in this generation."

No one matched Mott's energy for movement-building, but even he could not do everything at once. In 1904, he wrote to American heiress Grace Headley Dodge, asking her to fund the salary of a female organizer. "The world field is too large for me to cover properly," he explained. "Moreover there are certain problems and opportunities in work for women students which a woman can treat far better than a man. The woman's student field is enormous."[12] After re-

12. Quoted in Johanna M. Selles, *The World Student Christian Federation, 1895–1925: Motives, Methods, and Influential Women* (Eugene, OR: Pickwick, 2011), 66.

do thus in the early days in Rome? Were not many ladies there Christians, in the days of Jerome, long before the men had accepted Christianity?

What surprises me is that men unfriendly to Christianity will send their daughters to Christian schools knowing that six days in the week they will be taught Christianity & take part in Christian worship. The girls are expected to attend church & the majority come. As to one or two who have stayed away from church, I have thought it best not to make an issue. They study Christian books daily. Two of my girls come from a family once official & wealthy. They must have an escort to & from school daily, & are addressed as *Ku niang* (Miss). They are gentle, modest, well dressed & very eager, diligent students. One dear little girl, very quiet, sweet & gentle, has a grandfather with a high literary degree & a father who also has a degree, though not so high. So you see, our schools are growing in favor with the better class. One school is in my front yard. The girls study aloud according to Chinese custom. Their childish voices are musical to me because they tell of a new China, especially for girls & women.

And so, our "labor is not vain in the Lord." Thanks be to his Holy Name. The joy of the work grows day by day.

Keith Harper, ed., *Send the Light: Lottie Moon's Letters and Other Writings* (Macon, GA: Mercer University Press, 2002), 366–67.

ceiving assurance that the candidate for the position would have broad Christian sympathies and a capacious view of what constituted Christian mission, Dodge agreed to support Ruth Rouse as traveling secretary for the World Student Christian Federation (WSCF).

Rouse, born and educated in England, had already been involved with the SVM and the YWCA, and she had also spent two years as a missionary in India, before illness forced her to return to England. Rouse would spend the rest of her life performing tasks similar to those of Mott: traveling widely, giving speeches, raising money, running organizations, promoting international cooperation, and galvanizing Christian, humanitarian responses to the upheavals of war. Mott won the Nobel Peace Prize for this work in 1946. Rouse's name, by contrast, is hardly known outside the history of Christian missions.

According to historians of the WSCF, Rouse was able to accomplish as much as she did because she did not insist on equality. The men would have shut her down if she had. A female delegate to a WSCF conference in the Netherlands in 1905 wrote regarding the women's experience there, "We tried to behave very well and prove ourselves worthy; we lived submissively in a village a mile away from the men. We attended only such meetings as were open to us, and trooped out again obediently when they were over. We tried to win implacable enemies of women students, by being very discrete [sic] and 'womanly' and keeping silence as to any ideas that might be seething in our brains."[13] Historian Johanna Selles described the WSCF as modeled on a patriarchal family in which Mott, the father figure, brought in the biggest dona-tions and determined top-level goals, while Rouse, the mother figure, focused on communication, encouragement, and mediating among leaders. Despite their second-class status, though, women constituted some 60 percent of the American foreign mission force in the early 1900s. If American Protestant churchgoers in that era knew of any woman who spoke a foreign language, or had lived outside the United States, or was allowed to speak from the pulpit, she probably was a missionary.

"Re-thinkers": Sherwood Eddy and Pearl Buck

Mott's mode of organizing reached a crescendo at the 1910 World Missionary Conference in Edinburgh, Scotland. Mott chaired this meeting of 1,200 del-egates who gathered to celebrate a century of Christian growth—an estimated 35 percent of the global population professed Christianity in 1910, up from less than 25 percent in 1800—and to muster ecumenical strength for the century to come. Reflecting this widespread enthusiasm, a previously obscure Disciples of Christ magazine had even renamed itself the *Christian Century* in 1900, claiming, "The nineteenth century has witnessed an extraordinary growth in the extent of Christianity. Sixty per cent, or nearly nine hundred million of the world's population are governed by the Christian races. Christianity grew more in the past century than in all the preceding centuries since 'Christ died for our sins, according to the Scriptures.' May not the coming century be known as the Christian century?"[14] Rather than a stop on the way to greater heights, though, Edinburgh marked the peak of this phase of white, Protestant, English-speaking foreign missions. The climate for missions changed dramatically in the next few decades, and some missionaries also changed their minds, notably Sherwood Eddy and Pearl Buck.

Eddy, like Mott, was a midwestern boy who traveled east for an Ivy League education and then had a profound spiritual experience at one of Moody's Mount Hermon conferences. Affiliated with the SVM, the YMCA, and the ABCFM, he became a missionary to very poor, Tamil-speaking Indians. His initial impression

13. Quoted in Selles, *World Student Christian Federation*, 89.
14. C. A. Young, "The Christian Century," *Christian Century* 17, no. 1 (January 4, 1900): 4.

of India was dire; as he wrote in 1897, "*Heathenism* here is indescribable in its depths of degradation." He soon discovered, though, that addressing people as degraded heathens did not win many converts. It was more effective to present Christ as the fulfillment of their traditions rather than as a conqueror who wanted to smash everything they had believed. In 1914, he declared that Jesus "will never destroy one truth of the sages of the past. Buddha made a great contribution to the better life of India and Asia. Mohammed uplifted idolatrous Arabia. Confucius gave priceless teaching of personal, social and political ethics, and no one truth of the past will ever be lost or destroyed."[15] Eddy also became convinced that training and elevating Christian workers from within the various cultures would be far more effective than forever importing white missionaries. That idea, which originated with pioneering mission theorist Rufus Anderson in the mid-1800s, would become mainstream a few decades later.

Senior leaders at the 1920 SVM Quadrennial continued to present the "untamed world" as a wild place in need of "Christian civilization," but young people disillusioned by the Great War were unsure of this vision for global mission.

It was the West, rather than the East, that set about destroying its own truths in the Great War that lasted from the assassination of Austrian archduke Franz Ferdinand on June 28, 1914, to the armistice of November 11, 1918. Tragically, the war drew fuel from some of the same sources that had propelled the missions movement: dreams of extending God's kingdom on earth, the ideal of muscular manhood, international alliances, and civilizational confidence. Young men who boldly donned their nations' uniforms, anticipating glory, found slaughter and disease instead. The war directly claimed about twenty million lives, and the flu pandemic spread by wartime displacement and mobilization added as many as fifty million more fatalities. The death, destruction, and disillusionment were all significantly worse in Europe than in

15. Quoted in Rick Nutt, "G. Sherwood Eddy and the Attitudes of Protestants in the United States toward Global Mission," *Church History* 66, no. 3 (September 1997): 505, 511.

the United States, but even the internationally minded American students who gathered in Des Moines for the 1920 SVM Quadrennial Convention were not sure how to proceed. Some of them had, as Ezra Pound wrote in the haunting poem "Hugh Selwyn Mauberley," "walked eye-deep in hell / believing in old men's lies, then unbelieving / came home, home to a lie."[16] How could anyone move forward after an experience like that?

The elder statesmen of the SVM attempted to pick up where the war had forced them to leave off. Wilder organized the Quadrennial Convention, which Mott opened with a bracing address on "The World Opportunity." Eddy, who spoke toward the end of the gathering, struck a different tone, admitting that he had been asked by some of the students, "Why do you bring us this piffle, these old shibboleths, these old worn-out phrases, why are you talking to us about the living God and the divine Christ?" Eddy hoped that deeper faith and stronger character would carry the volunteers through, and indeed, the meeting was a numerical success—it tallied a record 6,899 delegates, 400 of them representing 39 foreign countries, and enlisted 637 volunteers for missions.[17] Nonetheless, a current of unease was building. The Harvard Crimson reported of the conference, "Men looked forward to a discussion of broad religious problems with their economic and political bearings. What they got, for the most part, from the speeches in the big Coliseum was narrow sectarian religion."[18]

Eddy heard these complaints grow louder after what he called the "insurgent revolution" in Des Moines, and he agreed with them. In the summer of 1922, he told the SVM executive committee that it had to decide whether to take "a more socialized and broader" approach to Christian mission, including taking a hard look at the failings of the United States, or become merely "a reactionary body unresponsive to the demands of the present student generation."[19] Students pushed the 1924 convention in the broader direction. While the banner over the gathering in Indianapolis still bore the watchwords "the evangelization of the world in this generation," student-led discussion groups grappled with lynching, the exploitation of workers, and the dangers of militarization. Though outnumbered, the voices of international students and American racial minorities were especially pointed in these discussions. One delegate, a Black student from New York City, recalled that he expected to hear "the usual superlatives about the splendor of Western civilization" contrasted with "the supposedly backward

16. Ezra Pound, Hugh Selwyn Mauberley (London: The Ovid Press, 1920), 12.
17. On the Des Moines convention, see Parker, Kingdom of Character, 147–50, the quote is from p. 149.
18. "The Des Moines Convention," Harvard Crimson, January 7, 1920.
19. Quoted in Nathan D. Showalter, The End of a Crusade: The Student Volunteer Movement for Foreign Missions and the Great War (Lanham, MD: Scarecrow, 1998), 96.

peoples of Asia and Africa," but instead he heard Chinese, Indian, and African students critiquing American short-comings and demanding that Americans show more respect for foreign cultures.[20] If Western civilization betrayed Christian values, then the project of spreading it around the world seemed much less compelling.

By 1932, the movement launched at Mount Hermon in 1886 had fizzled. The numbers of convention participants, new missionary volunteers, and dollars raised went sharply downhill after 1920. Eddy quit his position with the YMCA and identified as a Christian Socialist, pursuing the social welfare and social justice goals that had been present since

Pearl S. Buck's experiences as a missionary in China caused her to rethink her vocation and her faith. She left Christianity and became a celebrated writer, winning a Pulitzer Prize for her 1932 novel *The Good Earth*.

the founding of the YMCA and YWCA but had been sidelined within the SVM wing. Donors, led by John D. Rockefeller Jr., called for a thorough review of the American Protestant missionary enterprise. That study became the searching, occasionally scathing 1932 book *Re-Thinking Missions*, also known as the Hocking Report (named for the head of the study commission, Harvard philosophy professor William Ernest Hocking). Eddy, Rockefeller, and the members of the Hocking commission did not give up on Christian mission, but they wanted to see it changed, chastened, and rechanneled. The most celebrated missionary of the era, though, was ready to walk away.

Pearl Sydenstricker Buck's parents were Presbyterian missionaries in China. She grew up there, fluent in Chinese, then attended college in the United States before returning to China as a missionary herself in 1914. While her family held a higher view of Chinese culture than did many Western missionaries, she nonetheless complained in letters to relatives and friends in 1918 about "constant contact with the terrible degradation and wickedness of a heathen people," and she struggled with the burden of taking "*sole* charge of the evangelistic work for the women in a district of about two million people."[21] In addition to feeling unequal to this evangelistic task, she started to wonder whether it was even the

20. Quoted in Showalter, *End of a Crusade*, 104.

21. Quoted in Grant Wacker, "Pearl S. Buck and the Waning of the Missionary Impulse," *Church History* 72, no. 4 (December 2003): 857–58.

right task to undertake. "Too often we have tried to preach the gospel to people who were starving and cold and homeless, instead of first ministering to their physical needs," she mused.[22]

By the late 1920s, the political situation in China was deteriorating, and Buck's marriage, to a fellow missionary, was fraying. Seeking a new direction in life and a new source of income, she turned to writing. Her second novel, *The Good Earth*, told a story of hardship, ambition, and conflict within a Chinese family. The book was a bestseller in the United States for two years and earned the 1932 Pulitzer Prize for fiction, the first time that award was won by a woman. This acclaim led to numerous speaking engagements for the author. Missionaries played only a small, very negative role in the novel, but because that was Buck's background, and because missions were such a major mode of contact between the United States and China, Buck was asked to speak on that topic. In April 1932, at the Hotel Astor in New York City, she addressed an audience of two thousand Presbyterian women on the subject "Is There a Case for Foreign Missions?" Her answer was maybe, but only with radical changes in message and approach:

> I should like to see every missionary sent to satisfy a special need of a community—not the artificial need of a mission station for a clerical man or a woman evangelist or what not, but a real need of the people. I should like him to feel that in satisfying this need he was fulfilling the primary purpose of his religion, and not that he was to use it as a bait for enticing anyone into belief in a creed or into belonging to an organization. This, of course, changes at once the whole basis of missions. It shifts the emphasis from preaching *to* a people to sharing a life *with* them, the best life we know. It seems to me this is the only possible basis for missions. It removes from us the insufferable stigma of moral arrogance, and it gives us besides a test of our own worth. Before we can share anything with benefit we must have tried it ourselves.[23]

Backlash to Buck's speech was severe. J. Gresham Machen, a prominent conservative Presbyterian, demanded that the mission board denounce her. The board's leader, missiologist Robert E. Speer, publicly urged charity while privately speculating that Buck was psychologically unwell. Buck saved them the trouble of dealing with her by cutting ties to the church and sailing back to China.[24] In later years, she said, "I make it a policy never to associate myself with religious organizations," and she claimed to need no faith other than her

22. Quoted in Wacker, "Pearl S. Buck," 858–59.
23. Pearl S. Buck, "Is There a Case for Foreign Missions?," *Harper's Monthly Magazine*, January 1933, 154.
24. See Wacker, "Pearl S. Buck," 855.

faith in human beings.[25] She donated much of the money that she earned from her books to secular charities.

The rethinking that took place in the 1930s split the Protestant missionary movement into two broad trajectories. Liberal Protestants, such as Eddy, and post-Protestants, such as Buck, focused on this-worldly work. Some of the biggest donors followed the same turn. John D. Rockefeller Jr., for example, directed his family's millions toward education, the arts, national parks, and international diplomacy. The YMCA in the United States became known for providing recreation and cheap lodging; many Americans did not even realize that the "C" in the abbreviation stood for "Christian." Conservative Protestants, meanwhile, focused on evangelization, increasingly mobilizing through nondenominational faith missions rather than denominational mission boards (with the notable exception of Southern Baptists, who maintained a robust International Mission Board). Conservative Protestants did not ignore the bodily needs of people whom they began to call "unreached" rather than "heathen"; in fact, the evangelical organization World Vision is one of the biggest relief and development agencies on the planet. Rather, conservative Protestants prioritized direct evangelism, as in the mission statement of the organization Pioneers, Inc.: "Pioneers empowers gospel-driven Christians to go to the ends of the earth together in relentless pursuit of the unreached."

The SVM had attempted to harness all these impulses and energies in one global project. But the twentieth century did not become the imagined Christian century, under the benevolent governance of the "Christian races." It was, instead, an era of theological division, war, decolonization, and challenges to racial and gender hierarchies. Foreign missions alternately ameliorated and exacerbated these frictions. By the early twenty-first century, the United States was both the top missionary-sending country in the world and the country to which the highest number of foreign missionaries were sent. The evangelization of the world continued, long after and far beyond the Mount Hermon generation.

------▼------

Althea Brown, a Black woman from Alabama, graduated from Fisk University in 1901 and began a career as a missionary in Congo Free State the next year. There, she met and married fellow missionary Alonzo Edmiston, who had trained at Stillman College and Tuskegee Institute. The couple faced unique challenges on both sides of the Atlantic. Their predominantly white American mission board questioned their leadership, and they were deeply uneasy interacting with the brutal Belgian colonial regime. Some of the principles they had learned at their

25. Quoted in Wacker, "Pearl S. Buck," 864.

historically Black alma maters translated better to the African context than others. In a 1908 issue of the periodical the *American Missionary*, Althea used a few lines of a hymn to express the spirit with which she faced those challenges.

> Ill that He blesses is our good,
> And unblessed good is ill,
> And all is right that seems most wrong
> If it be His sweet will.[26]

FURTHER READING

Bays, Daniel H., and Grant Wacker, eds. *The Foreign Missionary Enterprise at Home: Explorations in North American Culture History*. Tuscaloosa: University of Alabama Press, 2003.

Corrigan, John, Melani McAlister, and Axel R. Schäfer, eds. *Global Faith, Worldly Power: Evangelical Internationalism and U.S. Empire*. Chapel Hill: University of North Carolina Press, 2022.

Gin Lum, Kathryn. *Heathen: Religion and Race in American History*. Cambridge, MA: Harvard University Press, 2022.

Hill, Kimberly D. *A Higher Mission: The Careers of Alonzo and Althea Brown Edmiston in Central Africa*. Lexington: University Press of Kentucky, 2020.

Hollinger, David A. *Protestants Abroad: How Missionaries Tried to Change the World but Changed American Culture*. Princeton: Princeton University Press, 2017.

Hutchison, William R. *Errand to the World: American Protestant Thought and Foreign Missions*. Chicago: University of Chicago Press, 1987.

Parker, Michael. *The Kingdom of Character: The Student Volunteer Movement for Foreign Missions (1886–1926)*. Lanham, MD: American Society of Missiology; University Press of America, 1998.

Robert, Dana L., ed. *Converting Colonialism: Visions and Realities in Mission History, 1706–1914*. Grand Rapids: Eerdmans, 2008.

Ruble, Sarah E. *The Gospel of Freedom and Power: Protestant Missionaries in American Culture after World War II*. Chapel Hill: University of North Carolina Press, 2012.

Showalter, Nathan D. *The End of a Crusade: The Student Volunteer Movement for Foreign Missions and the Great War*. Lanham, MD: Scarecrow, 1998.

---

26. Althea Brown Edmiston, "Missions in Congo Free State, Africa," *The American Missionary* (December 1908): 310.

10

Los Angeles Fire

Azusa Street Revival Catalyzes Pentecostalism, 1906

Although the Azusa Street revival departed very intentionally from the printed hymnals and preset orders of worship utilized in other churches, it developed its own sort of liturgy that included touchstone songs. Three hymns were sung nearly every day in the early months of the revival: "Heavenly Sunlight," "Under the Blood," and the song most often associated with the revival, "The Comforter Has Come." While the first two of these hymns emphasized salvation through Christ, the third conveyed the event's signature focus on the Holy Spirit.

> O spread the tidings 'round
> Wherever man is found,
> Wherever human hearts and human woes abound;
> Let every Christian tongue proclaim the joyful sound:
> The Comforter has come!
>
> [*refrain*] The Comforter has come, the Comforter has come!
> The Holy Ghost from heaven, the Father's promise given;
> O spread the tidings 'round wherever man is found:
> The Comforter has come![1]

1. Francis Bottome, "The Comforter Has Come," in *Redemption Hymnal* (London: Elim Publishing House, 1951), no. 227.

In June 1906, Clara E. Lum, a stenographer in Los Angeles, penned a letter to friends describing a recent religious experience. "The Lord is . . . pouring out Pentecost in old time power," she wrote. "I have never seen the power of God manifest in so many people, nor have I ever seen such manifestations of his power." She continued:

> He . . . gave me the baptism of the Holy Ghost. . . . It came in power thrilling me and remaining upon me in a power like electricity. He also gave me the gift of healing and casting out devils. He has used me to heal a few sick since then. He shows me he is going to use me to write in a different way than before. He also will not take this power from me. . . .
>
> The Lord is saving souls, sanctifying believers and baptizing them with the Holy Ghost. . . . They have spoken in Spanish, Chinese, Japanese, African dialects, Indian dialects, Esquimaux language is spoken by one; deaf mute language is spoken by one; Hebrew, Greek, Latin, a language of India, French, by others. . . .
>
> The Lord is giving the gift of prophecy . . . that a revival of the pure Gospel is to sweep over the land.[2]

Lum was describing the Azusa Street revival, an event with clear echoes of Acts 2, which contains the description of what many Christians consider the birth of the church. To call the 1906 revival the birth of Pentecostalism is complicated, because the event had important global antecedents and because many Christians in this lineage do not think of themselves as Pentecostals. Yet it is undeniable that a distinctive form of Christianity burst forth from a run-down building in Los Angeles to become, a century later, the second-most prevalent form of the faith globally, touching more than six hundred million souls. (The most prevalent form is Roman Catholicism, but substantial portions of that church feature Pentecostal inflections.) No other event in American church history has had such a far-reaching impact, which raises questions of how and why this happened.

Roads to Azusa Street

All of the beliefs and practices that came to be seen as Pentecostal hallmarks—including revivalism, miraculous healing, eschatological urgency, attention to personal holiness, energy for missions, and glossolalia, or speaking in tongues—

---

2. Letter published in *Missionary World*, August 1906; condensed in Gastón Espinosa, *William J. Seymour and the Origins of Global Pentecostalism: A Biography and Documentary History* (Durham, NC: Duke University Press, 2014), 332.

had appeared somewhere before 1906. Evangelicals had welcomed revivals since the 1730s (see chap. 4). Reports of miraculous healings cropped up throughout church history, from the New Testament forward. Belief that the world would end soon characterized the second-century Montanist movement, the twelfth-century thought of Joachim of Fiore, the Latter-day Saints in the 1830s, the Millerites (precursor to the Seventh-day Adventist Church) in the 1840s, and countless other groups. Emphasis on personal holiness was especially strong in German Pietism and Methodism. Fervor for missions and evangelism ran high throughout the English-speaking world at the turn of the twentieth century. Even the most distinctive aspect of early Pentecostal worship, speaking in tongues, had decades-old precedent. Spontaneous utterances in unknown languages, sometimes thought to be earthly languages that the speaker had never studied and sometimes thought to be heavenly, were documented in Glasgow, Scotland, in 1830 and in London the following year, with additional reports scattered across the nineteenth century.

The most immediate precursors to the Azusa Street revival occurred in three very different places. In January 1901, in Topeka, Kansas, a woman named Agnes Ozman asked her spiritual mentor, the evangelist Charles Fox Parham, to pray that she would be filled with the Holy Spirit and speak in tongues. When Parham did so, Ozman's fellow students at Parham's Bible college attested that they saw a halo around her face and she began speaking Chinese, a language she had never studied. In September 1904, evangelist Seth Joshua visited a church in New Quay, Wales, and wrote in his diary, "I have never seen the power of the Holy Spirit so powerfully manifested among the people as at this place just now."[3] Another evangelist, Evan Roberts, prayed that God would "give us 100,000 souls," and, by the end of the 1904–5 Welsh Revival, about that many people had been added to Welsh churches.[4] In January 1905, Bible teacher and activist Pandita Ramabai instituted morning prayer meetings at her Mukti Mission in India, where women asked for an outpouring of the Holy Spirit. Attendance at the prayer meetings swelled to five hundred women, weeping, praying, prophesying, and speaking in tongues. According to Ramabai, "Some have laughed at us, for we have become fools. The Spirit-filled girls cannot suppress their sorrow for sin or their joy in salvation. They burst into loud crying and laughing, they shake, they tremble, some of them dance with joy and almost pray simultaneously in loud voices."[5] It all looked, and sounded, a lot like Acts 2.

3. Quoted in Eifion Evans, *The Welsh Revival of 1904* (London: Evangelical Press, 1969), 59–60.
4. Evans, *Welsh Revival*, 79.
5. Quoted in Allan Heaton Anderson, *To the Ends of the Earth: Pentecostalism and the Transformation of World Christianity* (New York: Oxford University Press, 2013), 27.

These antecedents connected to Azusa Street through people and publications. After his school in Topeka failed, Parham relocated to Houston, where one of his students was the Black evangelist William J. Seymour. Seymour would go on to lead the Azusa Street revival. Another Los Angeles pastor, Joseph Smale, had already been trying to replicate what he saw in Wales, though with little success. Reports of the Welsh Revival also reached India, where they inspired Ramabai. One of the evangelists active in Wales, R. A. Torrey, subsequently conducted meetings in Australia, and Ramabai sent her daughter and a member of her mission staff, Minnie Abrams, there to see him. Reports on Ramabai's revival were then published around the world, and Abrams spread the word on trips back to the United States. A prolific chronicler of the Azusa Street revival, Frank Bartleman, famously wrote, "The present world-wide revival was rocked in the cradle of little Wales, it was 'brought up' in India, following; becoming full grown in Los Angeles later."[6]

Itinerant evangelism and heavy use of print media had propelled revivalism since the days of George Whitefield. Faster transportation and innovations in communications amplified these effects in the early twentieth century, making it possible for not just a transatlantic but a truly global network to emerge. Network connections did not, however, mean that Christians who shared some characteristic beliefs and practices agreed on everything or thought of themselves as part of a unified movement. A closer look at the Azusa Street revival reveals how the diversity that has always marked Pentecostal expressions of faith has been a source of both strength and conflict.

Race and Revival

William Seymour was an unlikely candidate to lead a world-altering event. He was born in 1870 in Louisiana, the son of formerly enslaved laborers, and in the 1890s he moved to Indianapolis and then Cincinnati, seeking work and relative safety from racial violence. Although he had been baptized as a baby and grew up attending churches, he converted to a different kind of Christianity in the Midwest. This region was home to many radical Holiness churches, offshoots of Methodism that taught Christians to seek a baptism from the Holy Spirit that would enable them to experience physical healing and spiritual perfection in advance of the imminent rapture of the saints. Seymour absorbed these ideas, attended a Bible school, and might have become a full-time preacher right away, but a smallpox infection left him blind in one eye, and

6. Frank Bartleman, *How Pentecost Came to Los Angeles: The Story behind the Azusa Street Revival* (Los Angeles: Gospel Publishing House, 1925), 21.

An abandoned African Methodist Episcopal Church on Azusa Street in Los Angeles became the generally recognized birthplace of Pentecostalism. People flocked to the simple building to partici-pate in, or gape at, the exuberant worship services held there.

he hesitated. In 1903, he moved back to the South, hoping to reconnect with relatives.

In Houston, Seymour interacted with many Holiness leaders, Black and white, mostly men but also a few women. He grew close to Charles Parham, who taught, controversially, that the only sure sign of Holy Spirit baptism was speaking in tongues. Seymour attended Parham's newly founded Bible school, sitting in a room separate from white students due to Texas's segregation laws. He sometimes engaged in evangelism with Parham, preaching to Black audi-ences while Parham addressed whites.

Parham's racial views were a source of friction between the two men. Parham believed that members of all races should be evangelized, but he also believed that Adam and Eve belonged to a white race that God created on the eighth day, superior to the other races that God had created on the sixth day. When Sey-mour learned of an opportunity to lead a Black Holiness church in Los Angeles, far from Parham, he was eager to take it. Parham initially objected, preferring to maintain oversight over the promising evangelist, but he eventually relented and even provided part of the funding for Seymour's journey.

A different aspect of Parham's theology created a barrier for Seymour after he arrived in Los Angeles in February 1906. The woman who had invited Sey-mour to lead her church, Mrs. Julia Hutchins, was put off by his claim that fully sanctified Christians should speak in tongues—a power that Seymour himself had not even attained. Less than two weeks after he started preaching in California, Hutchins padlocked the church door and expelled him from ministry. Seymour asked a member of the church, Edward Lee, for help and soon started over with a prayer meeting at Lee's cottage on Union Street. That group grew, adding some white members, and moved to a site on Bonnie Brae Street, still in a predominantly Black section of town.

On April 6, Seymour initiated a ten-day fast for revival, a practice that had been employed in Wales and elsewhere. Just three days later, Seymour prayed that Lee would receive the baptism of the Holy Spirit, and Lee immediately spoke in tongues. Seymour preached that night on Acts 2:4, cementing the connection between this event and the first Christian Pentecost. Seymour finally spoke in tongues on April 12, alongside a white man at the altar, a level of racial mixing that Parham never allowed. On April 15, meetings moved to an even larger venue, an abandoned African Methodist Episcopal Church on Azusa Street. That address has been used as shorthand for the revival ever since.

Exuberant, tongues-speaking spirituality was not common on the West Coast, and it attracted a lot of attention. On April 18, 1906, the *Los Angeles Daily Times* published a stacked headline that would become famous: "Weird Babel of Tongues. New Sect of Fanatics Is Breaking Loose. Wild Scene Last Night on Azusa Street. Gurgle of Wordless Talk by a Sister." The account was suffused with racism, highlighting Seymour's disability and charging him with exercising unwarranted authority. It read, "With his stony optic fixed on some luckless unbeliever, the old man yells his defiance and challenges an answer. Anathemas are heaped upon him who shall dare to gainsay the utterances of the preacher." A Black woman in the congregation was also caricatured, described as "an old colored 'mammy,'" swinging her arms and shouting incomprehensible syllables, "You-oo-oo gou-loo-loo come under the bloo-oo-oo boo-loo."[7]

Histories of Pentecostalism often cite this article to illustrate widespread mockery of the revival, but initially only the local press noticed. Some neighbors complained about the noise, as did the Los Angeles Ministerial Association, but the city made no moves to curtail the meetings. A few other newspapers with a connection to the event did eventually weigh in negatively, including the *Indianapolis Star*, with an article even more flagrantly racist than the one in the *Los Angeles Daily Times*, and the *Topeka Daily State Journal*, which played up Parham's role as founder of the "strange religious movement," calling its adherents "His Holy Rollers."[8]

7. "Weird Babel of Tongues," excerpted in Espinosa, *William J. Seymour*, 372–74.

8. "Negro Bluk Kissed," *Indianapolis Star*, June 3, 1907, in Espinosa, *William J. Seymour*, 376; "His Holy Rollers," *Topeka Daily State Journal*, July 25, 1906.

Answered Prayers

The Azusa Street publication, *The Apostolic Faith*, listed an array of spiritual manifestations in its first issue (September 1906), revealing much about the concerns and hopes of revival participants.

Many have laid aside their glasses and had their eye sight perfectly restored. The deaf have had their hearing restored.

A man was healed of asthma of twenty years standing. Many have been healed of heart trouble and lung trouble.

Many are saying that God has given the message that He is going to shake Los Angeles with an earthquake. First, there will be a revival to give all an opportunity to be saved. The revival is now in progress.

The Lord has given the gift of writing in unknown languages, also the gift of playing on instruments.

A little girl who walked with crutches and had tuberculosis of the bones, as the doctors declared, was healed and dropped her crutches and began to skip about the yard.

All over this city, God has been setting homes on fire and coming down and melting and saving and sanctifying and baptizing with the Holy Ghost.

Many churches have been praying for Pentecost, and Pentecost has come. The question is now, will they accept it?

Azusa Papers and Azusa Books, https://www.azusabooks.org/af/LA01.shtml.

The fiercest criticisms of Azusa Street appeared in other Christian periodicals, especially those representing the Holiness tradition from which Seymour had broken. These journals published articles with headlines such as "The Tongues Heresy," "Satan Transformed," "Gibberish," "Fanaticisms and Humbugs," "Given Over to Believe a Lie," and "It Is a Counterfeit Pentecost." Secular observers saw in ecstatic, mixed-gender, and interracial religious services a threat to the social order, echoing older critiques of Black churches, Quakers, Shakers, the First Great Awakening, and the Second Great Awakening. Holiness Christians, by contrast, felt betrayed by their closest kin. The country might not be big enough for both their churches and this new, as-yet-unnamed, tongues-speaking movement.[9]

9. Headlines from the *Rocky Mountain Pillar of Fire, Beulah Christian*, the *Burning Bush*, and the *Nazarene Messenger*, in Larry E. Martin, *Skeptics and Scoffers: The Religious World Looks at Azusa Street, 1906–1907* (Pensacola, FL: Christian Life Books, 2004).

To counteract the negative coverage and publicize accounts of the revival, attracting visitors and potentially sparking new revivals elsewhere, the mission at Azusa Street launched its own periodical, *The Apostolic Faith*. It had a lot of good news to report. Services grew in attendance and diversity, Blacks worshiping with whites, Swedes and Russians with Mexicans, Chinese, and Native Americans. Men prayed for women, and women prayed for men. Some people of higher social rank joined the predominantly working-class congregation. In the testimonies that constituted the bulk of each service, people spoke of miraculous healing and spiritual deliverance. Scores volunteered to be door-to-door evangelists or foreign missionaries—even Julia Hutchins, the woman who had locked Seymour out of her church, became convinced of his teaching and traveled as a missionary to Liberia. Many preachers visited, bringing their doubts but leaving convinced that this was the Spirit's work. (Preachers who were not convinced wrote many of those scathing articles in Christian periodicals.) According to Pentecostal historian Gastón Espinosa, by 1914 Azusa-inspired churches and missions could be found in every US city with a population over three thousand, plus hundreds of locations in other countries. The influence was swift and vast.[10]

Inevitably, a ministry growing so fast and deviating so sharply from churchly and cultural norms experienced both external attacks and internal tensions. The nature of these challenges at Azusa Street presaged the challenges faced later in the movement that was catalyzed there.

Six months into the revival, Charles Parham visited, and he later wrote, "Found conditions even worse than I anticipated." Shocked by the boisterous worship and erasure of the color line, he strode to the pulpit and announced, "God is sick at his stomach!" This declaration initiated a brief but intense campaign to siphon members from Seymour's mission and a much longer campaign to discredit him. Parham, with his doctrine of eighth-day white creation, could not abide the authority of a Black leader or behaviors he derided as "animalism." Many early white Pentecostals shared Parham's racism. Parham openly supported the Ku Klux Klan, and Klansmen—sometimes wearing their hoods— were welcome at Pentecostal meetings from California to West Virginia. (The same was true at many other white Protestant churches in this era.) Meanwhile, the Azusa mission initially forbade whites to serve as elders, and some Latinos and Native Americans felt that Seymour did not heed their concerns. Azusa had racial and ethnic diversity but fell short of equity.[11]

---

10. Espinosa, *William J. Seymour*, 70.

11. Espinosa, *William J. Seymour*, 96–101. On interactions between the Klan and early Pentecostals, see Brian C. Sears, "The Vanguard of God: Pentecostals and Charismatics in the Religious Right" (MA thesis, Baylor University, 2022). On entanglements between the Klan and other white

William Seymour, seated at center, led the Apostolic Faith Mission. Other members of the leadership team included Florence Crawford (standing behind Seymour) and Clara Lum (seated next to Seymour). The child in the front row is Crawford's daughter, Mildred.

A combination of growing pains and gender dynamics shook the Azusa mission the following year. Florence Crawford had been the first white woman to experience Holy Spirit baptism in the early days of the Azusa revival, and by summer she was part of its inner circle of leaders. In the fall, she felt called to preach the revival's message up the West Coast to Oregon. Seymour reluctantly agreed. Some of her meetings produced many conversions and Holy Spirit baptisms, but the local press responded with increasing hostility. By the time she got to Portland, in late December, city authorities were looking for a reason to shut her down. When Crawford's nine-year-old daughter, Mildred, spoke in tongues at a meeting, they found one. The local newspaper claimed that Crawford had allowed Mildred to become the "chief attraction" at her "fantastic orgies," and a judge in juvenile court threatened to take Mildred away. Crawford begrudgingly traveled back down the coast to Los Angeles but considered the episode a temporary setback. She was sure that God wanted her in Portland.[12]

churches, see Kelly J. Baker, *Gospel according to the Klan: The KKK's Appeal to Protestant America, 1915–1930* (Lawrence: University of Kansas Press, 2011).

12. Cecil M. Robeck Jr., "Florence Crawford: Apostolic Faith Pioneer," in *Portraits of a Generation: Early Pentecostal Leaders*, ed. James R. Goff Jr. and Grant Wacker (Fayetteville: University of Arkansas Press, 2002), 218–35.

Seymour generally supported women's leadership in ministry, but Crawford's case altered his stance. Crawford disagreed with Seymour on some minor points of belief and practice. Worse, Crawford's husband, Frank, did not support her work in Portland. The couple divorced, and Seymour sided with Frank, obliquely attacking Florence in print by writing, "Many homes today have been wrecked and brought to naught through false teaching. Wives have left husbands and gone off, claiming that the Lord has called her to do mission work, and to leave the little children at home to fare the best they can."[13] Crawford responded by cutting ties with Seymour, as well as with her husband, and starting a new denomination called Apostolic Faith. In this way, Crawford became a competitor in the religious market. Her position was strengthened when another member of the Azusa Street inner circle, Clara Lum, also bolted, bringing the Azusa Street publication and its valuable mailing list from Los Angeles to Portland.

All of these types of conflicts recurred in the history that followed Azusa Street: attempts to erode or reinforce racial and gender hierarchies; a desire to plant new churches and missions coexisting uneasily with a desire to maintain oversight; families strained by different perceptions of divine calling and children thrust into uncomfortable roles; a proliferation of denominations, along with fights for control over periodicals and other institutions. These conflicts were by no means unique to Pentecostalism, but they remained unusually prevalent as the energies unleashed at Azusa Street surged through three phases in the twentieth century: classical Pentecostalism, charismatic renewal, and the harder-to-define but much bigger neo-charismatic movement.

New Denominations

The portion of this story that scholars call the era of classical Pentecostalism consisted largely of denomination-building. Denominational history does not tend to be of much interest to people outside the denomination, but a brief look at this topic helps to explain the American religious landscape. Some of the denominations became quite large. The ways in which they were united and divided helps to clarify what was central to Pentecostalism and what was negotiable. A few leading figures attained notoriety far beyond the tradition, and some of the techniques that they pioneered were readily adopted by other churches.

The oldest large American Pentecostal denomination with a direct connection to the Azusa Street revival is the Church of God in Christ (COGIC), with headquarters in Memphis, Tennessee. It has been since its 1897 founding pre-

---

13. Quoted in Espinosa, *William J. Seymour*, 107.

dominantly Black. Its earliest leaders were part of the Holiness milieu in the South and Midwest that had nurtured William Seymour. When news of Seymour's revival reached them, one of the leaders, Charles Harrison Mason, was dispatched to investigate. In Los Angeles he received Holy Spirit baptism and spoke in tongues. When he returned and shared his experience, not all of the church leaders affirmed it, so the church split in 1907 into a Holiness faction, led by Charles Price Jones, and a Pentecostal faction, led by Mason.

Mason's vision was explicitly interracial. The church's 1917 manual stated, "The Church of God in Christ recognizes the fact that all believers are one in Christ Jesus and all its members have equal rights. Its Overseers, both colored and white, have equal power and authority in the church." But the COGIC struggled to recruit and retain white ministers. In 2020, the COGIC reported 8.8 million total members, including 5 million in the United States, with 84 percent of them Black and only 5 percent white.[14]

In 1914, approximately three hundred white ministers, many of them affiliated with the COGIC, met to organize their own Pentecostal denomination. They named it the Assemblies of God (AG), and it became the largest global Pentecostal denomination, with nearly seventy million members in 2020 (though only three million in the United States). Its US membership was 66 percent white, 25 percent Latino, and only 3 percent Black.[15] Aside from racial demographics, a notable difference between the COGIC and the AG is that the COGIC does not ordain women as ministers, while the AG does.

The AG did not initially draft a doctrinal statement, but it quickly divided over an elemental theological issue. Some of the founding ministers believed that God was not a Trinity but rather a single divine being manifested as Father, Son, and Holy Spirit at different points in human history. These ministers, who chose the term "Oneness" to describe their beliefs, baptized in the name of Jesus only, not using the words of the centuries-old trinitarian formula. The majority of the founding AG ministers considered this theology to be heresy. In 1916, the majority adopted a trinitarian "Statement of Fundamental Truths," and about one-third of the assembly left to form Oneness fellowships. After a series of mergers, the largest of these is the United Pentecostal Church International. It had 5.3 million members worldwide in 2020 and was predominantly white.

New Pentecostal denominations kept forming throughout the early twentieth century. The most famous founder of one of these was Aimee Semple

---

14. David D. Daniels, "Charles Harrison Mason: The Interracial Impulse of Early Pentecostalism," in Goff and Wacker, *Portraits of a Generation*, 254–70.

15. "Members of the Assemblies of God," Pew Research Center, Religious Landscape Study, https://www.pewresearch.org/religion/religious-landscape-study/religious-denomination/assemblies-of-god/.

Borderlands Ministry

Evangelists crossing between the United States and Mexico contributed greatly to the growth of Pentecostalism on both sides of the border. In this 1932 report for a denominational periodical, A. M. Lopez, the Texas-based superintendent of Mexican work for the Pentecostal Holiness Church, explained what he was doing and how readers could help.

> Port Isbell [Isabel] Church invited me to go and help in the work. Bro. Botello has a great work to do and he told me to go to that church which had not sufficient co-operation in its many needs. I take my family and go to that city and I work for two weeks and return to Weslaco [Texas]. I received a letter from Reynosa, Mexico, and the brother asked me to help in that work so it can be established according to the law of that Mexican city.
>
> I leave my family at Weslaco and I go to Reynosa City and work for God there. First, I was trying to reach the first class people, and I go out and see them. I also visit the city Mayor, Mr. Lauro Herrera, one of the best men I ever heard, and he was so nice to me. I talked to him in regard to the P.H. [Pentecostal Holiness] Church and he was surprised after I talked to him and told him about Rev. J.H. King our Gen. Supt., he said: I hope that man talk ▶

McPherson. Born in 1890 in Ontario, Canada, she was converted to Pentecostalism by a missionary in 1907, married the missionary, and traveled with him to China, where he died. She remarried in 1912, but, like Florence Crawford before her, she felt a call to ministry—preaching and healing at tent revivals across the United States—that her husband did not fully support. He filed for separation in 1918, the same year that she decided to anchor her ministry in Los Angeles. The 3,500-seat auditorium that she rented proved to be too small, so she raised money for a 5,300-seat domed structure, the Angelus Temple, which opened in 1923. It was not the first megachurch—a title sometimes bestowed on Charles Haddon Spurgeon's 6,000-capacity Metropolitan Tabernacle, which opened in London in 1861—but it was unlike anything previously built in the United States. It was shaped like an auditorium, not a cathedral, and fully equipped for both theatrical spectacle and radio broadcast.

Even in a tradition full of colorful figures, Sister Aimee stood out. Her services featured costumes, elaborate props (such as a motorcycle), and live animals. She delivered up to twenty-two sermons a week. She published a weekly newspaper and a monthly magazine, and she was the second woman in the over our Radio Station. This is one of the best ways to reach the high class people of Mexico, also if you can do this work for the Mexican people you may have more and more co-operation by the local laws of the small cities.

We have the permit to work among the people and hundreds of people come and hear the Gospel in the small hall we get for the revival. In one week's work God saved fifty-five souls, forty-six were sanctified and on the 31st of Jan. we organized the work in the church and more than four hundred people were there present. Also our people there, that is, the congregation desires to build a church and we got a good lot. I send the petition according to the Mexican law to Mexico City, so we can get a permit to build our church.

This service moved my heart when I see the brothers without sufficient clothing on their body, crying to God to help so they can get the building they need. I was crying too and saying: I hope some of our American people could see these services. The ladies said, we have no money but we can work for the glory of God, and they said, "Bro. Lopez, please help us so we can just get something to eat and we can build the church for God." Some people come from big ranches about thirty miles and they want some man to go there and preach to the people who are living there. Mexican people are hungry now.

A. M. Lopez, "Mexican Work," *Pentecostal Holiness Advocate*, February 25, 1932, 7–10.

country to attain a broadcast license for a radio station. She was photographed constantly and courted media attention. Journalists turned against her, however, in 1926, when she disappeared from a beach in Santa Monica, California, and then reappeared more than a month later in a hospital in Douglas, Arizona, saying that she had been kidnapped. Reporters suspected that she had faked the kidnapping, possibly to enjoy a getaway with a lover, and they passed information supporting this theory to the police. McPherson was charged with conspiracy, perjury, and obstruction of justice, but she insisted that she had truly been kidnapped. She won in court, with all charges dropped, but she lost in the court of public opinion. Nonetheless, the denomination that she founded, the Foursquare Church (so named for its theology of Jesus Christ as savior, baptizer, healer, and soon-coming king), persisted, claiming 8.8 million members in 2020.

To call all these churches—COGIC, AG, Oneness, Foursquare—Pentecostal is to make claims about the essence and boundaries of the movement. Speaking in tongues was the dividing line between these churches and the Holiness tradition, but they differed among themselves on major questions, such as the nature of God, the ministerial role of women, and separation from versus engagement with the wider world. Theologian Douglas Jacobsen wrote, "In a general sense, being pentecostal means that one is committed to a Spirit-centered, miracle-affirming, praise-oriented version of the Christian faith."[16] Pentecostal scholar Allan Heaton Anderson further clarified, "*Classical pentecostals* are those whose faith can be shown to have originated in the evangelical revival and missionary movements of the early twentieth century, particularly in the Western world."[17] The term "Pentecostal" is somewhat analogous to the term "Protestant," then, distinguishing a form of Christianity that emerged from a particular set of conflicts at a particular time but grew to encompass immense variety. That variety increased in the mid-twentieth century, as Spirit-centered beliefs and practices spilled out of classical Pentecostal denominations into other churches.

"It Is in Our Midst"

In June 1958, Henry P. Van Dusen, the president of Union Theological Seminary in New York, belatedly informed the readers of *Life* magazine about a "Third Force in Christendom," the article's subtitle reading, "Gospel-singing, Doomsday-preaching Sects Emerge as a Mighty Movement in World Religion."[18] Pictures embedded in the article showed smiling congregants raising hands in worship, some people lying on the floor while others prayed for them, healer Oral Roberts with his hands on the head of a sick child, a Puerto Rico–born pastor ministering in Harlem, and an Atlanta bakery owner stating from behind a stack of packaged buns, "The Lord wants us to prosper." *Life*'s approach was friendlier and more nuanced than the "Weird Babel of Tongues" story published in the *Los Angeles Daily Times* fifty years earlier, but it still presented Pentecostals as an exotic fringe group, muscling in on territory previously divided between the first two forces of Christendom, Protestants and Catholics.

Alarming as the third-force Christians might seem, Van Dusen counseled that other Christians had a lot to learn from them. "Many features of this 'new Christianity' bear striking resemblance to the life of the earliest Christian churches," he wrote. The groups (among which he curiously included not just classical Pentecostals but several Holiness churches, Seventh-day Adventists, and Jehovah's Witnesses) preached a readily understood gospel, promised "an immediate life-transforming experience of the living-God-in-Christ," and made great

16. Quoted in Anderson, *To the Ends of the Earth*, 5.
17. Anderson, *To the Ends of the Earth*, 5.
18. Henry P. Van Dusen, "The Third Force in Christendom," *Life*, June 9, 1958, 113–24.

effort to bring new people into their fellowship rather than passively waiting for visitors to find them.[19] Among his own kind of Christians, the tradition that would soon be labeled "the Protestant mainline," the tendency to dismiss the third force as a wild fad was "being replaced by a chastened readiness to investigate the secrets of its mighty sweep, especially to learn if it may not have important, neglected elements in a full and true Christian witness."[20]

A 1946 Pentecostal service in Harlan County, Kentucky, featured healing by the laying on of hands.

Some mainline Protestants, and Roman Catholics, did more than just investigate Pentecostalism. On April 3, 1960, Episcopal priest Dennis J. Bennett of St. Mark's Episcopal Church in Van Nuys, California, announced from the pulpit that he had received Holy Spirit baptism the previous fall and spoken in tongues. Some parishioners in his 2,500-member congregation supported him, but most did not. The vestry asked for his resignation, which he provided, and the bishop sent a new priest to the church with instructions that speaking in tongues would not be allowed. That summer, the Episcopal magazine *Living Church* opined,

> [Speaking in tongues] no longer is a phenomenon of some odd sect across the street—it is in our midst, and it is being practiced by clergy and laity who have stature and good reputation in the Church. . . . Humanly, one might hope this speaking in tongues would prove to have no relevance to the Christian life of today. Its widespread introduction would jar against our aesthetic sense and some of our most strongly entrenched preconceptions. But—and this is a very large "but" indeed—we know that neither our aesthetic preferences nor our preconceptions control God Almighty. And we know that we are members of a Church which definitely needs jarring.[21]

Bennett left California but stayed within the Episcopal Church, becoming rector of St. Luke's in Seattle. That church had been about to close, but under his leadership it grew almost as large as the church he had left. He became known as the father of charismatic renewal in his denomination.

19. Van Dusen, "Third Force in Christendom," 122.
20. Van Dusen, "Third Force in Christendom," 124.
21. "Pentecostal Voices," *Living Church*, July 17, 1960, 9.

Unlike early twentieth-century Pentecostalism, which spawned new denominations, the midcentury charismatic movement was a more diffuse phenomenon by which some ideas and practices associated with Pentecostalism gained traction in established denominations. Some ministers and congregations, such as Bennett's church in Seattle, formally allied with charismatic renewal, but many more Christians participated less formally through conferences and retreats, revival meetings, and print or broadcast media. These Christians did not necessarily expect to speak in tongues, as classical Pentecostals did, nor were they as driven by end-times urgency. Instead, they were most likely to encounter enhanced attention to the Holy Spirit; intense, ecstatic worship; and faith healing.

Religion scholar Amy Artman identified faith healer Kathryn Kuhlman as a key figure in the diffusion and gentrification of Pentecostalism. Kuhlman was born in 1907, the year after the Azusa Street revival, in Concordia, Missouri. She grew up attending a Methodist church and at age fourteen had a spiritually charged conversion experience during the closing hymn of a worship service. "I began to shake so hard that I could no longer hold the hymnal in my hand," she said. "This was my first contact with the Third Person of the Trinity, and in that moment I knew I needed Jesus to forgive my sins."[22] This conversion narrative was more typically evangelical than specifically Pentecostal, as it did not involve speaking in tongues. Kuhlman's older sister, however, adopted a more Pentecostal form of faith and married a traveling evangelist. The couple invited the teenage Kuhlman to travel with them. Their mentor, Charles Price, had attended one of Aimee Semple McPherson's revivals in 1921, arriving as a skeptic and leaving as a believer. Deeply influenced by McPherson, albeit indirectly, Kuhlman launched her own career as an itinerant revivalist at the age of twenty-one.

Kuhlman was very young but by no means the youngest "girl evangelist" of her era. Uldine Utley, another person who had been converted at one of McPherson's services, was just eleven when she started preaching in 1924. By 1926, she was a national sensation, addressing crowds of thousands at Madison Square Garden in New York, but the pressure led to mental collapse a decade later. Kuhlman initially kept a much lower profile, preaching at small churches in the Northwest accompanied by another young woman, who played piano. Even on this small scale, itinerant evangelism was a tiring, stressful lifestyle. After a few years, Kuhlman settled in Denver, establishing the Denver Revival Tabernacle—she did not call it a church, uncomfortable with the idea of a woman as pastor—and a radio broadcast, titled *Smiling Through*.

---

22. Quoted in Amy Artman, *The Miracle Lady: Kathryn Kuhlman and the Transformation of Charismatic Christianity* (Grand Rapids: Eerdmans, 2019), 16.

Kuhlman's unfailing positivity, conveyed in the title of her radio program and her later, much more successful television program, *I Believe in Miracles*, helped her build an audience without the hard-hitting tactics of some other preachers. She consistently projected a gentle image, dressing in feminine pastels and keeping her voice calmer than the rapid-fire style of her male counterparts. She healed with words rather than the forceful laying on of hands. For years, she did not televise the healings that made her famous and drew prodigious crowds; instead, on a set like that of a talk show, she interviewed people who had been healed, drawing out the stories of their transformed lives. Despite a brief, disastrous marriage to another evangelist in the 1940s, she also avoided the sexual and financial scandals that plagued many TV preachers. Millions of Christians outside Pentecostal denominations who would never go near a loud preacher who laid hands on bodies to heal them (such as the man who claimed to be her successor, Benny Hinn) might tune into Kuhlman's show, read one of her books, or even attend one of her services.

Charismatic revival proceeded somewhat differently within Roman Catholicism. Pope John XXIII, who convened the Second Vatican Council in 1962, prayed that the Holy Spirit would "renew Your wonders in our time, as though by a new Pentecost."[23] The council opened the Catholic Church to new expressions of faith, empowerment of laity, and engagement with Christians in other traditions. Amid this ferment, a small group of faculty and students at Duquesne University in Pittsburgh read some Pentecostal literature and participated in an interdenominational charismatic prayer meeting. At a 1967 retreat, known as the Duquesne Weekend, several members had transformative experiences. Participant Patti Gallagher Mansfield recalled, "God sovereignly drew many of the students into the chapel. Some were laughing, others crying. Some prayed in tongues, others (like me) felt a burning sensation coursing through their hands. One of the professors walked in and exclaimed, 'What is the Bishop going to say when he hears that all these kids have been baptized in the Holy Spirit!' Yes, there was a birthday party that night, God had planned it in the Upper Room Chapel. It was the birth of the Catholic Charismatic Renewal!"[24]

From Duquesne, the renewal spread to Notre Dame University and the University of Michigan before quickly gaining international interest, especially in Latin America. It was from the beginning a predominantly lay movement with support from some church leaders and opposition from others. In 1975, the movement got a warm reception in Rome as ten thousand people from sixty-one

23. Pope John XXIII, *Humanae Salutis*, in *Documents of Vatican II*, ed. Walter M. Abbott, SJ, trans. Joseph Gallagher (New York: Guild, 1966), 709.
24. Patti Gallagher Mansfield, "The Duquesne Weekend," Catholic Charismatic Renewal, http://www.ccr.org.uk/about-ccr/about/the-duquesne-weekend/.

countries gathered for an international conference of charismatic Catholics, called by Pope Paul VI. The conference featured a charismatic Mass in St. Peter's Square and workshops that blended historically Pentecostal emphases, such as prayer and healing, with historically Catholic emphases, such as family life and sacramental renewal. The workshop on healing was especially popular.

Christians who participated in charismatic renewal had several religious options. Some stayed in their churches but adopted blended identities, such as charismatic Catholic. (More than half of Hispanic Catholics in the United States identified as charismatics at the end of the twentieth century, as well as 12 percent of white, non-Hispanic Catholics.)[25] A small number joined classical Pentecostal churches. A few formed new denominations that retained elements of their old denominations, such as the Charismatic Episcopal Church, founded in 1992. A larger number found their way to neo-charismatic churches, such as the Calvary Chapel Association (founded 1965) and the Association of Vineyard Churches (founded 1982), or joined charismatic nondenominational churches. All these developments blurred religious categories while expanding the influence of Azusa Street.

The Third Wave

Look Out! The Pentecostals Are Coming proclaimed the title of a 1973 book by C. Peter Wagner, a professor of church growth at Fuller Seminary's School of World Mission.[26] Before becoming a professor at the flagship evangelical seminary, Wagner had spent decades as a missionary in Latin America, where, by his count, Protestant Christianity had exploded from just fifty thousand adherents in 1900 to twenty million in the 1970s. Though his own background was Congregational, he had to admit that a different kind of Protestantism was responsible for nearly all of this growth: Pentecostalism. Like Van Dusen, Wagner wanted to plumb the secrets of Pentecostal success and replicate them.

Wagner became a leading theorist of and evangelist for what he dubbed the third wave of Pentecostalism. In 1987 he wrote,

> There is no question that a new and exciting era has come upon Christianity in the twentieth century. It started with the Pentecostal movement at the beginning of the century, a movement which continues to multiply under God's blessing.

25. Luis Lugo et al., "A Portrait of American Catholics on the Eve of Pope Benedict's Visit to the U.S.," Pew Research Center, March 27, 2008, https://www.pewresearch.org/religion/2008/03/27/a-portrait-of-american-catholics-on-the-eve-of-pope-benedicts-visit-to-the-us-2/.

26. C. Peter Wagner, *Look Out! The Pentecostals Are Coming* (Carol Stream, IL: Creation House, 1973), 25.

It was joined by the charismatic movement soon after mid-century. And now in these latter decades the Spirit is moving in what some of us like to call the third wave where we are seeing the miraculous works of God operating as they have been in the other movements in churches which have not been nor intend to be either Pentecostal or charismatic.[27]

In some ways, it is inapt to center a white, North American man in a discussion of this phase of Pentecostal history. The third wave was spectacularly diverse in terms of gender, race, and location. Nonetheless, Wagner's trajectory offers a framework for understanding a sprawling and still-developing story.

Wagner was initially interested not in Pentecostalism per se but in church growth, and he came to see supernatural manifestations as the most effective means to that end. Controversially, he partnered with pastor John Wimber, from the neo-charismatic Vineyard Movement, for a class at Fuller that endeavored to teach students how to bring New Testament signs and wonders into their ministries. This move was both a callback to Azusa Street and an acknowledgment that, in most of the world, reports of interactions with the supernatural—healings, curses, demon possession, visions, and more—were commonplace. Wagner highlighted the supernatural in books with titles such as *Spiritual Power and Church Growth* (1986) and *Signs and Wonders Today* (1987).

There is no doubt that the third wave of Spirit-centered Christianity led to growth. By the late twentieth century, postdenominational and independent charismatic groups had more adherents than the first or second waves. A preponderance of the biggest, wealthiest megachurches in the United States and abroad could be categorized as third-wave. Enhanced emphasis on, and expanded range of, signs and wonders also characterized this form of Christianity. For example, a revival known as the Toronto Blessing, which began at a Vineyard church in 1994, was marked by uncontrollable "holy laughter" and animal sounds, as well as dozens of participants who claimed that they miraculously received gold or silver fillings in their teeth. The expectation that God will bestow health and wealth on the faithful—commonly referred to as the "prosperity gospel"—inspires many third-wave believers.

In addition to church growth and signs and wonders, third-wave Christianity has been characterized by heightened attention to spiritual leaders, some of whom became celebrities. In his book *Leading Your Church to Growth*, Wagner sharply delineated the roles of leader and follower, lamenting that

27. C. Peter Wagner, introduction to *Signs and Wonders Today: The Story of Fuller Theological Seminary's Remarkable Course on Spiritual Power*, ed. C. Peter Wagner (Altamonte Springs, FL: Creation House, 1987), 11.

Television broadcasts, such as Kenneth and Gloria Copeland's "Believer's Voice of Victory" (shown here in 2011), greatly enhanced the visibility of Pentecostal and charismatic Christianity starting in the 1950s.

pastors' authority was being eroded by antiauthoritarianism and democratic culture. God called a pastor to a church, Wagner wrote, not the congregation. A pastor who had to ask church members for authority clearly did not have any. Wagner approvingly quoted Black church executive Joseph H. Jackson as saying, "Every pastor's a king, and you don't mess with his crown."[28]

This tendency to elevate pastoral authority, which was characteristic of though not unique to neo-charismatic Christianity, was especially pronounced in the shepherding movement of the 1970s. The five members of a charismatic Bible study that met in Fort Lauderdale, Florida, decided that the solution to shallow faith was strict accountability in a pyramid-shaped structure with themselves, as apostles, at the top; other leaders that they discipled in ranks below; and, at the bottom, followers who submitted to their local shepherds on all major life decisions. Tithes and donations were supposed to flow up through the shepherding structure, not to local churches or media ministries. Other charismatic leaders, notably Pat Robertson, opposed this movement as being ripe for abuse (and a threat to their own livelihoods). The movement faded after about a decade, but its influence continued in some American, British, and Australian charismatic churches.

To these elements, Wagner later added a focus on spiritual warfare. This turn was evident in his 1992 book *Warfare Prayer: How to Seek God's Power and Protection in the Battle to Build His Kingdom.* American interest in spiritual warfare had been heightened by bestselling thrillers *This Present Darkness* (1986) and *Piercing the Darkness* (1989) by Pentecostal novelist Frank Peretti. Meanwhile, conservative American politicians increasingly used the rhetoric of "culture wars," in which political conflict was recast as a cosmic battle of good versus evil. Whereas Wagner once saw signs and wonders as a means to the end of church growth, in *Warfare Prayer* even church growth had become a means to an end, conquering earthly territory for God. That theology is known as dominionism. Wagner labeled the movement that would combine

28. C. Peter Wagner, *Leading Your Church to Growth: The Secret of Pastor/People Partnership in Dynamic Church Growth* (Ventura, CA: Regal Books, 1984), 127.

all of his ideas and would work toward this ultimate goal "the New Apostolic Reformation."

Many Americans got their first introduction to this movement the day after the 2020 presidential election when Paula White, a megachurch pastor and televangelist, prayed in a live-streamed service that supernatural powers would come to the aid of incumbent Donald Trump, for whom White served as a spiritual adviser. Votes were still being counted, but data analysis indicated that Trump had lost to challenger Joseph Biden. At this incredibly fraught moment, White promised, "I hear a sound of victory, the Lord says it is done. For angels have even been dispatched from Africa right now. . . . In the name of Jesus, from South America they're coming here." Interspersed with these statements, White spoke in tongues.[29] Mainstream observers mocked the video, and a writer for the small collective Pentecostals & Charismatics for Peace & Justice called it one of the five most embarrassing evangelical responses to the election.[30] But White was only doing what Wagner had recommended: invoking territorial spirits in order to defeat not a seventy-seven-year-old human man but the "demonic confederacies" who were conspiring to "steal the election."[31]

Impact

The Azusa Street revival altered the course of American church history. Fifty years after Van Dusen's article in *Life*, a report from the Barna Group asked, "Is American Christianity Turning Charismatic?"[32] Barna research found that 36 percent of Americans identified as Pentecostal or charismatic, including about half of evangelicals and over one-third of Catholics. One in four American Protestant congregations was charismatic or Pentecostal, including 16 percent of predominantly white congregations and 65 percent of predominantly Black congregations. A different survey found in 2022 that 25 percent of American evangelicals had spoken in tongues, reflecting both (1) the propensity of some Christians in historically Pentecostal churches to also identify as evangelical

29. Wyatte Grantham-Philips, "Pastor Paula White Calls on Angels from Africa and South America to Bring Trump Victory," *USA Today*, November 5, 2020, https://www.usatoday.com/story/news/nation/2020/11/05/paula-white-trumps-spiritual-adviser-african-south-american-angels/6173576002/.

30. Micael Grenholm, "The Five Most Embarrassing Evangelical Reactions to the Election Results," Pentecostals & Charismatics for Peace & Justice, November 14, 2020, https://pcpj.org/2020/11/14/the-five-most-embarrassing-evangelical-reactions-to-the-election-results/comment-page-1/.

31. Grantham-Philips, "Pastor Paula White Calls on Angels."

32. Barna Group, "Is American Christianity Turning Charismatic?," January 7, 2008, https://www.barna.com/research/is-american-christianity-turning-charismatic/.

and (2) the diffusion of this quintessentially Pentecostal practice into evangelical churches.[33] Other typically but not exclusively Pentecostal or charismatic practices, such as singing praise choruses and raising hands in worship, were even more widespread in American churches by the early twenty-first century. If American Christianity had not fully turned charismatic, it had certainly absorbed a charismatic flavor.

The global impact was even more significant. Combining Pentecostal and charismatic traditions under the common label "renewalists," a ten-country study found in 2006 that renewalists constituted 60 percent of the population of Guatemala, 56 percent of the population of Kenya, 49 percent of the population of Brazil, and 44 percent of the population of the Philippines.[34] The largest church in the world was Yoido Full Gospel Church, an Assemblies of God congregation in Seoul, South Korea, with membership estimates hovering around half a million. More than a century after the Azusa Street revival, the biggest story in American church history kept getting bigger.

In 1927, the *Pentecostal Evangel* published an extended poem by F. M. Lehman in which the author reflects on his experience of what he calls the "Second Blessing Movement." One paragraph of the piece expresses a prayer for ongoing sanctification.

> *Lord, dear Lord!—Thou great Baptizer, send us now the "latter rain"! Empty us that we may never, never yield to Self again. Take the emptied, broken vessel—mend and make it Thine to-day; fill it with Thy holy presence—yielding, Thou shalt have Thy way. Let the Upper Room enduement now our waiting hearts inspire—emptied, yielded, baptized, Jesus, with the Holy Ghost and fire.*[35]

FURTHER READING

Anderson, Allan Heaton. *An Introduction to Pentecostalism.* 2nd ed. Cambridge: Cambridge University Press, 2014.

———. *To the Ends of the Earth: Pentecostalism and the Transformation of World Christianity.* New York: Oxford University Press, 2013.

33. Infinity Concepts and Grey Matter Research, "The Renewalists: Pentecostal and Charismatic Evangelicals," 2022, https://www.infinityconcepts.com/wp-content/uploads/2022/08/The-Renewalists-Downloadable.pdf.

34. Luis Lugo, "Spirit and Power—A 10-Country Survey of Pentecostals," Pew Research Center, October 5, 2006, https://www.pewresearch.org/religion/2006/10/05/spirit-and-power/.

35. F. M. Lehman, "Self and Grace," *Pentecostal Evangel*, September 24, 1927, 6.

Artman, Amy Collier. *The Miracle Lady: Kathryn Kuhlman and the Transformation of Charismatic Christianity*. Grand Rapids: Eerdmans, 2019.

Bowler, Kate. *Blessed: A History of the American Prosperity Gospel*. New York: Oxford University Press, 2013.

Christerson, Brad, and Richard Flory. *The Rise of Network Christianity: How Independent Leaders Are Changing the Religious Landscape*. New York: Oxford University Press, 2017.

Espinosa, Gastón. *William J. Seymour and the Origins of Global Pentecostalism*. Durham, NC: Duke University Press, 2014.

Goff, James R., Jr., and Grant Wacker, eds. *Portraits of a Generation: Early Pentecostal Leaders*. Fayetteville: University of Arkansas Press, 2002.

Sutton, Matthew Avery. *Aimee Semple McPherson and the Resurrection of Christian America*. Cambridge, MA: Harvard University Press, 2009.

Wacker, Grant. *Heaven Below: Early Pentecostals and American Culture*. Cambridge, MA: Harvard University Press, 2001.

Walsh, Arlene M. Sánchez. *Latino Pentecostal Identity: Evangelical Faith, Self, and Society*. New York: Columbia University Press, 2003.

11

Science versus Religion?

The Scopes "Monkey" Trial, 1925

Countless revival meetings and church services in the early twentieth century featured the hymn "The Old Rugged Cross," written in 1913 by midwestern Methodist minister George Bennard. Fundamentalist preachers, such as Bob Jones, utilized the hymn to express continuity with the past and detachment from the surrounding culture.

> 1. On a hill far away stood an old rugged cross,
> the emblem of suffering and shame;
> and I love that old cross where the dearest and best
> for a world of lost sinners was slain.
>
> [*refrain*] So I'll cherish the old rugged cross,
> till my trophies at last I lay down;
> I will cling to the old rugged cross,
> and exchange it some day for a crown.
>
> 4. To that old rugged cross I will ever be true,
> its shame and reproach gladly bear;
> then he'll call me some day to my home far away,
> where his glory forever I'll share. [*refrain*][1]

1. This version is from the *United Methodist Hymnal* (Nashville: United Methodist Publishing House, 1989), no. 504.

By the time they faced off at the Scopes Trial, Clarence Darrow (left) and William Jennings Bryan (right) had been acquainted for years. Darrow had supported Bryan's first presidential campaign, in 1896, but he had little use for Bryan's religious beliefs.

The case officially known as *The State of Tennessee v. John Thomas Scopes* turned the town of Dayton into a zoo. Ostensibly a test of the state's ban on teaching evolution, in political cartoons and the popular imagination the trial hinged on the question of whether monkeys were the biological ancestors of human beings. Among the hundreds of reporters and gawkers who crowded into the town of eighteen hundred residents for the "Trial of the Century" were numerous owners of pet primates, offering their animals as evidence on one side of the debate or the other. Joe Mendi, the "chimpanzee with the intelligence of a five-year-old child," came all the way from New York to dazzle locals by playing a tiny piano while wearing a three-piece suit. His promoters encouraged audiences to "Take a look at 'Joe'" so that everyone could "decide for himself as to whether his [own] 'family tree' bore cocoanuts or not." Meanwhile, the Dayton Hotel put up a gorilla display in the lobby, and fashionable young women made a brief fad of wearing toy monkeys as fur stoles.[2]

Beneath this over-the-top ballyhoo of the Roaring Twenties lurked deep anxieties. John Scopes faced trial for teaching human evolution in a public high school. Evolution was still a relatively new concept in the United States, as was public high school, and both made some people extremely nervous. Everything about the trial exposed a fault line in American culture, between secular and sacred, rural and urban, common folks and elites, whites and people of color, conservative and liberal, young and old. The real issue was not monkeys but truth and authority. Who got to make what kinds of claims in the public sphere, and on what basis? What would a nation built on any of those competing claims look like?

The Scopes Trial was a turning point in American church history not because it started or settled these questions but because it cranked up preexisting conflicts and disabled mechanisms that might have smoothed them out afterward. There were many possible trajectories for the interaction of science, education,

2. Jeffrey P. Moran, *The Scopes Trial: A Brief History with Documents* (New York: Palgrave, 2002), 1.

and Christianity in the United States in the twentieth century. This 1925 spectacle dug the trenches for a century of culture wars.

Finch Beaks and Bibles

Alleged hostility between Christianity and science, or between sacred and secular knowledge, was by no means new in the 1920s. Around AD 200, the North African Christian apologist Tertullian famously asked, "What indeed has Athens to do with Jerusalem? What concord is there between the Academy and the Church?"[3] About one thousand years later, when the first European universities were founded, the main perceived antagonist to Christian thinking was Aristotle, whose works had been preserved by Muslim scholars and finally rediscovered in the West. Aristotle emphasized empirical observation as the route to truth, a "seeing is believing" approach foundational to the scientific method. This approach threatened belief in miracles and ran counter to a definition of faith as "the evidence of things not seen" (Heb. 11:1). The thirteenth-century theologian Thomas Aquinas labored to reconcile the Aristotelian science and Catholic religion of his day, arguing that human reason and divine revelation were both valid ways of knowing and would, if followed faithfully, lead to the same conclusions. Some Christians agreed with him, but many did not. In 1633, Galileo Galilei was sentenced to house arrest for teaching that the Earth revolves around the sun. Church authorities deemed this scientific discovery heretical, on the grounds that it contradicted both Scripture and the writings of respected theologians.[4]

By the turn of the twentieth century, the scientist provoking the most angst among British and American Christians was Charles Darwin. In his 1859 book *On the Origin of Species*, Darwin argued that the observable diversity among living and fossilized creatures resulted from natural selection, the propensity over generations of reproduction for traits to emerge that gave some organisms a competitive advantage. If, say, a certain beak shape made it easier for a finch to eat the food prevalent on a specific island, then finches that happened to be born with that beak shape were more likely to survive to mating age and produce babies with the same trait. Over millions of years, the random, undirected process of natural selection produced not just different-looking finches but all of the variety within and among species. Darwin could not explain exactly how this process worked, but he made enough observations to be persuaded that his was the best explanation for why the natural world looked the way it did.

---

3. Tertullian, *Prescription Against Heretics* 7.22, in *Ante-Nicene Fathers*, ed. Philip Schaff, trans. Peter Holmes, Christian Classics Ethereal Library, available at https://www.ccel.org/fathers.

4. See Ronald L. Numbers, *Galileo Goes to Jail and Other Myths about Science and Religion* (Cambridge, MA: Harvard University Press, 2010).

Although Darwin had been drifting from the Anglican Christianity of his youth for many years, he did not propose his theory of natural selection in order to destroy faith in a creator God. As he wrote in an 1860 letter to the American Presbyterian botanist Asa Gray:

> With respect to the theological view of the question; this is always painful to me.—I am bewildered.—I had no intention to write atheistically. But I own that I cannot see, as plainly as others do, & as I [should] wish to do, evidence of design & beneficence on all sides of us. There seems to me too much misery in the world. . . . I feel most deeply that the whole subject is too profound for the human intellect. A dog might as well speculate on the mind of [Isaac] Newton.—Let each man hope & believe what he can.[5]

Gray found it possible to reconcile his own Christian faith with Darwin's scientific findings, as did many other churchmen of the era, but cultural waters grew murkier when debate about Darwin's work spilled out of scholarly journals and into the rough-and-tumble world of partisan discourse.

Part of the problem was how easily Darwin's ideas could be deployed in other arguments. In correspondence with geologist Charles Lyell, who had earlier sparked debate with his claims that the Earth was much, much older than the few thousand years derived from counting biblical generations, Darwin wrote that a book review in a Manchester newspaper showed "that I have proved 'might is right', & therefore that Napoleon is right & every cheating Tradesman is also right."[6] Darwin had not asserted that might makes right, nor even used the phrase that became shorthand for his concept of the natural world, "survival of the fittest." (That phrase was coined by English biologist Herbert Spencer in 1864 and not used by Darwin until the fifth edition of his book, in 1869.) But in the late nineteenth century, as industrialization exacerbated social inequality and Western nations competed for imperial supremacy, a cutthroat cosmology made sense. Darwin's analysis of finch beaks sent the same message that people heard all around them: The world is a cold, hard place. Use every advantage. Only the strong survive.

These messages emanated from the grueling experience of trying to eke out a living in the mines or the filthy cities or the brutal colonies but also from the arguments of men such as Spencer who used the theory of natural selection

5. Charles Darwin to Asa Gray, May 22, 1860, University of Cambridge, Darwin Correspondence Project, letter 2814, https://www.darwinproject.ac.uk/letter/?docId=letters/DCP-LETT-2814.xml&query=2814.

6. Charles Darwin to Charles Lyell, May 4, 1860, University of Cambridge, Darwin Correspondence Project, letter 2782, https://www.darwinproject.ac.uk/letter/?docId=letters/DCP-LETT-2782.xml&query=2782.

to justify exploitation of the poor and persons believed to be of lesser races. If the fittest survive, this argument ran, then those who do not survive must be unfit, and there is nothing that the fit can or should do to help them. Some humans were born to rule, and others were born to serve. A whole scientific movement, eugenics, sprang up to promote breeding among the "better sort" of humans while segregating, incarcerating, sterilizing, or annihilating the allegedly inferior stock. Public policies rooted in this hypercompetitive view of humanity became known as social Darwinism. In the United States, these policies produced results such as coercive residential schools for Native American children (see chap. 3) and laissez-faire economics, which allowed individuals and corporations to amass as much wealth as they possibly could with minimal taxation or regulation. In other places, such as the Ottoman Empire and Nazi Germany, social Darwinism inspired genocide.

For decades, as other scientists continued to debate Darwin's biological theories and politicians enacted policies that Darwin never proposed, the conversation also got mixed in with heightened concern about the reliability of biblical texts. In the nineteenth century, a method of analyzing the Bible known as higher criticism spread from Germany to England and the United States. Also called the historical-critical method, this approach endeavored to analyze the Bible the same way scholars might analyze any ancient text, attending to the historical context in which it was written; considering how it was constructed, edited, and transmitted; categorizing its literary forms; and comparing it to other works. Higher criticism elicited strong reactions. Some Christians perceived it as an attack on the uniqueness of the Bible, by extension an affront to God's holiness, and basically an all-out campaign to undermine doctrine. Other Christians viewed it as their best chance to determine what the Bible really meant, enabling them to peel away centuries of misinterpretation to find a pure, enduring religious message.

The scriptural account of creation became hotly contested territory in this biblical-studies war. In 1873, the redoubtable Princeton Seminary theologian Charles Hodge wrote that the entire Bible was both divinely inspired and infallible, accurate not only regarding "moral and religious truths" but also regarding "statements of facts, whether scientific, historical, or geographical," indeed "everything which any sacred writer asserts to be true."[7] This posture created problems for interpreting passages such as Genesis 1 and 2, which gave different timelines for creation (whether humans appeared before or after trees, for example), featured highly poetic rather than technical language, and had not previously been read by most Christians as statements of scientific fact. Rather,

---

7. Charles Hodge, *Systematic Theology*, vol. 1 (New York: Charles Scribner, 1940), 163.

Two Views on the Challenge of Science

Early twentieth-century modernists, such as Baptist minister Harry Emerson Fosdick, and fundamentalists, such as Presbyterian theologian J. Gresham Machen, agreed that modern science posed a challenge to Christianity, but they defined that challenge in opposite ways. Did churches need to adapt to the ascendant scientific mindset or resist it?

From Harry Emerson Fosdick's sermon "Shall the Fundamentalists Win?" (1922):

> As I plead thus for an intellectually hospitable, tolerant, liberty-loving church, I am, of course, thinking primarily about this new generation. We have boys and girls growing up in our homes and schools, and because we love them we may well wonder about the church which will be waiting to receive them. Now, the worst kind of church that can possibly be offered to the allegiance of the new generation is an intolerant church.
>
> Ministers often bewail the fact that young people turn from religion to science for the regulative ideas of their lives. But this is easily explicable. Science treats a young man's mind as though it were really important. A scientist says to a young man, "Here is the universe challenging our investigation. Here are the truths which we have seen, so far. Come, study with us! See what we already have seen and then look further to see more, for science is an intellectual adventure for the truth." Can you imagine any man who is worthwhile turning from that call to the church if the church seems to him to say, "Come, and we will feed you opinions from a spoon. No thinking is allowed here except such as brings you to certain specified, predetermined conclusions. These prescribed opinions we will give you in advance of your thinking; now think, but only so as to reach these results."
>
> My friends, nothing in all the world is so much worth thinking of as God, Christ, the Bible, sin and salvation, the divine purposes for humankind, life everlasting. But you cannot challenge the dedicated thinking of this ▶

the prevailing view of this passage from the early church through the nineteenth century was that it told a story in terms intelligible to ancient humans, leaving many technical questions to be answered by other sources of knowledge. That perspective continued to be held by figures such as American Congregational minister Henry Ward Beecher, who wrote, "That the whole world and the universe were the creation of God is the testimony of the whole Bible, both Jewish and Christian; but how he made them—whether by the direct force generation to these sublime themes upon any such terms as are laid down by an intolerant church.

Harry Emerson Fosdick, "Shall the Fundamentalists Win?" *Christian Work* 102 (June 10, 1922): 716–22.

From J. Gresham Machen, *Christianity and Liberalism* (1923):

The application of modern scientific methods is almost as broad as the universe in which we live. Though the most palpable achievements are in the sphere of physics and chemistry, the sphere of human life cannot be isolated from the rest. And with the other sciences, there has appeared a modern science of history, for example. Along with psychology, sociology, and the like, it claims full equality with its sister sciences, even if it does not deserve it. No department of knowledge can maintain its isolation from the modern lust for scientific conquest. Inviolable treaties, though hallowed by all the sanctions of age-long tradition, are being flung ruthlessly to the winds.

In such an age, it is obvious that every inheritance from the past must be subject to searching criticism. As a matter of fact, some convictions of the human race have crumbled to pieces in the test. Indeed, the dependence of any institution on the past is now regarded as furnishing a presumption, not in favor of the institution, but against it. So many convictions have had to be abandoned, men sometimes believe that all convictions must go.

If such an attitude is justifiable, then no institution is faced by a stronger hostile presumption than the institution of the Christian religion. . . . May Christianity be maintained in a scientific age? . . . It is not the Christianity of the New Testament which is in conflict with science, but the supposed Christianity of the modern liberal Church. The real city of God, and that city alone, has defenses which are capable of warding off the assaults of modern unbelief.

J. Gresham Machen, *Christianity and Liberalism* (New York: Macmillan, 1923), 3–4, 7.

of a creative will or indirectly through a long series of gradual changes—the Scriptures do not declare."[8] By the time Beecher wrote that sentence, though, in his 1885 book *Evolution and Religion*, those were fighting words, not merely reflecting long Christian tradition but directed against the new, hard-edged, anti-Darwin position espoused by figures such as Hodge.

8. Henry Ward Beecher, "The Two Revelations," in *Evolution and Religion, Part I: Eight Sermons, Discussing the Bearings of the Evolutionary Philosophy on the Fundamental Doctrines of Evangelical Christianity* (New York: Fords, Howard & Hulbert, 1885), 44.

Biblical scholars and other churchmen who saw promise in emerging science and higher criticism became known as modernists. Biblical scholars and other churchmen who perceived both of these developments as dire threats became known as fundamentalists, taking their name from a series of pamphlets published between 1910 and 1915. (The protagonists with the most institutional power on both sides were men, although there were also women involved at lower positions of leadership and at the grassroots.) Battles raged at sites including theology journals, seminaries, high-profile pulpits, missionary societies, and denominational heresy trials. Deep-pocketed backers on both sides, led by John D. Rockefeller Sr. and Jr. for the modernists and by Lyman and Milton Stewart for the fundamentalists, funded efforts to publicize and institutionalize their positions. Rockefeller Sr. built the University of Chicago as a modernist stronghold, and his son bankrolled New York's Riverside Church and its eloquent modernist pastor, Harry Emerson Fosdick. The Stewarts anonymously funded publication of *The Fundamentals*, and Lyman built the Bible Institute of Los Angeles (now Biola University). Americans who were affiliated with none of these institutions and read none of the related literature likely had some awareness of the controversy. For arguments about Darwinism and Genesis to erupt into the Trial of the Century, though, required a confluence of additional factors: racial anxieties, social change, and the rise of the public high school.

The Roiling '20s

The United States of the 1920s looked a lot different than it had a generation earlier. Total population swelled from about 63 million in 1890 to nearly 106 million in 1920. This increase included 15 million immigrants who arrived between 1900 and 1915, the same number as had come in the previous forty years combined.[9] The majority of the newer immigrants came from southern or eastern Europe; most were Roman Catholic or Jewish, and many did not speak English. Immigration from Asia had been curtailed by the 1882 Chinese Exclusion Act and other forms of hostility, but migration across the southern US border was boosted both by the reduction of Asian laborers and by the Mexican Revolution, which began in 1910. The US census counted just 78,000 ethnic Mexicans in 1890, but that number increased to 486,000 in 1920. Most of the ethnic Mexicans lived in Texas and California, while the European immigrants

9. "Immigrants in the Progressive Era," Library of Congress, https://www.loc.gov/classroom
-materials/united-states-history-primary-source-timeline/progressive-era-to-new-era-1900-1929
/immigrants-in-progressive-era/.

were concentrated in cities such as New York, Chicago, Philadelphia, and Boston.[10] In 1920, for the first time in US history, more people lived in urban areas than in rural areas. All these developments led some Americans, including native-born white Americans in small towns like Dayton, Tennessee, to feel that the country they knew was slipping away, and they needed to find some way to put the brakes on.

Little of this demographic change directly affected Tennessee or the rest of the Southeast, however. There, the color line ran between white and Black, with Jim Crow laws and episodic violence enforcing Black subjugation. The Ku Klux Klan had been founded by embittered Confederate veterans in Pulaski, Tennessee, in 1865, and Tennessee had 214 confirmed lynchings between 1882 and 1930, with 177 Black victims and 37 white victims.[11] Although white observers of the Scopes Trial and most histories of the event downplayed race, Black observers at the time asserted that white Southern opposition to evolution, much stronger than opposition in the North, was rooted in racial anxiety. An editorial in the *Chicago Defender*, a Black newspaper, surmised that the Tennessee legislators who passed the law against teaching evolution had never read Darwin, "and all they know about the subject is that the entire human race is supposed to have started from a common origin. Therein lies their difficulty. Admit that premise and they will have to admit that there is no fundamental difference between themselves and the race they pretend to despise."[12] Many white Southerners preferred the theory of polygenesis, championed by Mobile, Alabama, physician Josiah Clark Nott, which held that God had created multiple human species separately, each with a different skin color and suited to life in a different region of the planet. The logic of polygenesis supported laws to keep the races separate and prevent them from marrying, while the logic of Darwinism threatened to undercut the Southern social order. If there was no biological basis for racial segregation, only bald prejudice (rooted in bad readings of biblical texts) remained.

Social change created a backlash of social control legislation. The marquee example was Prohibition, a ban on the production, transport, or sale of alcohol that was ushered in by the Volstead Act in 1919. Crusades to curb drinking had begun in the nineteenth century (see chap. 7), but they gained traction by associating drunkenness with immigrants and urban crime. When the United

10. Ramón Gutiérrez, "Mexican Immigration to the United States," Oxford Research Encyclopedia, July 29, 2019, https://doi.org/10.1093/acrefore/9780199329175.013.146.

11. Kathy Bennett, "Lynching," Tennessee Encyclopedia, http://tennesseeencyclopedia.net/entries/lynching/.

12. "If Monkeys Could Speak," *Chicago Defender*, May 23, 1925, quoted in "Scopes Trial," Historical Thinking Matters, https://historicalthinkingmatters.org/scopestrial/1/sources/43/index.html.

States went to war against Germany, a country known for its beer-making and beer-drinking, abstinence from alcohol finally became national law.

Meanwhile, World War I and the 1917 Bolshevik Revolution in Russia increased native-born Americans' fears of immigrants and the importation of "foreign" ideas, such as socialism and labor unions. Antiforeigner sentiment, or nativism, coupled with wartime fervor led to laws limiting speech, assembly, and, eventually, immigration itself. An ethnic quota system imposed in 1924, heavily influenced by eugenics, reduced overall immigration by more than 80 percent and shifted the countries of origin back to northwestern Europe. (Prior to 1924, with a few exceptions such as the Chinese Exclusion Act, there was no such thing as "illegal immigration"; people just came, over a border or an ocean, and were almost always allowed to stay.) Social legislation and policies also targeted movies, music, flirting, "petting," and other behaviors. New Orleans—of all places—banned jazz music and dancing in high schools in 1922. The same year, several major banks, including the Federal Reserve Bank of New York, issued strict new rules for what female employees could wear, down to dress patterns and stockings. "Big Business Banishes the Flapper," headlines announced, to the dismay of women who did not want to wear—and could not afford—an entirely new, dowdier wardrobe. "They'll be putting us in gunnysacks with nothing but our hands sticking out the next thing you know," one young woman complained.[13]

It was difficult to regulate how people behaved in movie theaters or the back seats of automobiles (an invention sweeping the nation in the 1920s), but one place where concerned adults could continue to exert a strong influence over young women and men was the public high school. Only about 5 percent of American children attended secondary school in the late nineteenth century, but demand for better-trained professionals and factory workers spurred a movement to expand high school education. Attendance quadrupled between 1900 and 1920, to a total enrollment of more than two million teenagers.[14] American schooling had always proceeded with a high degree of local control, so curricula across these schools varied, and there were often heated fights about what was appropriate for students to learn. Shakespeare or stenography? "Civil War" or "War for Southern Independence"? And, in biology class, Genesis or Darwin?

High schools got squeezed in a vise. Pressure to accept evolution pushed down from the elite ranks of universities, while pressure to halt social change pushed up from communities. Many of the same people who had fought for a

13. "Big Business Banishes the Flapper," *South Bend News-Times*, June 23, 1922, 22.
14. Paul Beston, "When High Schools Shaped America's Destiny," *City Journal*, 2017, https://www.city-journal.org/article/when-high-schools-shaped-americas-destiny.

local option to ban alcohol, and then advocated a nationwide prohibition, fought for their local schools, and then their states, to ban the teaching of evolution. "The early 1920s were still heady days for the prohibition experiment," noted historian Jeffrey P. Moran, "and the antievolution crusade not only repeated the temperance movement's own progress from voluntarism to coercion but drew its leadership and much of its support from the same source."[15] Three states—Tennessee, Mississippi, and Arkansas—passed laws making the teaching of evolution a crime, while Oklahoma banned textbooks that taught evolution, and Florida condemned (but did not criminalize) the teaching of Darwinism as "improper and subversive." In all, the anti-evolution movement promoted at least fifty-three bills in twenty-one state legislatures, plus two proposed federal laws that would apply to the District of Columbia.[16]

As in the Manchester newspaper review of *On the Origin of Species*, American attacks on evolution readily linked Darwinism to other concerns. In an oft-repeated 1924 sermon, for example, the prominent Baptist evangelist Mordecai Ham declared, "Evolution is a lie out of Hell that has never produced anything but infidelity." He blamed Germans, the United States' World War I enemy, for mixing the Bible and Darwinism. He also identified evolution with "anti-Christ Bolshevism" and accused "so-called Christian colleges" of spreading the pernicious ideology. He closed the sermon by warning, "The day is not distant when you will be in the grip of the Red Terror and your children will be taught free love by the damnable theory of evolution."[17] Speeches like this (and there were hundreds more examples, delivered by preachers and politicians alike) were intended to provoke alarm and action, and they did, culminating outside a Tennessee courthouse in the summer of 1925.

The Trial

Tennessee's ban on teaching evolution—named the Butler Act for the Primitive Baptist preacher John Washington Butler, who proposed it in the state house of representatives—was very popular with voters, but it bothered activists at the American Civil Liberties Union (ACLU). The ACLU, founded in 1920, opposed the laws curbing speech, assembly, and individual freedoms that proliferated during World War I and the years afterward. To fight the Butler Act, the ACLU

15. Moran, *Scopes Trial*, 21.

16. Adam Laats, *Fundamentalism and Education in the Scopes Era: God, Darwin, and the Roots of America's Culture Wars* (New York: Palgrave Macmillan, 2010), 4.

17. Quotations from William B. Gatewood Jr., *Preachers, Pedagogues and Politicians: The Evolution Controversy in North Carolina, 1920–1927* (Chapel Hill: University of North Carolina Press, 1966), 44–45.

advertised for a Tennessee teacher who was willing to defy it publicly and stand trial. John Scopes was a single, young, substitute teacher whose father was a Socialist labor organizer. Scopes had little to lose by standing trial, and he believed in the value of taking unpopular but principled stances. Several of the leading citizens of Dayton encouraged Scopes to volunteer for the ACLU test case, not because they supported evolution but because they wanted to bring publicity to a town that was down on its economic luck. Scopes duly confessed to a constable that he had taught a lesson from Tennessee's approved, pro-evolution textbook, then he assumed a minor role in a show that was designed from the beginning to play to a national audience.[18]

Fundamentalists recruited William Jennings Bryan to lead the prosecution of Scopes. Bryan was a spellbinding speaker and three-time presidential candidate, known as the Great Commoner for his populist identification with the interests of common folks against the power of elites. He had supported progressive causes such as higher wages and women's right to vote, but he vigorously opposed Darwinism on the grounds that it contradicted Christianity and led to the cruel policies of eugenics and social Darwinism. On the defense side, the notorious and usually high-priced lawyer Clarence Darrow offered his services for free. More accustomed to defending striking laborers, alleged bombers, and confessed murderers, Darrow took Scopes's case because he wanted an opportunity to debate Bryan about science and religion. Both lawyers reveled in the hype surrounding the trial.

Scopes never testified on his own behalf. Instead, in an unorthodox move that suited both lawyers' larger agendas, Darrow called Bryan to the stand. By this point, the seventh day of the trial, the crowds of journalists and spectators had grown so large that the judge moved proceedings to an outdoor platform. Thousands more Americans were able to follow along on the radio, as Chicago station WGN produced the first-ever live broadcast of a trial, and millions read the daily dispatches from print journalists. For two hours, under a blazing sun, the men traded jabs about topics such as Jonah and the whale, the tower of Babel, the age of the earth, and whether it was possible, as recorded in the book of Joshua, for the sun to stand still. Several times, Darrow forced Bryan to admit that the Bible raised questions he could not answer, as when Darrow asked, "Did you ever discover where Cain got his wife?" and Bryan replied, "No, sir; I leave the agnostics to hunt for her."[19] Eventually, the exasperated state

18. It was unclear whether Scopes actually taught the lesson from the book or whether the information in the book actually broke Tennessee's law. Those details did not matter in the court case.

19. In Genesis 4, Cain, son of the first man and woman (Adam and Eve), murders his brother Abel, is banished to another land, marries a woman, and has a son. Because Adam, Eve, Cain,

attorney general objected, asking, "What is the purpose of this examination?" His question led to the following exchange:

BRYAN: The purpose is to cast ridicule on everybody who believes in the Bible, and I am perfectly willing that the world shall know that these gentlemen have no other purpose than ridiculing every Christian who believes in the Bible.

DARROW: We have the purpose of preventing bigots and ignoramuses from controlling the education of the United States, and you know it, and that is all.

BRYAN: I am glad to bring out that statement. I want the world to know that this evidence is not for the view Mr. Darrow and his associates have filed affidavits here stating, the purpose which, as I understand it, is to show that the Bible story is not true.

DUDLEY FIELD MALONE [DEFENSE EXPERT]: Mr. Bryan seems anxious to get some evidence in the record that would tend to show that those affidavits are not true.

BRYAN: I am not trying to get anything into the record. I am simply trying to protect the word of God against the greatest atheist or agnostic in the United States. [*prolonged applause*] I want the papers to know I am not afraid to get on the stand in front of him and let him do his worst! I want the world to know that agnosticism is trying to force agnosticism on our colleges and on our schools, and the people of Tennessee will not permit it to be done. [*prolonged applause*]

DARROW: I wish I could get a picture of these claquers.[20]

Claquers were people hired by managers of French opera houses and theaters to sit in the audience and applaud. In other words, Darrow derided Bryan's supporters as shills, clapping on command. Some out-of-town reporters went further, not just dismissing the crowd's enthusiasm but claiming that spectators laughed at Bryan. When Bryan unexpectedly died in his sleep a few days after his testimony, a narrative arose that Darrow had broken Bryan by exposing his most cherished beliefs as a wobbly pile of contradictions. But the crowd, and the judge, genuinely sided with Bryan. Scopes was convicted and fined,

---

and Abel are the only humans named in the Genesis narrative to this point, it is unclear how Cain found a woman outside his own family to marry.

20. Some published versions of the trial transcript have "clappers," and there are other minor variations among versions. No audio recording of the trial was preserved.

although the conviction was later overturned on a technicality, and the Butler Act remained the law in Tennessee until it was repealed in 1967.

The Long Shadow of Scopes

The Scopes Trial has been credited with a number of far-reaching effects. Some of the alleged effects are better attested in the historical record than others.

For years, many political historians cast the trial as an embarrassing defeat for fundamentalists, who retreated from the public arena until reappearing as the Moral Majority in the 1970s. That is not quite what happened, though. Fundamentalists did redirect some of their energies away from public fights and toward, as historian Joel Carpenter wrote, cultivating "distinctive religious communities, or 'shelter belts' as one person called them, to provide some respite from the gales of modern secularity and a home base from which to launch evangelistic campaigns."[21] They built Bible colleges, summer camps, publishing houses, lecture circuits, and radio programs, a network invisible to and thus easily dismissed by outsiders. But they did not stop voting or trying to influence law and policy. More recent scholarship has shown that fundamentalists vehemently opposed the New Deal in the 1930s, setting up a pattern of conservative political activism that persisted through the twentieth century.[22]

One reason that some scholars missed this longer pattern was that the label "fundamentalism" faded after the Scopes Trial. Historian Adam Laats, who has written extensively on the trial and its aftermath, argued that campaigns to outlaw the teaching of evolution tore the fundamentalist movement apart. Some fundamentalists relished these campaigns, which continued after 1925, and even leaned into the "Southern bumpkin" stereotype that was so prevalent in the trial coverage. Like William Jennings Bryan, they took pride in being mocked for their beliefs. Others longed to return to the broader and more respectable fundamentalism of The Fundamentals, which had included erudite essays by prominent men on both sides of the Atlantic. (Only one woman wrote for the series, the Welsh author Jessie Penn-Lewis.) By 1930, Laats wrote, Christians in this second group, "finding it impossible to maintain a fundamentalist movement wider than the Scopes-trial stereotype . . . drifted away from fundamentalism. They often continued their educational campaigns, especially those that had

21. Joel A. Carpenter, *Revive Us Again: The Reawakening of American Fundamentalism* (New York: Oxford University Press, 1997), 3.

22. For an example of the newer scholarship, see Matthew Avery Sutton, "Was FDR the Antichrist? The Birth of Fundamentalist Antiliberalism in a Global Age," *Journal of American History* 98, no. 4 (March 2012): 1052–74.

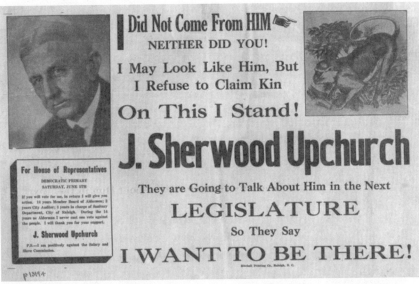

UNC Chapel Hill: Documenting the American South

In 1925, J. Sherwood Upchurch of Raleigh, North Carolina, touted his anti-evolution beliefs in a campaign for the North Carolina House of Representatives. Upchurch lost that election, but he ran successfully in 1929 and 1931.

not been associated in the public mind with fundamentalism, but they usually refrained from identifying themselves or their campaigns as 'fundamentalist.'"[23] In the 1940s, the wing of the movement that continued to uphold key fundamentalist doctrines—the inerrancy of the Bible, the virgin birth of Christ, salvation through substitutionary atonement, the bodily resurrection of Christ, and the historicity of biblical miracles—but disdained the militant, bumpkin posture rebranded itself as evangelical.[24]

Evolution serves as a marker of the contrast and continuity between fundamentalism and American evangelicalism. Billy Graham, a world-famous evangelist and leader of the American evangelical movement for much of the twentieth century, made his "decision for Christ" (his phrase for Christian conversion) at a revival led by Mordecai Ham in 1934. In his own preaching, Graham continued to emphasize personal conversion and conviction of sin, and he also retained Ham's animus toward communism. But Graham held a

23. Laats, *Fundamentalism and Education in the Scopes Era*, 6.
24. This is the most commonly referenced list of key fundamentalist beliefs, derived from a decision of the 1910 Presbyterian General Assembly. Substitutionary atonement is the teaching that humans are saved from damnation because Jesus Christ suffered and died in their place. Other explanations of salvation have put forth in church history, such as that humans are saved by following Christ's moral example or that humans are saved because Christ defeated the devil.

very different view of science. As he told British journalist David Frost in the 1960s,

> I don't think that there's any conflict at all between science today and the Scriptures. I think that we have misinterpreted the Scriptures many times and we've tried to make the Scriptures say things they weren't meant to say, and I think we have made a mistake by thinking that the Bible is a scientific book.
>
> The Bible is not a book of science. The Bible is a book of redemption, and of course, I accept the Creation story. I believe that God did create the universe. I believe He created man, and whether it came by an evolutionary process and at a certain point He took this person or being and made him a living soul or not, does not change the fact that God did create man.[25]

Not all American evangelicals agreed with Graham on this topic. His alma mater, the evangelical flagship Wheaton College, attempted in 1993 to mandate that all faculty members affirm that human beings were directly created by God and did not evolve from other forms of life. Faculty members asserted academic freedom to hold a wider range of views, and the mandate was diluted to allow belief that humans might have evolved from earlier hominids. Graham's statements and the Wheaton faculty stance demonstrated that evangelicalism could accommodate belief in evolution, albeit uneasily, while fundamentalism made rejection of evolution a core value.

Another realm in which scholars have traced the long shadow of the Scopes Trial is American science education, and there the effects—not just of the trial but of anti-evolution campaigns more broadly—have been profound. Most upper-level science textbooks in the early twentieth century presented evolution as settled fact. One went so far as to claim, "There is no rival hypothesis to evolution, except the out-worn and completely refuted one of special creation, now retained only by the ignorant, dogmatic, and the prejudiced."[26] But the successful prosecution of Scopes made textbook publishers and school boards wary while emboldening anti-evolutionists. New editions of some textbooks dropped the chapter on evolution. Other books published in the decade after Scopes downplayed evolution, presented it as a theory rather than a fact, described natural selection without using the words "Darwin" or "evolution," or even asserted that Darwinism had been discredited by subsequent scientists. The few books that continued to present evolution as a central concept in biology

25. David Frost, *Billy Graham: Personal Thoughts of a Public Man* (Colorado Springs: Chariot Victor, 1997), 73.

26. H. H. Newman, *Outlines of General Zoology* (1924), quoted in Randy Moore, "The Lingering Impact of the Scopes Trial on High School Biology Textbooks," *BioScience* 51, no. 9 (September 2001): 791.

struggled for market share. Teaching on evolution never entirely disappeared from US high schools, but it receded.

This tide began to turn in the late 1950s, owing to a new confluence of social factors. On October 4, 1957, the Soviet Union launched Sputnik, the first artificial Earth satellite. Panicked that the United States was falling behind in the "space race," Americans invested heavily in science and technology, including science education. Scientists tasked with producing new textbooks were stunned at the mismatch between knowledge that was used every day

In this famous 1922 cartoon, doubts about the Genesis narrative of creation mark the first steps toward atheism. William Jennings Bryan used the cartoon in one of his books.

in laboratories—where Darwinism had never been discredited—and the narratives taught to American students. "One hundred years without Darwin are enough," announced biologist H. J. Muller in 1959.[27] As evolution was reemphasized in American classrooms, fundamentalists fought back again, but this time they were not as successful. It was harder to whip up public opinion against textbooks when science education was portrayed as a matter of national defense against an enemy even more fearsome than evolution, communism. The US Supreme Court ruled bans on teaching evolution unconstitutional in 1968, which did not stop anti-evolution campaigns but forced campaigners to change tactics. In the 1970s and following, efforts were made to mandate the teaching of biblical creation alongside evolution, and there was also a shift in the primary target, from evolution to sex education. Republican politicians have supported these campaigns, and several state Republican party platforms endorse creationism.

Nothing like any of this happened in other developed countries. Where human evolution did not get politicized or arouse the opposition of a major religious faction, the concept was widely accepted. A 2005 study of thirty-two European countries, the United States, and Japan found that American adults were far less likely than adults in any other surveyed country, except Turkey, to agree with the statement "Human beings, as we know them, developed from earlier species of animals." In several European countries, more than 80 percent of adults agreed

27. H. J. Muller, "One Hundred Years without Darwin Are Enough," *School Science Mathematics* 59 (1959): 304–5.

CLASSROOM IN PROPOSED BRYAN UNIVERSITY OF TENNESSEE

A 1925 cartoon predicts abandonment of truth and loss of academic freedom at the imagined "Bryan University of Tennessee."

with the statement, as did 78 percent of adults in Japan. In the United States, however, only 40 percent agreed (down from 45 percent in 1985), while 39 percent disagreed and 21 percent said they were unsure. In Turkey, a Muslim-majority country, 25 percent of adults agreed with the statement and 75 percent rejected it. One of the study's coauthors, political scientist Jon Miller, concluded, "American Protestantism is more fundamentalist than anybody except perhaps the Islamic fundamentalist, which is why Turkey and we are so close."[28]

Culture Wars

While the political and pedagogical effects of the Scopes Trial continue to be debated, there is no question that it became an iconic episode in American history, representing a mode of conflict that sociologist James Davison Hunter labeled "culture wars." According to Hunter, culture wars involve "our most fundamental ideas about who we are as Americans," and they are waged by factions whose differences are primarily not demographic (e.g., race, class, gender, age) but ideological. The antagonists have "different systems of moral understanding," and their goal is not compromise or coexistence but domination. Highly publicized battles such as the Scopes Trial do not conjure such massive conflicts out of nothing, but culture-war differences "are often intensified and aggravated by the way they are presented to the public."[29] Phrases pulled out of context take on a life of their own, and familiar battle plans get reused again and again in new circumstances.

Providing a stark example of this phenomenon, what many Americans believe they know about the Scopes Trial actually comes from the 1955 play, made

28. Ker Than, "U.S. Lags World in Grasp of Genetics and Acceptance of Evolution," *Live Science*, August 10, 2006, https://www.livescience.com/963-lags-world-grasp-genetics-acceptance -evolution.html. A 2020 update of the same survey found that US acceptance of the statement had risen to 54 percent, but international comparisons were not available for that year.

29. James Davison Hunter, *Culture Wars: The Struggle to Define America* (New York: Basic Books, 1991), 34, 42. Hunter's work has been strongly critiqued, but its key concepts remain widely used.

into a 1960 movie, *Inherit the Wind*. Its authors used the trial as a parable for McCarthyism, suggesting parallels between 1920s campaigns against evolution and 1950s campaigns against communism. Playwright Arthur Miller used the Salem witch trials in the same way in his 1953 play *The Crucible*, which then shaped what countless Americans thought they knew about seventeenth-century Puritanism. *Inherit the Wind*, like Mordecai Ham's anti-evolution sermon, was uninterested in nuance or historical accuracy. It revived the dynamic of Darrow's questioning of Bryan and made sure that Darrow's side attained the moral victory. The movie version lodged so deeply in viewers' minds that Bryan is widely quoted as having said, "The Rock of Ages is more important than the age of rocks!" But those were the words of the movie character based on him. What Bryan actually said, in the final speech before he died, was more conciliatory: "Christians desire that their children shall be taught all the sciences, but they do not want them to lose sight of the Rock of Ages while they study the age of rocks."[30]

Perhaps, if the Scopes Trial had not become so iconic, there would not have arisen among both Darrow's and Bryan's heirs the notion that science education was a prime legal battlefield, or that the United States is populated by two kinds of people: atheists and bigoted ignoramuses. Other countries, including many with majority-Christian populations, did not get mired in that particular conflict. Historians call this phenomenon contingency—the idea that historical developments were not inevitable but occurred for context-specific reasons. What if Darrow had not called Bryan to the stand? What if there had been less media coverage of the trial? What if Congress had not overridden President Woodrow Wilson's veto of the Volstead Act, forcing supporters of Prohibition to keep working on that issue rather than pivoting to evolution? There is no way to know.

------ ▼ ------

Although women were involved in the anti-evolution movement and other fights against modernists, women in conservative Protestant denominations tended to be more open than fundamentalist men to collaboration with other Christians, particularly on issues such as foreign missions and world peace. For example, the September 24, 1925, issue of the Baptist periodical the *Watchman-Examiner* featured a report on women's peace meetings on both sides of the Atlantic. This prayer from the Washington, DC, meeting was led by Lucy Whitehead McGill Waterbury Peabody, a prominent missions promoter and publisher of missionary

---

30. William Jennings Bryan, *The Last Message of William Jennings Bryan* (London: Fleming H. Revell, 1925), 52.

literature who was identified in print (as was customary in that era) using her husband's name, as Mrs. Henry W. Peabody.

Our Father, for whom the whole family in heaven and earth is named, we come to Thee in deep humility to ask Thy forgiveness for the sin of war.

Show us, Thy children, we pray Thee, a better way for the settlement of differences between men and nations. Thou alone, O Lord of love and peace, canst give to men that spirit of patience, tolerance, and good will which will overcome the evil spirit of fear and greed and lust of power leading to hatred and revenge.

We ask that Thou wilt grant Thy wisdom and blessing to all rulers who seek a plan which shall end war. We pray for our President, our Secretary of State, our Congress and all who guide the affairs of this nation, that they may not be hindered in the accomplishment of this task. Deliver us, O God, from a narrow, selfish nationalism and establish a golden rule of nations which will lead to mutual trust and friendship.[31]

FURTHER READING

Bare, Daniel R. *Black Fundamentalists: Conservative Christianity and Racial Identity in the Segregation Era.* New York: New York University Press, 2021.

Bendroth, Margaret Lamberts. *Fundamentalism and Gender, 1875 to the Present.* New Haven: Yale University Press, 1993.

Gloege, Timothy E. W. *Guaranteed Pure: The Moody Bible Institute, Business, and the Making of Modern Evangelicalism.* Chapel Hill: University of North Carolina Press, 2015.

Kazin, Michael. *A Godly Hero: The Life of William Jennings Bryan.* New York: Knopf, 2006.

Laats, Adam. *Fundamentalism and Education in the Scopes Era: God, Darwin, and the Roots of America's Culture Wars.* New York: Palgrave Macmillan, 2010.

Larson, Edward J. *Summer for the Gods: The Scopes Trial and America's Continuing Debate over Science and Religion.* New York: Basic Books, 1997.

Lienesch, Michael. *In the Beginning: Fundamentalism, the Scopes Trial, and the Making of the Antievolution Movement.* Chapel Hill: University of North Carolina Press, 1997.

Numbers, Ronald L. *Darwinism Comes to America.* Cambridge, MA: Harvard University Press, 1998.

Shapiro, Adam R. *Trying Biology: The Scopes Trial, Textbooks, and the Antievolution Movement in American Schools.* Chicago: University of Chicago Press, 2013.

Weinberg, Carl R. *Red Dynamite: Creationism, Culture Wars, and Anticommunism in America.* Ithaca, NY: Cornell University Press, 2021.

---

31. "Report of the Conference on the Cause and Cure of War," Washington, DC, January 18–24, 1925, 6.

12

Civil Rights and Uncivil Religion

Sixteenth Street Baptist Church Bombing, Birmingham, 1963

In 1900, James Weldon Johnson, a teacher at a Black preparatory school in Jacksonville, Florida, wrote a poem for students to recite when renowned educator Booker T. Washington came to visit on Abraham Lincoln's birthday. Johnson's younger brother, a composer, later set the words to music. The National Association for the Advancement of Colored People (NAACP) promoted the song as the "Negro National Anthem," and it became a staple of the mid-twentieth-century civil rights movement. Johnson went on to be an NAACP officer, civil rights activist, and professor of creative literature at Fisk University. His anthem can be found in dozens of hymnals as "Lift Every Voice and Sing," but many white Americans heard it for the first time at rallies held after the murder of George Floyd in 2020.

> Lift ev'ry voice and sing,
> Till earth and heaven ring,
> Ring with the harmonies of liberty.
> Let our rejoicing rise
> High as the listening skies,
> Let it resound loud as the rolling sea.
> Sing a song full of the faith that the dark past has taught us,
> Sing a song full of the hope that the present has brought us.

Facing the rising sun of our new day begun,
Let us march on till victory is won.[1]

———————▼———————

It can be tempting to see Martin Luther King Jr.'s "I Have a Dream" speech, one of the most famous speeches in US history, as the turning point in the civil rights movement. By the time he spoke those stirring words during the March on Washington for Jobs and Freedom, held on August 28, 1963, Black Americans had been fighting nearly a century for the equality promised to them in the Fourteenth Amendment. An audience of 250,000 peaceful demonstrators heard the Baptist preacher proclaim, in the tradition that scholars call civil religion, "Now is the time to make real the promises of democracy. Now is the time to rise from the dark and desolate valley of segregation to the sunlit path of racial justice. Now is the time to lift our nation from the quicksands of racial injustice to the solid rock of brotherhood. Now is the time to make justice a reality for all of God's children."[2] Three thousand journalists carried the message across the country and around the world. Surely it would make a difference. Surely change would come.

But words were not enough.

The turning point came just a few weeks later, on a Sunday morning in Birmingham, Alabama. It was fitting, in a way, that the climactic event occurred in a church, because the contest between segregationists and supporters of racial justice was preeminently a contest between different kinds of American Christians. Not soaring rhetoric but appalling violence began to convince just enough white Christians that their Black brethren were right—that the brutality and intransigence of segregationists were unacceptable and that laws needed to change, even if hearts were sluggish. The Birmingham church bombing did not by any means effect all of this change swiftly or easily, but it shifted momentum, finally, toward justice.

Bombingham

Bombings were not uncommon in what was, in 1960, the largest city in Alabama. What turned the city into a war zone nicknamed "Bombingham" was segregation—not just the indignity of having to use a different water fountain or sit at the back of the bus but a whole system built by white people to determine where and how Black people could live. As in many cities all over the

---

1. This version is from *Voices Together* (Harrisonburg, VA: Menno Media, 2020), no. 611.
2. A transcript of the entire speech is available online at University of Minnesota Human Rights Library, http://hrlibrary.umn.edu/education/lutherspeech.html.

Partial Timeline of Civil Rights-Era Violence

August 1955 — Murder of fourteen-year-old Emmett Till in Mississippi

September 1957 — Little Rock Nine (Black students attempting to integrate Central High School) attacked by mob

May 1961 — Freedom Riders on bus in Alabama bombed, beaten

May 1963 — Attack dogs and firehoses set on marching children in Birmingham, Alabama

September 1963 — Birmingham church bombing

June 1964 — Three volunteers helping to register voters in Mississippi kidnapped and killed

February 1965 — Malcolm X assassinated in New York City

March 1965 — "Bloody Sunday"—marching protesters beaten and teargassed on Edmund Pettus Bridge in Selma, Alabama

August 1965 — Traffic stop in Watts section of Los Angeles turns violent, sparking six days of rioting

April 1968 — Martin Luther King Jr. assassinated in Memphis

United States, a succession of laws, zoning plans, and lending practices had drawn sharp racial divisions on the local map. When Black residents, who constituted about 40 percent of the population of Birmingham, attempted to move into areas that white residents wanted to reserve for themselves, white vigilantes shot at their houses or bombed them. Desegregation activists, of any color, got the same treatment. There were fifty racially motivated bombings in Birmingham between 1947 and 1966, several in a contested neighborhood that came to be called Dynamite Hill. As urban-planning scholar Charles E. Connerly wrote, "City planning did not bomb the Sixteenth Street Baptist Church, but it was used to codify the segregation that those who bombed Dynamite Hill were attempting to preserve."[3] Noonday city planning meetings and midnight violence were the civil and uncivil means to the same end: the maintenance of white privilege.

3. Charles E. Connerly, *"The Most Segregated City in America": City Planning and Civil Rights in Birmingham, 1920–1980* (Charlottesville: University of Virginia Press, 2005), 3.

Rosa Parks Papers / Library of Congress

Rev. Fred Shuttlesworth led Bethel Baptist Church in Birmingham, Alabama, at the height of the civil rights movement.

On two occasions, the target of the bombings was the Rev. Fred Shuttlesworth. Born in 1922 in tiny Mount Meigs, Alabama, Shuttlesworth was licensed and ordained a Baptist minister in 1948. He ministered first in Selma and then, in 1953, was called to Bethel Baptist Church in Birmingham. Bethel, located in a Black section of north Birmingham, had an aging congregation and had never been a hotbed of activism, but it also had a cohort of young World War II veterans who were emboldened by President Harry Truman's 1948 desegregation of the armed forces. This cohort helped convince the church to take a chance on the young Shuttlesworth, hoping that he would attract new members.

Shuttlesworth quickly established himself as an engaging preacher and a strong leader. He also encouraged church members to register to vote, a rare and difficult step. Of the 121,667 Black residents of Jefferson County (where Birmingham is located) who were old enough to vote in 1956, just seven thousand, or 5.8 percent, were registered. When Shuttlesworth first tried to transfer his own registration to Jefferson County, the registrar told him, "Boy, I don't think I want you to register right now; I want you to come back at a later time."[4] Jefferson was one of the hardest counties for a Black voter to register in, though it was not one of the three Alabama counties that refused to register Black voters at all.

Following the 1954 Supreme Court decision *Brown v. Board of Education of Topeka*, which ruled segregation in public schools unconstitutional, Shuttlesworth accelerated and expanded his civil rights activism. He convinced other ministers in the city to sign petitions requesting Black police officers, new recreational areas for Black residents to use, and restrictions on liquor licenses in high-crime neighborhoods. The city commission accepted the petitions but refused to act on them. Shuttlesworth concluded that Southern politicians "smile and say 'yes' when they really mean 'hell no.'"[5] He also accompanied Autherine

---

4. Quoted in Andrew M. Manis, *A Fire You Can't Put Out: The Civil Rights Life of Birmingham's Reverend Fred Shuttlesworth* (Tuscaloosa: University of Alabama Press, 1999), 75; voting statistics from C. G. Gomillion, "The Negro Voter in Alabama," *Journal of Negro Education* 26, no. 3 (Summer 1957): 281–86.

5. Quoted in Manis, *Fire You Can't Put Out*, 86.

Lucy to the University of Alabama campus when she became the first Black student to enroll there, in February 1956. White students rioted, and Lucy was suspended over safety concerns. Soon afterward, assailants threw bricks through the window of Shuttlesworth's parsonage.

Shuttlesworth was committed to Mahatma Gandhi's principles of nonviolent action, but his opponents were not. One of the key nonviolent actions of the civil rights movement was the Montgomery bus boycott, sparked when Rosa Parks refused to give up her seat. Shuttlesworth applauded that campaign and said to the Black activists of Montgomery, "Because of you, instead of burning crosses, we shall bear our crosses; instead of throwing bombs, we'll throw truth. You have taught us that our greatest contribution must be to bring social change without violence."[6] In December 1956, when a Supreme Court decision struck down segregation on public buses, he announced his intention to integrate Birmingham buses right after Christmas. On Christmas Eve, however, would-be assassins bombed his house with between six and sixteen sticks of dynamite. The blast destroyed the house, but Shuttlesworth, his wife and four children, and their guests were only lightly injured. A white police officer who responded to the explosion told the pastor, "I didn't think they would go this far. I know these people. Reverend, if I were you, I'd get out of town as fast as I could." Shuttlesworth replied, "Officer, you are not me. You see God saving me through all this. So you go back and tell your Klan brethren that if God could keep me through all this, then I'm here for the duration."[7]

Shuttlesworth survived two more violent attacks. In 1957, when he and his wife, Ruby, attempted to enroll their daughters in a previously all-white high school, a mob of Klansmen beat Fred with baseball bats and chains, and Ruby was stabbed in the hip while trying to get the girls back to the car. One daughter, Ruby Fredericka, got a broken ankle when the car door slammed on her leg. The next year, a bomb was placed at his church in the middle of the night. Fortunately, a man guarding the church saw smoke, grabbed the can full of explosives, and moved it to the middle of the street before diving for cover. The police accused members of the church of setting the bomb as a publicity stunt, although officers knew who was actually responsible, had collaborated with the bomber, and were in fact arguing with him that night about payment for the botched attack. That truth finally came out when the bomber was convicted in 1980.

The congregation at Bethel Baptist came to admire their pastor's tenacity, which made him a rising star in the civil rights movement. White authorities in Birmingham, by contrast, despised his audacity, and some other Black civil

6. Quoted in Manis, *Fire You Can't Put Out*, 105.
7. Quoted in Manis, *Fire You Can't Put Out*, 110.

As schools across the country began to desegregate, white parents protested, sometimes with words and sometimes with violence. One of the signs at this 1959 protest at the Arkansas state capitol in Little Rock called race-mixing the "march of the antichrist."

rights leaders also wondered if he was pushing too far, too fast. The word "civil" in civil rights meant legal, government-granted, but civility also encompasses notions of deference, decorousness, and propriety. It was hard for some Black Americans, and for nearly all white Americans, to accept acts of civil disobedience as steps toward a better social order. The Ku Klux Klan, of course, was troubled by no such qualms about its members' own actions. The Klan proclaimed its religiosity openly and flouted laws just as openly. Yet it was Black Christian activists whose civility was stringently policed.

Strategies and Coalitions

All eras of Black history featured a range of approaches to the quest for fair treatment. As seen in previous chapters, some enslaved Black preachers ministered with the enslavers' permission, some preached in secret, and a few led rebellions. The early nineteenth century spawned organizations promoting immediate abolition of slavery, or gradual abolition, or the transport of all Black people to Africa. Around the turn of the twentieth century, educator Booker T. Washington told Black Americans that if they worked hard enough, they could earn white respect, while figures such as scholar W. E. B. DuBois and journalist Ida B. Wells argued that recognition would never be granted but had to be claimed. White Americans frequently praised meek approaches while castigating any hint of Black assertiveness, and even the Black leaders whom white Americans preferred had to walk a fine line. For example, when President Theodore Roosevelt invited Booker T. Washington to dine at the White House in 1901, the meal triggered ferocious backlash. Washington faced death threats, and a Southern newspaper editor declared Roosevelt "the worst enemy to his race of any white man who has ever occupied so high a place in this republic."[8]

By 1960, there was a complex network of civil rights figures and organizations navigating relationships among themselves and with white power structures. Shuttlesworth was most involved with the Alabama Christian Movement for Human Rights, which he founded when the NAACP was banned from Alabama in 1956, and with the Southern Christian Leadership Conference (SCLC), of which he was a cofounder along with Martin Luther King Jr., Ralph Abernathy, Bayard Rustin, and Joseph Lowery. Of those five men, all but Rustin were ministers, and the organization positioned itself as the political arm of the Black church. King was the group's first president. Much of the group's behind-the-scenes organizing was done by experienced activist Ella Baker.

The SCLC was among the more staid civil rights organizations, as well as the most explicitly Christian. It endeavored, according to its motto, to "redeem the soul of America." Baker found it stodgy and sexist; she left in 1960 to help launch the more radical Student Nonviolent Coordinating Committee (SNCC). At the same time, though, many members of Black churches deemed the SCLC too political, and these critics included members of the founders' own congregations. Clergymen often hesitated to risk their positions and families, while college students had less to lose. The spectrum of Black approaches to liberation ranged beyond these organizations to include Black nationalists and the Nation of Islam, but those groups generally did not coordinate with the NAACP, SCLC, or even SNCC.

Contrasting visions for activism came into conflict in 1961. That year, the SNCC and another organization, the Congress of Racial Equality (CORE), mounted Freedom Rides across the South. Public buses were supposed to be desegregated by then, but it remained perilous for Black Americans to travel. To call attention to this reality, interracial groups of Freedom Riders boarded buses on routes where they knew they were likely to be mistreated, jailed, beaten, or worse. Stories of such mistreatment would no longer just circulate in hushed tones within Black communities; the violence would be public, irrefutable.

---

8. *Daily Picayune* (New Orleans), March 8, 1903, quoted in C. Vann Woodward, *Origins of the New South, 1877–1913* (Baton Rouge: Louisiana State University Press, 1951), 465.

Diversity and the participation of children gave momentum to civil rights demonstrations. The front line of a 1965 Selma-to-Montgomery march for voting rights included Unitarian minister James Reeb; Dr. Martin Luther King Jr. and his wife, Coretta Scott King; and Dr. Ralph Abernathy and his children. Reeb was murdered by white supremacists just hours after this photo was taken.

Freedom Riders hoped that either the administration of the recently elected, progressive president John F. Kennedy or a national outcry would force segregationists to stand down.

Since the period before the Civil War, white Southerners had complained about outside agitators coming into their territory to stir up trouble. Many of the Freedom Riders really were outside agitators. One group, which rode from Atlanta to Montgomery, consisted largely of faculty from Yale and Wesleyan, universities in Connecticut. Two members of the Catholic Worker movement, one from Chicago and one from Staten Island, were both arrested in Jackson, Mississippi, and imprisoned in the notorious Parchman penitentiary. The all-clergy Interfaith Freedom Ride from Washington, DC, to Tallahassee, Florida, included rabbis from Jewish congregations in New Jersey, New York, and Pennsylvania, along with white and Black Protestant ministers from the same region. These ecumenical and interfaith Freedom Rides illustrated what sociologist Robert Wuthnow identified as a shift in the latter twentieth century from strong denominational identities to a two-party system in American religion.[9] Activists realized

9. Robert Wuthnow, *The Restructuring of American Religion: Society and Faith Since World War II* (Princeton: Princeton University Press, 1988).

that they often had more in common with other activists, across confessional lines, than with more conservative members of their own religious communities. It came to matter less whether a person was a Methodist, or a Lutheran, or a Catholic than which side that person took on issues such as racial justice.

Southern Black churches, including Bethel Baptist, provided financial and logistical support for the Freedom Rides, but the actions put leaders such as Shuttlesworth in a difficult position. Shuttlesworth had plenty of experience already going toe-to-toe with the bombastic, flagrantly racist head of law enforcement in Birmingham, Eugene "Bull" Connor, but an intentionally high-profile demonstration staged by people from outside the community raised the stakes considerably. Shuttlesworth did not know what would happen on May 14, 1961, when he was scheduled to deliver a Mother's Day sermon and the first busload of Freedom Riders was scheduled to arrive en route from Washington, DC, to New Orleans. On the bus would be white retirees from Michigan, CORE officers from New York, a Baptist seminarian, a Congregational minister, and several students from historically Black colleges and universities. Shuttlesworth prayed for their safety and prepared for a fight.

Nine Freedom Riders were injured that day in two separate attacks. A mob of fifty armed Klansmen smashed the bus when it arrived in Anniston, Alabama. Police pretended to escort the bus to a safe location but instead abandoned it at the city limits, where another mob attempted to burn its occupants alive. An exploding fuel tank enabled the riders to get out of the bus, but the mob continued to beat them until police finally intervened.

When Shuttlesworth learned of the attacks, he dispatched cars to pick up the stranded and wounded riders, ordering drivers not to take guns on the dangerous errand. "You must trust God and have faith," he admonished them.[10] One rider who was brought, bleeding, to Bethel Baptist was James Peck, a white, forty-six-year-old activist who had been beaten so badly that Shuttlesworth could see his skull through a gash in his forehead. Police officers, who had done so little to protect the riders, showed up at Shuttlesworth's home to try to arrest them. Shuttlesworth rebuffed the police, got an ambulance for Peck, and eventually gathered the remaining riders and members of his community for a revival service. "This is the greatest thing that has ever happened in Alabama, and it has been good for the nation," he proclaimed. "It was a wonderful thing to see these young students—Negro and white—come, even after the mobs and the bus burning. When white and black men are willing to be beaten up together, it is a sure sign they will soon walk together as brothers."[11]

10. Quoted in Manis, *Fire You Can't Put Out*, 264.
11. Quoted in Manis, *Fire You Can't Put Out*, 266–67.

Such statements endeared Shuttlesworth to the younger, more radical wing of the movement but alienated older or more cautious figures, as well as members of both the Black and the white middle class. King, for example, was younger than Shuttlesworth but was more educated and came from a wealthier family. When student activists pressed him to participate in Freedom Rides, he declined, telling them that he had to choose "the when and where of his own Golgotha."[12] As news coverage of the rides prompted widespread indignation, though, King publicly encouraged the riders while privately negotiating with the Kennedy administration for federal protection. Later events in Birmingham and elsewhere would prod King in a more confrontational direction. White and Black Americans kept getting beaten up together, but brotherhood kept getting deferred.

Project C

On January 14, 1963, Alabama's newly elected governor, George Wallace, claimed the mantle of the Confederacy and declared in his inaugural address, "In the name of the greatest people that have ever trod this earth, I draw the line in the dust and toss the gauntlet before the feet of tyranny, and I say segregation now, segregation tomorrow, segregation forever."[13] That sentiment was prevalent among white Southerners, including clergy. In a 1960 Easter sermon, which was broadcast on the radio and then distributed as a booklet, evangelist and university founder Bob Jones Sr. considered the question "Is Segregation Scriptural?" He answered that it was, because God created the races to be separate, setting each within the "bounds of their habitation." White enslavers may have erred by bringing Africans to the United States, he admitted, but Black Americans should be happy that slavery enabled them to become Christians, and they should accept the racial boundaries that persisted after enslavement. "If we would just listen to the Word of God and not try to overthrow God's established order," Jones claimed, "we would not have any trouble. God never meant for America to be a melting pot to rub out the lines between the nations. . . . When someone goes to overthrowing His established order and goes around preaching pious sermons about it, that makes me sick."[14]

12. Adam Fairclough, *To Redeem the Soul of America: The Southern Christian Leadership Conference and Martin Luther King, Jr.* (Athens: University of Georgia Press, 1987), 80.

13. A transcript of the inaugural address is available online at Alabama Department of Archives and History, https://digital.archives.alabama.gov/digital/collection/voices/id/2952/.

14. Bob Jones Sr., "Is Segregation Scriptural?" A transcript of this sermon is available at https://www.drslewis.org/camille/2013/03/15/is-segregation-scriptural-by-bob-jones-sr-1960/.

Jones's attitude was not fringe. Based on her research on white evangelicals in Mississippi, historian Carolyn Renée Dupont wrote,

> Fixated on the potential advent of black equality, white Christians joined the fight to preserve white power and privilege in all its forms. . . . In their religious world, racial integration represented a heinous moral evil—and they fought it as if against the devil himself. White Mississippians' fierce and tenacious defense of their segregated society relied heavily on religious ideas and frames of reference. Their segregationist polemics employed biblical apologetics, but religion figured in the defense of the racial hierarchy in other far more significant ways, including the overt sanctification of a political philosophy that underpinned segregation. And evangelicals went well beyond rhetoric. They marshaled the power of the state, warred against their own denominations, caucused and organized, and ejected black worshippers from their sanctuaries.[15]

Although there were a few white Southern Christians who supported civil rights, and a small minority of Southerners who were not Christians, the fight to desegregate the South is rightly understood as a contest between white and Black Christians, with churches as key battle sites.

The same day that Wallace promised "segregation forever," King began a fundraising tour for Project C, which he called "the most difficult campaign I have yet undertaken."[16] "C" stood for "Confrontation," and its epicenter would be Birmingham, where Shuttlesworth and activist Wyatt Tee Walker were laying the groundwork for an escalating series of nonviolent actions. As with the Freedom Rides, the goal was to provoke a heavy-handed response from segregationists, filling local jails with protestors and blanketing the country with disturbing images. The architects of Project C hoped to prick the conscience of any persuadable white person and goad the federal government (the "tyranny" to which Wallace referred) into taking stronger measures. As Shuttlesworth told an audience of potential supporters in the New York apartment of musician Harry Belafonte, "Birmingham's Negroes have endured too much for too long. If freedom doesn't come now, it may be too late for it ever to come." Linking the campaign to the Easter season, when it would begin, Shuttlesworth closed by saying, "You have to be prepared to die before you can live."[17]

On April 3, 1963, Shuttlesworth announced that boycotts, sit-ins, and other peaceful actions would commence in Birmingham and last until a list of demands was met. Demands included desegregation of stores and public facilities,

---

15. Carolyn Renée Dupont, *Mississippi Praying: Southern White Evangelicals and the Civil Rights Movement, 1945–1975* (New York: New York University Press, 2013).

16. Quoted in Manis, *Fire You Can't Put Out*, 333.

17. Quoted in Manis, *Fire You Can't Put Out*, 342.

Moderation and Frustration

On April 12, 1963, eight white Alabama clergymen (seven church officials and one rabbi) responded to the start of Project C demonstrations with a public statement aimed at Martin Luther King Jr. It read, in part:

> We are now confronted by a series of demonstrations by some of our Negro citizens, directed and led in part by outsiders. We recognize the natural impatience of people who feel that their hopes are slow in being realized. But we are convinced that these demonstrations are unwise and untimely.
>
> We agree rather with certain local Negro leadership which has called for honest and open negotiation of racial issues in our area. And we believe this kind of facing of issues can best be accomplished by citizens of our own metropolitan area, white and Negro, meeting with their knowledge and experience of the local situation. All of us need to face that responsibility and find proper channels for its accomplishment.[a]

King's lengthy letter of response, written on April 16, explained why he and other "outsiders" had come to Birmingham and why their nonviolent, yet confrontational, approach was necessary. This oft-cited passage communicated his frustration with white notions of civility.

> I must make two honest confessions to you, my Christian and Jewish brothers. First, I must confess that over the past few years I have been gravely disappointed with the white moderate. I have almost reached the regrettable conclusion that the Negro's great stumbling block in his stride toward freedom is not the White Citizen's Counciler or the Ku Klux Klanner, but ▶

fair hiring and advancement policies for Black workers, and dismissal of charges against people who had taken part in previous protests. By the end of a week of actions, no demands had been met, but 150 protestors had been arrested, and Bull Connor had obtained a court injunction barring further demonstrations. Shuttlesworth and King both took leading roles in the demonstrations, which continued despite the injunction, and both were jailed for their participation. It was this imprisonment, one of many over his career, that led to King's famous "Letter from a Birmingham Jail" (see a portion of the text in the sidebar titled "Moderation and Frustration").

Negotiations involving Governor Wallace, Attorney General Robert Kennedy, and Black leaders stalled, so organizers mounted a new round of marches the white moderate, who is more devoted to "order" than to justice; who prefers a negative peace which is the absence of tension to a positive peace which is the presence of justice; who constantly says: "I agree with you in the goal you seek, but I cannot agree with your methods of direct action"; who paternalistically believes he can set the timetable for another man's freedom; who lives by a mythical concept of time and who constantly advises the Negro to wait for a "more convenient season." Shallow understanding from people of good will is more frustrating than absolute misunderstanding from people of ill will. Lukewarm acceptance is much more bewildering than outright rejection. . . .

I had hoped that the white moderate would understand that the present tension in the South is a necessary phase of the transition from an obnoxious negative peace, in which the Negro passively accepted his unjust plight, to a substantive and positive peace, in which all men will respect the dignity and worth of human personality. Actually, we who engage in nonviolent direct action are not the creators of tension. We merely bring to the surface the hidden tension that is already alive. We bring it out in the open, where it can be seen and dealt with. Like a boil that can never be cured so long as it is covered up but must be opened with all its ugliness to the natural medicines of air and light, injustice must be exposed, with all the tension its exposure creates, to the light of human conscience and the air of national opinion before it can be cured.[b]

a. "Statement by Alabama Clergymen, April 12, 1963," King Institute, Stanford University, https://kinginstitute.stanford.edu/sites/mlk/files/lesson-activities/clergybirmingham1963.pdf.
b. Martin Luther King Jr., "Letter from a Birmingham Jail," African Studies Center, University of Pennsylvania, https://www.africa.upenn.edu/Articles_Gen/Letter_Birmingham.html.

and demonstrations during the first week of May. This time, marches would feature hundreds of high school students and younger children who, organizers believed, would bring energy and publicity to the marches without having to risk losing their livelihoods, because they did not yet have jobs. By eight o'clock on the morning of May 2, Shuttlesworth was preaching to a full crowd of students gathered at Sixteenth Street Baptist Church and listening as they sang the old spiritual "Woke Up This Morning with My Mind Stayed on Freedom." When the young people marched from the church to a nearby park, Connor's police force sprayed them with firehoses and arrested so many that they had to be transported to the jail in school buses. The next day, more waves of young people marched again, only to be met by hoses and attack dogs. Associated

Press photos of the clash became some of the most iconic images of the civil rights era. The students' resolve helped to convince some white observers that fervor for justice was not the result of outside agitation but a deep-seated force within their own community. Some local white leaders became more open to negotiation, while others doubled down on violent resistance. King called for a halt to the demonstrations in order to facilitate negotiations; Shuttlesworth wanted more action but reluctantly agreed to back off.

The upswell of energy in Birmingham propelled plans for a massive march on Washington, DC, in August. The march brought together all wings of the civil rights movement, from the stolid NAACP to the edgy SNCC, and included other organizations, both religious (National Council of Churches, National Catholic Conference for Interracial Justice, American Jewish Committee) and secular (United Auto Workers). Six buses carried 260 demonstrators from Birmingham, bringing, a *New York Times* reporter wrote, "picnic baskets, water jugs, Bibles and a major weapon—their willingness to march, sing and pray in protest against discrimination."[18] Following jubilant hours of speeches and songs on the Capitol mall, leaders traveled to the White House to discuss civil rights legislation with President Kennedy and Vice President Lyndon Baines Johnson. The day was entirely peaceful, but more violence loomed on the path to legislative progress, some of it back in Birmingham.

"The Blood of Four Little Children"

September 15, 1963, was Youth Sunday at Sixteenth Street Baptist Church. The most elegant of Birmingham's Black churches, it had shied away from taking a leading role in activism, though it had, five years earlier, exchanged Sunday visits with a white church, Thirty-fifth Avenue Baptist. Four Klansmen at the white church were so incensed by the exchange that they denounced their pastor as a communist—a common accusation leveled at anyone working for racial justice. One of the men, Robert Chambliss, refused to go to church ever again. But he did go to Sixteenth Street that morning in September, to plant a bomb.[19]

Excited to participate in the morning's service, four young women were fixing up their hair and dresses in the women's lounge in the basement. Three of them, all fourteen years old, wore white, in preparation to serve as ushers: Addie Mae Collins, Carole Robertson, and Cynthia Wesley. Just as Addie was tying the sash on the purple dress of a younger girl, eleven-year-old Denise McNair, there was,

18. Fred Powledge, "Alabamians Gay on Bus Journey," *New York Times*, August 28, 1963, 21.
19. Diane McWhorter, *Carry Me Home: Birmingham, Alabama; The Climactic Battle of the Civil Rights Revolution* (New York: Simon & Schuster, 2001), 519–20.

in the words of journalist Diane McWhorter, "a resonant thud, as if someone had hit the world's largest washtub, followed by a ripping blast that sent a streak of fire above the church. Closed doors flew open, and the walls shook. As a stale-smelling white fog filled the church, a blizzard of debris—brick, stone, wire, glass—pelted the neighborhood." Twelve-year-old Sarah Collins, who survived the blast but was blinded in one eye, vainly called out to her sister, "Addie, Addie, Addie."[20]

The bomb detonated at Sixteenth Street Baptist Church in September 1963 obliterated the face of Jesus in a stained-glass window.

Shock, sorrow, and outrage followed the deaths. Martin Luther King Jr., who learned of the bombing as he was about to step into his pulpit at Ebenezer Baptist Church in Atlanta, sent a furious telegram to Governor Wallace, telling him that "the blood of four little children . . . is on your hands. Your irresponsible and misguided actions have created in Birmingham and Alabama the atmosphere that has induced continued violence and now murder."[21] King's tone at the funeral for three of the girls on September 18 was softer, when he said, "In spite of the darkness of this hour, we must not despair. We must not become bitter, nor must we harbor the desire to retaliate with violence. No, we must not lose faith in our white brothers. Somehow we must believe that the most misguided among them can learn to respect the dignity and the worth of all human personality."[22] The next day, King and Shuttlesworth led a delegation of Black ministers to the White House, asking for federal intervention to stave off what King said would be the "worst racial holocaust this nation has ever seen."[23]

Several of the white Alabama clergymen who had written an open letter to King in April, urging moderation, also visited the White House. They all expressed a desire to ease racial tensions in Birmingham but complained that

20. McWhorter, *Carry Me Home*, 522–23.

21. "Six Dead after Church Bombing," *Washington Post*, September 16, 1963, https://www.washingtonpost.com/wp-srv/national/longterm/churches/archives1.htm. In addition to the four young women killed at the church, two Black teenage boys were shot in separate incidents later in the day.

22. Martin Luther King Jr., "Death of Illusions," in *The Autobiography of Martin Luther King, Jr.*, ed. Clayborne Carson (New York: Grand Central Publishing, 2001). Available online at https://kinginstitute.stanford.edu/chapter-21-death-illusions.

23. McWhorter, *Carry Me Home*, 530.

King's actions prevented them from exercising the spiritual leadership they thought was their due. Kennedy found their position naive and warned, "You have no idea what's waiting in the wings. If King fails, you won't have much of a city to save." Catholic bishop Joseph Durick had an interesting suggestion for the country's first Catholic president: Might Kennedy use his influence to ask the white, Baptist evangelist Billy Graham to hold an "ecumenical, interracial revival in the city"?[24] Graham had refused to participate in the March on Washington and had disparaged pastors who made "the race issue their gospel," but he was shaken by the Sixteenth Street church bombing and was helping to raise funds for rebuilding.[25] Kennedy and Graham were not close, though, and the evangelist did not hold an interracial gathering in Birmingham until Easter 1964.

As President Kennedy weighed religious leaders' calls for bold or incremental interventions, he also had to consider the international implications of the racial turmoil in Birmingham. In the Cold War context of the later twentieth century, the United States and its communist rival, the Soviet Union, vied for the allegiance of nations in Central and South America, Africa, the Middle East, and Asia, many of them just emerging from European colonization. Images of violence against dark-skinned people in the United States made good propaganda for the Soviets, who could argue, plausibly, that any nation that treated its own citizens so badly was no reliable ally. According to a June 1963 intelligence briefing, Soviets had broadcast 1,420 commentaries on the American racial crisis just in the period May 14–26, emphasizing "the hypocrisy of US claims to leadership of the free world." The briefing reported that the amount of coverage was seven times what the Soviets gave to the embattled enrollment of Black student James Meredith at the University of Mississippi in the autumn of 1962 and nine times the amount given to the Freedom Riders.[26] Racism was a rising foreign policy crisis as well as a domestic emergency.

It took all of these factors, combined, to set in motion meaningful progress toward civil rights—pain, pleas, guilt, protest, negotiation, strategy. The Civil Rights Act that Kennedy was working to pass when he was assassinated in November 1963 was muscled through Congress by his successor, Lyndon Johnson, and passed in 1964. It was followed by a landmark Voting Rights Act in 1965. All

24. S. Jonathan Bass, *Blessed Are the Peacemakers: Martin Luther King Jr., Eight White Religious Leaders, and the "Letter from the Birmingham Jail"* (Baton Rouge: Louisiana State University Press, 2001), 186–87.

25. William Martin, *A Prophet with Honor: The Billy Graham Story* (New York: William Morrow, 1991), 296.

26. Department of State Bureau of Intelligence and Research, Thomas L. Hughes to the Secretary, research memorandum, June 14, 1963, John F. Kennedy Presidential Library and Museum, https://archiveblog.jfklibrary.org/2013/07/newly-digitized-material-subject-series-of-the-national-security-files/jfknsf-295-016-p0018/.

of that progress was hard-fought, and none of it was sufficient. As Black historian Jemar Tisby reflected in 2019, "The 'Whites Only' and 'No Negroes Allowed' signs have been taken down, but schools remain segregated. People of color are incarcerated at dispropor- tionately high rates. Black unemployment re- mains double that of whites. Most poignantly, churches remain largely segregated. The re- luctance to reckon with racism has led to a chasm between black and white Christians in theology, politics, and culture. This chasm only makes it harder to productively com- municate and take effective action around racial issues."[27]

Activist Fannie Lou Hamer, speaking at the Democratic National Conven- tion in 1964.

In terms of turning points, then, the Bir- mingham church bombing can be viewed two ways. In the assessment of many schol- ars, the attack changed the course of the civil rights movement and bent the arc of US history toward justice. There had been many other horrific tragedies in Black history, many other calls for intervention; this one got more traction among a wide range of white powerbrokers, without whom structural change could not occur. But events in Birmingham in the early 1960s also significantly affected the shift to the two-party system in American religion. Religious Ameri- cans either agreed with Black activists that racial justice was an urgent, moral issue, or they did not. Individuals, congregations, and denominations took sides. Often, support for racial justice went along with support for women's liberation and opposition to the Vietnam War, while outright opposition or a go-slow posture regarding civil rights went along with a preference for male headship and support for the Vietnam War. Those divisions cleaved deep and ranged far beyond the haltingly desegregating South.

A 1966 documentary made clear the ways in which churches would continue to be frontline sites in the long fight for racial equality. Titled *A Time for Burning*, the film depicts the attempt by a white pastor, Rev. Bill Youngdahl, to lead his all-white congregation, Augustana Lutheran Church in Omaha, Nebraska, into some kind of relationship with Black Lutherans across town. Despite their dated apparel, the people and their perspectives remained all too familiar decades

27. Jemar Tisby, *The Color of Compromise: The Truth about the American Church's Complicity in Racism* (Grand Rapids: Zondervan, 2019), 192.

Born in the Mess

For her work helping Black Americans vote and participate in politics, activist Fannie Lou Hamer was threatened, shot at, attacked by mobs, sexually assaulted, and nearly beaten to death in jail. When she spoke, as at the 1964 mass meeting in Indianola, Mississippi, excerpted here, she often employed the cadences of Black preaching, rich in references to Scripture and to the community's embodied experience.

> This is one of the next things that I don't like: every church door in the state of Mississippi should be open for these meetings; but preachers have preached for years what he didn't believe himself. And if he's willing to trust God, if he's willing to trust God, he won't mind opening the church door. Because the first words of Jesus's public ministry was: "The spirit of the Lord is upon me because he has anointed me to preach the gospel to the poor. He has sent me to proclaim and bring relief to the captive." And you know we are living in a captivated society today. And we know the things we doing is right. The thirty-seventh of Psalms said, "Fret not thouselves because of evildoers, neither be thy envious against the workers of iniquity for they shall be cut down like the green grass and wither away as the green herb. Delight thouselves in the Lord and verily thou shalt be filled." And we are determined to be filled in Mississippi today. ▶

later. Members of the white congregation expressed discomfort with sharing pews or social spaces with Black people. They complained about the pace of social change and fretted about their property values. A Black activist filmed at the barbershop, Ernest Chambers (who went on to serve several terms in the Nebraska legislature), told Youngdahl, "As far as we're concerned, your Jesus is contaminated, just like everything else you've tried to force upon us is contaminated." Members of the Black youth group voiced frustration that neither pastors in churches nor teachers in school were brave enough to confront race prejudice. By the end, just one white congregational leader, Ray Christensen, had come to see the urgency of racism, and Youngdahl resigned his pastorate in defeat. When interviewed in July 2020, filmmaker Bill Jersey said, "There's nothing in that film that would not happen now."[28]

---

28. Robert Edwards, "America against Itself: A Time for Burning (Again)," *Medium*, July 7, 2020, https://edwardsrobt.medium.com/america-against-itself-a-time-for-burning-again-bd37baf10905.

Some of the white people will tell us, "Well, I just don't believe in integration." But he been integrating at night a long time! If he hadn't been, it wouldn't be as many light-skinned Negroes as it is in here. The seventeenth chapter of Acts and the twenty-sixth verse said: "Has made of one blood all nations." So whether you black as a skillet or white as a sheet, we are made from the same blood and we are on our way!

We know, we know we have a long fight because the leaders like the preachers and the teachers, they are failing to stand up today. But we know some of the reasons for that. This brainwashed education that the teachers have got, he know that if he had to get a job as a janitor in this missile base that they are be building he'd probably turn something over and blow up the place because he wouldn't know what it was.

Righteousness exalts a nation, but sin is a reproach to any people. Sin is beginning to reproach America today and we want what is rightfully ours. And it's no need of running and no need of saying, "Honey, I'm not going to get in the mess," because if you were born in America with a black face, you were born in the mess.

> Fannie Lou Hamer, "We're on Our Way," in *The Speeches of Fannie Lou Hamer: To Tell It Like It Is*, ed. Maegan Parker Brooks and Davis W. Houck (Jackson: University Press of Mississippi, 2011), 49.

Theologian, pastor, and mystic Howard Thurman (1899–1981) was a mentor to many civil rights leaders. King often carried a much-read copy of Thurman's 1949 book *Jesus and the Disinherited*. This portion of a longer prayer, "O God, I Need Thee," comes from another of his books, *Deep Is the Hunger: Meditations for Apostles of Sensitiveness*.

> *I Need Thy Sense of the Future*
> *Teach me to know that life is ever*
> *On the side of the future.*
> *Keep alive in me the forward look, the high hope,*
> *The onward surge. Let me not be frozen*
> *Either by the past or the present.*
> *Grant me, O patient Father, Thy sense of the future*
> *Without which all life would sicken and die.*[29]

29. The poem "Oh God, I Need Thee," is excerpted from Howard Thurman, *Deep Is the Hunger: Meditation for Apostles of Sensitiveness* (New York: Harper, 1951), 204–5. Used by permission of Friends United Press. All rights reserved.

──────────────── **FURTHER READING** ────────────────

Bell, Janet Dewart. *Lighting the Fires of Freedom: African American Women in the Civil Rights Movement*. New York: New Press, 2019.

Curtis, Jesse. *The Myth of Colorblind Christians: Evangelicals and White Supremacy in the Civil Rights Era*. New York: New York University Press, 2021.

Harvey, Jennifer. *Dear White Christians: For Those Still Longing for Racial Reconciliation*. Grand Rapids: Eerdmans, 2014.

Hawkins, J. Russell. *The Bible Told Them So: How Southern Evangelicals Fought to Preserve White Supremacy*. New York: Oxford University Press, 2021.

Jones, Doug, with Greg Truman. *Bending toward Justice: The Birmingham Church Bombing That Changed the Course of Civil Rights*. New York: All Points Books, 2019.

King, Martin Luther, Jr. *Stride toward Freedom: The Montgomery Story*. New York: Harper & Row, 1958.

Marsh, Charles. *God's Long Summer: Stories of Faith and Civil Rights*. Princeton: Princeton University Press, 1997.

Theoharis, Jeanne. *A More Beautiful and Terrible History: The Uses and Misuses of Civil Rights History*. Boston: Beacon, 2018.

13

Religion Moves Right

Ronald Reagan Elected President, 1980

Episcopal priest Daniel C. Roberts (1841–1907) wrote the hymn "God of Our Fathers" for a national centennial celebration in Vermont in 1876. A new arrangement of the hymn was played by the US Marine Band at Ronald Reagan's first inauguration, and it became a staple at Republican inaugurations afterward. The tune, with recurring trumpet fanfare, emphasizes the martial and regal tones of the text. Democratic presidents since Reagan have tended to select milder inaugural hymns, such as "America, the Beautiful," "My Country, 'Tis of Thee," or "American Anthem."

> God of our fathers, whose almighty hand
> Leads forth in beauty all the starry band
> Of shining worlds in splendor thro' the skies,
> Our grateful songs before Thy throne arise.
>
> Thy love divine hath led us in the past,
> In this free land by thee our lot is cast;
> Be thou our ruler, guardian, guide, and stay,
> Thy word our law, thy paths our chosen way.[1]

---

1. This version is from the *United Methodist Hymnal* (Nashville: United Methodist Publishing House, 1989), no. 704.

"Born Again!" proclaimed the cover of the October 25, 1976, issue of *Newsweek* magazine, with a photo of a pastor laying his hand on a man's head in church. Published just a few weeks before that year's presidential election, the article, subtitled "The Year of the Evangelicals," cast both Democrat Jimmy Carter and Republican Gerald Ford as evangelicals. Carter had the stronger claim to the identity—the "best-known Baptist deacon in America" was running on a promise to return honesty to a White House stained by the Watergate scandal. He had even, controversially, explained his religious beliefs and practices at length in an interview with *Playboy* magazine. But Ford had evangelical credentials as well. According to the *Newsweek* article, Ford, although a member of the not-notably-evangelical Episcopal Church, "says that he reads the Bible daily, often prays in the Oval Office and has had his life transformed by Jesus Christ."[2] Additionally, Ford's son attended an evangelical seminary, Gordon-Conwell, and Ford had just been endorsed by Rev. W. A. Criswell, the pastor of the world's largest Southern Baptist Church, in Dallas.

The US Constitution specifies that no religious test can be required for holding public office. In other words, presidential candidates do not have to declare a religion, much less speak extensively about it. Why, then, would it be a major news story for both candidates to identify so publicly as evangelicals, a label unfamiliar enough to *Newsweek* readers that author Kenneth Woodward felt a need to define it (as "the religion you get when you 'get' religion")?[3]

In a word, polling. Evangelical pollster George Gallup had just published a study showing that 34 percent of all Americans, or fifty million adults, said that they had been "born again," meaning that they had experienced a particular kind of Christian conversion. While that experience of conversion was significantly more common among Protestants than Catholics (48 percent compared to 18 percent), 31 percent of Catholics, along with 46 percent of Protestants, held the belief that every word of the Bible was literally true. Also, 38 percent of Catholics and 58 percent of Protestants had "witnessed" to someone in an attempt to convert them. Gallup classed all these traits as evangelical. Christians who answered yes to these poll questions had not previously functioned as a voting bloc, but with other typical influences on voting (especially region) in flux, the potential was suddenly there. "There is a hidden religious power base in American culture which our secular biases prevent many of us from noticing," conservative Catholic theologian Michael Novak told *Newsweek*. "Jimmy Carter has found it."[4]

---

2. Kenneth L. Woodward, "Born Again: The Year of the Evangelicals," *Newsweek*, October 25, 1976, 68.

3. Woodward, "Born Again," 68.

4. Woodward, "Born Again," 68.

Baptist minister Jerry Falwell, founder of the Moral Majority political organization, led rallies (such as this one in 1980) fusing faith and patriotism. This mobilization of conservative Christians bolstered the Republican party.

Novak was right on the first part of that statement but wrong on the second. Carter did, narrowly, win the 1976 election, but evangelicals never really warmed to him, and neither did anyone else. When he ran for reelection in 1980, he faced former movie star and governor of California Ronald Reagan, whose evangelical bona fides were much weaker than Carter's or Ford's—he was divorced and remarried, rarely attended church, and had worked in an industry that most conservative Christians considered decadent—but he had a masterful way of relating to evangelicals. At an ostensibly nonpartisan event in Dallas, attended by Criswell, Moral Majority founder Jerry Falwell, religious broadcasting mogul Pat Robertson, Catholic antifeminism activist Phyllis Schlafly, and fifteen thousand other conservative Christians, Reagan famously said, "I know you can't endorse me, but . . . I want you to know that I endorse you and what you're doing." The *New York Times* headlined its coverage of the speech as "Reagan Backs Evangelicals in Their Political Activities."[5] Reagan won the 1980 election by a landslide, and conservative Christians (evangelical and Catholic) have been overwhelmingly allied with the Republican Party ever since.

Among scholars, Reagan's capture of the conservative Christian vote is almost universally regarded as a major turning point in American religious and political

5. Howell Raines, "Reagan Backs Evangelicals in Their Political Activities," *New York Times*, August 23, 1980.

history. But this story is so big, so historically recent, and so polarizing that there is no consensus on why it happened or how best to understand its ongoing ramifications. Therefore, instead of offering a single analysis, this chapter will include views from insiders who perceived what is often called "the rise of the religious right" as a triumph, as well as more critical views. The chapter will also bring in more work by journalists and social scientists who generate the early records that other scholars can use as historical distance grows.

"Religious America Is Awakening"

Reagan told the 1980 Dallas audience that "religious America is awakening, perhaps just in time for our country's sake."[6] That single line combined four emphases that resonated with his audience and helped to forge a durable coalition: an appeal to religious America, contrasted with secularism; hope for awakening, or revival; fearful urgency; and the goal of saving the nation.

During the Cold War period, from the end of World War II through the early 1990s, the United States portrayed its geopolitical rival, the Soviet Union, as a bastion of "godless communism." From 1946 to 1972, there was even a propaganda comic series called "This Godless Communism" distributed to students in American Catholic schools. As Catholic congressman Louis Rabaut put it in 1954, "You may argue from dawn to dusk about differing political, economic, and social systems, but the fundamental issue which is the unbridgeable gap between America and Communist Russia is a belief in Almighty God. From the root of atheism stems the evil weed of communism and its branches of materialism and political dictatorship. Unless we are willing to affirm our belief in the existence of God and His creator-creature relation to man, we drop man himself to the significance of a grain of sand and open the floodgates to tyranny and oppression."[7] Rabaut is best known for introducing legislation to add the words "under God" to the Pledge of Allegiance.

Reagan and his conservative Christian supporters wanted to reinforce the religious character of the United States in numerous ways. In the 1960s, the Supreme Court had ruled mandatory prayer and Bible reading in public schools unconstitutional, but Reagan vowed to bring the practices back. This promise was extremely popular with his religious base. Many of his other policy initiatives countered popular perception of communist Russia, as seen in the words

6. Ronald Reagan, "National Affairs Campaign Address on Religious Liberty," American Rhetoric, https://www.americanrhetoric.com/speeches/ronaldreaganreligiousliberty.htm.

7. Louis C. Rabaut, speaking in favor of "House Joint Resolution 243, To Amend the Pledge of Allegiance to Include the Phrase 'Under God,'" February 12, 1954, *Congressional Record* 100, part 2, February 8–March 8, 1954, 1700.

of Rabaut and countless similar speeches, point for point. Instead of the wealth redistribution intrinsic to communism, Reagan's economic strategy cut taxes for the rich and slashed welfare programs. To combat materialism, Reagan supported the teaching of creationism alongside evolution in schools. And to stave off political dictatorship, Reagan pledged to shrink the federal government (excepting the Department of Defense, the budget for which he more than doubled). "In this present crisis," he said in his first inaugural address, "government is not the solution to our problem; government is the problem." What the crisis required instead was "our willingness to believe in ourselves and to believe in our capacity to perform great deeds, to believe that together with God's help we can and will resolve the problems which now confront us."[8]

Awakening could take a secular or religious meaning in Reagan's speeches. A television ad for his 1984 reelection campaign memorably began, "It's morning again in America," before touting high rates of employment, marriage, and home ownership. Reagan also spoke often of a need for religious revival. Bob Slosser, a columnist for Pat Robertson's Christian Broadcasting Network, collected a long list of examples that demonstrated that Reagan usually linked revival with the past. Reagan spoke of "a spiritual rebirth, a rededication to the moral precepts which guided us for so much of our past," and "a great spiritual awakening in America—a renewal of the traditional values that have been the bedrock of America's goodness and greatness." As evidence that revival was happening during his presidency, he referenced polling data showing that Americans were "far more religious" than residents of other countries, reporting near universal belief in God and the Ten Commandments.[9]

Fearful urgency—the notion that there might be just enough time to avert calamity—could also take secular or religious meaning. Both the United States and the Soviet Union possessed nuclear weapons capable of ending millions of lives within minutes, perhaps obliterating all life on the planet. The popular genre of disaster movies served up fictionalized versions of perils familiar from the news: terrorist attacks, killer viruses, plane crashes, and nuclear meltdown. Many conservative American Protestants, who subscribed to a theology known as dispensational premillennialism, saw events like these as evidence that Jesus Christ would soon return to earth to save (rapture) the faithful before catastrophe struck. They sang the Larry Norman song "I Wish We'd All Been Ready" and read Hal Lindsey's 1970 book *The Late Great Planet Earth*. That book, which rooted contemporary events in biblical prophecies, sold millions of copies. Another of Lindsey's books, *The 1980's: Countdown to Armageddon*,

8. Ronald Reagan, inaugural address, January 20, 1981, Ronald Regan Presidential Foundation & Institute, https://www.reaganfoundation.org/media/128614/inaguration.pdf.

9. Bob Slosser, *Reagan Inside Out* (Waco: Word, 1984), 156.

Opposition to Communism was central to Ronald Reagan's appeal and to his warm relationship with Pope John Paul II, who grew up in the shadow of the Soviet Union.

predicted that "the decade of the 1980's could very well be the last decade of history as we know it."[10] When that deadline passed, he published *Planet Earth—2000 A.D.: Will Mankind Survive?*

Catholics, for the most part, did not engage in such speculation about Armageddon or rapture. While conservative Catholics and evangelical Protestants blended in many areas, this was not one of them. Also, some evangelicals, such as Billy Graham, saw in the prospect of a looming end of days a heightened need for personal salvation rather than a political program. Near the end of his 1983 book *Approaching Hoofbeats: The Four Horsemen of the Apocalypse*, Graham wrote, "Thank God, the Messiah is coming. He saves individuals today."[11]

Reagan and figures such as Falwell and Robertson, however, more readily saw awakening and urgency in national terms. Slosser, the CBN columnist, quoted both the president and his Christian supporters on this theme. At his 1972 Governor's Prayer Breakfast, Reagan announced, "The time has come to turn back to God and reassert our trust in Him for the healing of America." Reagan applied God's words in 2 Chronicles 7:14 to the United States: "If my people, who are called by my name, will humble themselves and pray and seek my face and turn from their wicked ways, then I will hear from heaven, and I will forgive their sin and will heal their land" (NIV). Shirley Boone, wife of Christian singer and movie star Pat Boone, told Slosser that the revival spoken of by the president was happening. "I believe we're seeing the glory of God," she said. "I've spoken at the leadership conferences for women in the Washington for Jesus Rally in 1980 . . . and I'll never forget when we stood out on that mall and prayed and tore the strongholds down, and I know that was a turning point. When all of us went there and really started seeking God for our nation, and taking it seriously, look what happened."[12] Another Christian entertainer, Roy Rogers, when asked if national salvation was possible, replied yes, "if we keep getting leaders of a high caliber who are not afraid to

10. Hal Lindsey, *The 1980's: Countdown to Armageddon* (King of Prussia, PA: Westgate, 1980), 8.
11. Billy Graham, *Approaching Hoofbeats: The Four Horsemen of the Apocalypse* (Minneapolis: Grason, 1983), 231.
12. Slosser, *Reagan Inside Out*, 158.

stand up there and talk about it." He saw Reagan as such a leader and said, "If they'll just give him another four years, I think he'll get our country back together."[13]

On some metrics, Reagan succeeded at bringing the country together. In the 1984 election, he won all of the electoral college votes except those from Minnesota (his opponent's home state) and the District of Columbia. His party won the Senate majority for the first time in decades and made major gains in the House. His approval ratings over eight years were middling, an overall average of 53 percent, but his stature rose in hindsight. By 2001, 74 percent of Americans viewed him favorably, making him the second-most popular president, after John F. Kennedy, of the previous forty years.

But Reagan's overall approval rating masked a deep partisan divide. Over his eight years in office, 83 percent of Republicans approved of him, but just 31 percent of Democrats did. This was the widest partisan gap in polling to that point, and it only grew in years afterward. Democratic president Barack Obama (served 2008–16) averaged 81 percent approval from Democrats and 14 percent from Republicans. Republican Donald Trump (served 2016–20) averaged 87 percent approval from Republicans and just 6 percent from Democrats. Instead of unity, the Reagan years initiated an era of fracture and increased polarization.[14]

Presidential polling would not necessarily be relevant to American *church* history, but in this case it is, for at least three reasons. First, although many people understand and inhabit "evangelical" as a theological category, since 1976 pollsters, journalists, politicians, and social scientists have typically understood it as a religio-political identity, a mélange of beliefs, practices, demographic identifiers, and political preferences.[15] Evangelicals, in the latter rendering, are white, conservative Christians, probably Protestant, who vote Republican. Accurate or not, that definition is as relevant to church history as to political history. Second, and related to the first reason, as religio-political evangelicalism, operationalized as the religious right, grew more powerful in the United States,

13. Slosser, *Reagan Inside Out*, 163.

14. Amina Dunn, "Trump's Approval Ratings So Far Are Unusually Stable—and Deeply Partisan," Pew Research Center, August 24, 2020, https://www.pewresearch.org/fact-tank/2020/08/24/trumps-approval-ratings-so-far-are-unusually-stable-and-deeply-partisan/.

15. Definitions of evangelicalism are legion and hotly contested. Polls tend to use one of three approaches: self-identification (Does the person claim to be evangelical or born again?), church affiliation (Does the person belong to a church that social scientists count as evangelical, such as the Lutheran Church–Missouri Synod or the Assemblies of God?), or answers to questions about beliefs and practices. The 1976 Gallup survey combined self-identification with questions about the Bible and witnessing. For a primer on definitions, see Daniel Silliman, "An Evangelical Is Anyone Who Likes Billy Graham," *Church History* 90, no. 3 (September 2021): 621–43.

American religious affiliation declined. This rise of the "nones"—people who answer "none" when asked what religion they follow—was multifaceted, but many scholars posit that backlash against the religious right was a significant contributing cause.[16] If evangelicalism was, as *Newsweek* suggested, "the religion you get when you 'get' religion," a substantial number of Americans (nearly 30 percent in 2021) did not want religion at all. Third, the same power struggles and polarization that took place in the American political sphere from the late 1970s onward were also happening in American churches, frequently led by the same people. The remainder of the chapter will take that angle on the story, turning (as much as possible) away from Washington, DC, to look instead at churches and other Christian institutions.

Case Study: Southern Baptists

The Southern Baptist Convention (SBC), which formed in 1845 when Baptists split over slavery, is the largest Protestant denomination in the United States. Not all Southern Baptists consider themselves evangelical (one SBC leader famously called evangelical a "Yankee word"), but social scientists include the denomination in that category. More than 80 percent of SBC members are white, and more than 80 percent live in the South. For the century after the Civil War, white Southerners nearly always voted Democrat, but after Democratic president Lyndon B. Johnson signed major civil rights legislation in the 1960s, Republicans actively courted these voters in a project known as the Southern Strategy. The strategy worked, and the "solid South" flipped from electoral blue to red. Many Southern Baptist leaders welcomed and helped to hasten the change, as seen in W. A. Criswell's endorsement of Gerald Ford and his enthusiastic hosting of then-candidate Ronald Reagan in Dallas. Jerry Falwell was also Southern and a Baptist, though he and his 22,000-member Virginia church did not affiliate with the denomination until 1996. Trends in Reagan's Republican Party were mirrored or magnified in the SBC, in a movement called the "conservative resurgence."

The year before Reagan's big speech in Dallas, fifteen thousand Southern Baptist messengers (delegates) gathered in Houston to elect a president for the denomination. They selected Adrian Rogers, pastor of a massive church in Memphis who aligned with the fundamentalist wing of the denomination and promised to rescue it from liberals. One of his touchstone issues was biblical inerrancy, by which he meant the same thing that Charles Hodge (see chap. 11)

---

16. Michael Hout and Claude S. Fischer, "Why More Americans Have No Religious Preference," *American Sociological Review* 67, no. 2 (April 2002): 165–90.

meant in the late nineteenth century: every word of the Bible was historically, scientifically, and prophetically accurate. But, as in Hodge's day, this argument did not arise solely within the field of biblical studies. Rogers's statements about biblical inerrancy came in the context of specific cultural battles, preeminently regarding gender and sexuality.

The 1970s in the United States saw several changes in the status of women that were advocated by feminists. An Equal Rights Amendment (ERA) to the Constitution, stating, "Equality of rights under the law shall not be denied or abridged by the United States or by any State on account of sex," passed both houses of Congress and proceeded to the states, where it was expected to win ratification. Another piece of federal legislation, known as Title IX, addressed sex discrimination in schools. Its initial impact was most visible in school sports, where female participation soared. In later decades, Title IX became the basis for requiring schools to protect students from sexual assault and harassment. In the realm of reproductive rights, a 1972 Supreme Court decision enabled unmarried women to access contraception, and the more famous 1973 case *Roe v. Wade* legalized some abortions. The decade also saw numerous feminist publications, such as *Ms.* magazine and the book *Beyond God the Father: Toward a Philosophy of Women's Liberation* by radical theologian Mary Daly.

Rogers was one of many American Christians, men and women, who saw feminist gains as a threat. As he told an audience of four thousand at a women's conference organized by his wife in 1980 (his raised voice rendered here in small capital letters):

WHAT IS HAPPENING TO AMERICA IS NOT "JUST HAPPENING." It is the result of a well orchestrated plan with Satan waving the flag. FEMINIST THINKERS ARE OUT TO SUBVERT YOUR WOMEN AND TO BRING IN THEIR HEATHEN HEAVEN to do this through a HUMANIST/FEMINIST/SOCIALIST [sic]. There is a move to deny God, debase man, destroy the family, the world. Their plan is to free your children from the [sic] of their puritanical parents. . . . IN A WORLD GONE MAD I THANK GOD FOR SOME CONCERNED WOMEN WHO ARE SAYING "BACK TO THE BIBLE." STAND UP AND BE COUNTED BEFORE THE TIME RUNS OUT FOR AMERICA.[17]

With the urgency of Reagan's Cold War rhetoric, these words from Rogers indicated why he thought it was important to attend more closely to the Bible: to combat feminists' satanic plot to ruin the United States. It was unsurprising,

17. Adrian Rogers, "Welcome to the Women's Concerns Conference," *Bellevue Messenger*, May 16, 1980, 1, quoted in Elizabeth H. Flowers, *Into the Pulpit: Southern Baptist Women and Power since World War II* (Chapel Hill: University of North Carolina Press, 2012), 86.

Southern Baptist Women in Ministry

As SBC policy curtailed their roles, Southern Baptist women who were engaged in ministry launched a mutual support organization, Southern Baptist Women in Ministry (SBWIM). Its newsletter, *Folio*, was a place for them to share their stories and their ideas about the Bible and Christian service. In the winter 1989 issue, president Betty Winstead McGary described what women like her were and were not trying to do, and how those efforts were perceived by others.

> Since I've been involved with Women in Ministry I've discovered that the subject evokes many different responses from women. To some the thought of women ministers creates images of "angry feminists." Others think we are trying to be "one of the boys." Some perceive that we are implying that all women should work outside the home, or that women who choose to be homemakers have somehow made a lesser choice. Some think we've traded servanthood for ambition. To some, we have abandoned our sacred role as peacemakers by stirring up controversy. On the other hand, many are grateful for the ministry of women and find hope in a new vision of inclusiveness in the church and the world. ▶

then, that for Rogers and the wing of his church that supported his presidency, hallmarks of going "back to the Bible" included reading the Bible in such a way as to bolster men and the family, as well as ensuring men's authority as preachers and Bible teachers.

Resolutions passed at SBC annual meetings took increasingly firm stances on issues related to the Bible, authority, and gender and sexuality. The 1980 meeting stated opposition to the ERA, denounced homosexuality, and changed the denomination's position on abortion from seeing it as a matter of serious, moral concern but permissible in a wide range of circumstances, to seeing it as a violation of Scripture that should be prohibited by law except to save the life of the mother. All of these stances matched Republican Party positions. A 1983 resolution praised "women who serve the Lord as homemakers,"[18] while also expressing support for women who worked outside the home, including in churches, but a 1984 resolution cited several verses from the New Testament to assert, "The Scriptures teach that women are not in public worship to assume a

---

18. Southern Baptist Convention, "Resolution on Women," June 1, 1983, https://www.sbc.net/resource-library/resolutions/resolution-on-women-3/.

In reality, we clergywomen are no more or less perfect than our brothers in ministry. We are all flawed carriers of the holy vision. We come in all human varieties and have the usual assortment of strengths and weaknesses, and we vacillate between low self-esteem and "thinking more highly of ourselves than we ought to think."

Considering all that we are and are not, I am convinced beyond a doubt that we are God's beloved daughters and that we have been called to servant ministry. We've also been called to bring a prophetic vision of inclusiveness to our denomination and the world.

We are not about "equal pay for equal work," "pro- or anti-choice," "home-making or career," "day-care" . . . though all of these matters are worthy of concern. It is the "spiritual thing" that we are about—the spiritual reality that we are made in the image of Creator God who speaks to and through men and women and calls us to be all we can be in ministry and service.

In our struggle, I hope we won't lose sight of the meaning of what we are doing. I hope we will not grow weary as we wait for the blessing and encouragement of "mother church." God hasn't finished the new creation yet. In the meantime, there is so much love for us to share and there are so many who need it.

Betty Winstead McGary, "It's a Spiritual Thing," *Folio* 7, no. 3 (Winter 1989): 2.

role of authority over men lest confusion reign in the local church."[19] Hundreds of women had been ordained in the SBC, more than a dozen served as pastors, and scores more were enrolled in SBC seminaries, but those doors soon closed. Women faculty members at SBC seminaries were fired, as were male faculty members who supported women's ordination. Churches with female pastors were disfellowshiped.

Supporters of these shifts framed them as biblical faithfulness. Because the apostle Paul taught that man is to be the head of woman (1 Cor. 11:3), and women are not to speak in church (14:34), anyone who argued for women's equality to men or ability to serve as pastors was disobeying the Bible and "God's delegated order of authority."[20]

Members who opposed the shifts, as well as many scholars inside and outside the church, interpreted them differently. Jimmy Carter eventually left the

19. Southern Baptist Convention, "Resolution on Ordination and the Role of Women in Ministry," June 1, 1984, https://www.sbc.net/resource-library/resolutions/resolution-on-ordination-and-the-role-of-women-in-ministry/.
20. Southern Baptist Convention, "Resolution on Ordination."

SBC for the moderate Cooperative Baptist Fellowship because he could not accept the SBC's new emphasis on women's subordination. He wrote in 2009, "The truth is that male religious leaders have had—and still have—an option to interpret holy teachings either to exalt or subjugate women. They have, for their own selfish ends, overwhelmingly chosen the latter."[21] Baptist historian Elizabeth Flowers saw the SBC's attachment to a gendered order of authority as a response to changing mores regarding race. In regard to a denomination founded by enslavers and generally opposed to the civil rights movement, she wrote, "A more constrained view of womanhood and women's ministry replaced hardened notions of race and attitudes toward racial desegregation, which fell out of favor after the 1960s."[22] Overall, Flowers noted, "Southern Baptist conservatives conflated the religious right's fight for American culture with the denominational battles," a strategy that enabled them to "access the passion of the culture wars rhetoric, including its antifeminist invectives."[23] Southern Baptist moderates and progressives were soon reduced to a powerless minority in the SBC, much like Democrats across most of the South.

Case Study: Roman Catholics

Contrary to expectations, the Equal Rights Amendment fell short of ratification by the states. The person most responsible for its failure was Phyllis Schlafly, a Roman Catholic laywoman who had built credibility in conservative circles for her militant opposition to communism and her knack for grassroots organizing. Her Eagle Forum political-interest group aimed to neutralize feminists' National Organization for Women, and its members mobilized to STOP ERA. Schlafly believed that the amendment would erode families, erase all differences between men and women, increase rates of divorce and abortion, and open the door to equal rights for homosexuals. Like Adrian Rogers, she said that feminists were plotting against the nation. As she told the evangelical magazine *Moody Monthly* in 1978, "The feminists are making our laws. They are taking over our educational system and the media and they are going to get all the male jobs, too. This is their goal."[24]

21. Jimmy Carter, "The Words of God Do Not Justify Cruelty to Women," *The Observer*, July 12, 2009, available online at https://www.cartercenter.org/news/editorials_speeches/observer _071209.html.

22. Flowers, *Into the Pulpit*, 4.

23. Flowers, *Into the Pulpit*, 11.

24. Gary L. Wall, "The Equal Rights Amendment," *Moody Monthly*, November 1978, reprinted in Matthew Avery Sutton, ed., *Jerry Falwell and the Rise of the Religious Right: A Brief History with Documents* (Boston: Bedford/St. Martin's, 2013), 117.

That a significant portion of the American Catholic Church would make common political cause with Southern Baptists and other conservative American Protestants was also somewhat surprising. When Democrat John F. Kennedy campaigned to become the country's first Catholic president in 1960, an assembly of 150 Protestant clergy and laymen, calling themselves Citizens for Religious Freedom, issued a statement that read in part, "It is inconceivable

Catholic laywoman Phyllis Schlafly cast the Equal Rights Amendment as a menace to women and families. As a result of her efforts, the amendment fell short of ratification by the states.

that a Roman Catholic President would not be under extreme pressure by the hierarchy of his church to accede to its policies with respect to foreign relations, including representation to the Vatican. . . . Is it reasonable to assume that a Roman Catholic President would be able to withstand altogether the determined efforts of the hierarchy to gain further funds and favors for its schools and institutions, and otherwise breach the wall of separation of church and state?"[25] American Protestants had been airing similar suspicions of Catholics throughout the nation's history. Kennedy went out of his way to assure Protestants that he would not take orders from the pope, and some believed him. Still, Kennedy won just 38 percent of the Protestant vote. What put him over the top in a very tight election was winning support from 80 percent of Catholic voters.[26]

Much had changed within American Catholicism by the 1980s. The pope in 1960 was the progressive John XXIII, who convened the Second Vatican Council to update church structures, liturgy, and teachings. The pope in 1980 was the more conservative John Paul II, whose fierce opposition to communism (born of his experience living in Soviet-controlled Poland) and traditionalist views on gender and sexuality endeared him to the same Protestants who admired Ronald Reagan. Kennedy had to maintain his distance from the papacy, lest he seem to bear out his critics' fears of Vatican meddling, while Reagan was free to meet with and express his esteem for John Paul II frequently. A journalist who wrote glowingly of their relationship called them "men of the same moment."[27]

25. "The Power of Negative Thinking," *Time*, September 19, 1960, 21.

26. Bill Schneider, "The Role of Catholic Voters," CNN, April 8, 2005, https://www.cnn.com /2005/POLITICS/04/08/catholic.voters/index.html.

27. Craig Shirley, "Another President, Another Pope: Ronald Reagan and Pope John Paul II Set the Standard for Presidential-Papal Collaboration," *U.S. News & World Report*, September 24,

Granted, progressive or conservative leaning in American Catholicism was vastly more complicated than in a Protestant body like the Southern Baptist Church. Pope John Paul II espoused many positions, such as opposition to the death penalty and support for debt forgiveness, that contravened positions taken by the SBC and the Republican Party. Whereas communism was a far-off, abstract enemy for most Americans, the Roman Catholic Church, being a global entity, included millions of people either suffering under communist rule or, particularly in Latin America, adapting ideas associated with communism into a religious movement—liberation theology—that sought economic equality and resisted dictatorships. The Catholic Church in the United States was larger than any Protestant church and one of the most racially and ethnically diverse American denominations, a development boosted by rising immigration following the Immigration and Naturalization Act of 1965. Its membership was geographically and socioeconomically diverse too. Additionally, owing to a much more complex and hierarchical structure than that of any Protestant church, American Catholicism could not shift suddenly in any ideological direction. Shifts could happen, but they would proceed more slowly, and there would be pockets of resistance in places such as religious orders and universities.

Nonetheless, the post–World War II sorting of American Christians into what sociologist Robert Wuthnow identified as a religious two-party system affected American Catholics profoundly. These effects could be seen in the rise of special-purpose groups that drew like-minded Catholics and Protestants together as well as the rise of conservative Catholic media ventures that paralleled ventures in the conservative Protestant world.

Special-purpose groups, a major development in later twentieth-century American church history, in some ways recalled the organizations of the "benevolent empire" in the early nineteenth century (see chap. 7). Wuthnow wrote, "Their causes range from nuclear arms control to liturgical renewal, from gender equality to cult surveillance, from healing ministries to evangelism. They address issues both specific to the churches and of more general concern to the broader society. Yet they are clearly rooted in the religious realm. They take their legitimating slogans from religious creeds. And they draw their organizational resources, leadership, and personnel largely from churches and ecclesiastical agencies."[28] Legally classified as nonprofit organizations, these groups benefited from Republican policies that favored voluntarism over "big government." Specifically, tax cuts reduced funding for welfare

---

2015, https://www.usnews.com/opinion/articles/2015/09/24/ronald-reagan-pope-john-paul-ii
-and-the-alliance-that-won-the-cold-war.

28. Robert Wuthnow, *The Restructuring of American Religion: Society and Faith Since World War II* (Princeton: Princeton University Press, 1988), 100–101.

programs while leaving Americans more money to donate to their preferred causes. Historian Peter Dobkin Hall called the nonprofit sector "the opening frontier of public life in the 1980s and 1990s . . . the common meeting ground where the real decisions about the future of American society and institutions would be made."[29]

The most visible cause drawing conservative Catholics and Protestants into cooperative action was opposition to abortion, also called the pro-life movement. (How to label partisans on both sides of that issue is one of the many things those partisans disagree on.) The oldest and largest organization in this movement, the National Right to Life Committee, grew out of an initiative among American Catholic bishops but established organizational distance from the church in order to attract Protestants. Other pro-life organizations, such as the more radical Operation Rescue, were launched by Protestant laypeople. The founder of Operation Rescue, Randall Terry, frequently campaigned with conservative Protestant leaders such as Pat Robertson and James Dobson, but eventually he converted to Catholicism. Overall, the pro-life movement blurred denominational boundaries in favor of shining a bright light on a single political issue. That approach created hosts of single-issue voters to whom Republican politicians could appeal and also, though to a lesser extent, rallied pro-choice voters from a variety of religious and nonreligious backgrounds to support Democrats.

In other realms, conservative Catholic mobilization was more separate from though parallel to conservative Protestant mobilization. A key example here is media. Owing to technological and regulatory changes, as well as infusions of cash, the 1980s were boom years for conservative Christian television. On the Protestant side, Pat Robertson's Christian Broadcasting Network launched the first basic cable channel delivered by satellite in 1977, and by 1983 its audience had grown to 17 million. Robertson used the platform to announce his (unsuccessful) Republican presidential campaign in 1988. On the Catholic side, a conservative nun, Mother Angelica, formed her own network, Eternal Word Television Network (EWTN), dedicated to "teaching the truth as defined by the magisterium of the Roman Catholic Church."[30] She initially used a monastery garage as a studio. EWTN launched in 1981 with four hours of programming that could reach 300,000 cable subscribers. Thirty years later, it presented twenty-four-hour programming in 140 countries, available to as many as 228 million homes, in addition to extensive print and online offerings.

29. Peter Dobkin Hall, *Inventing the Nonprofit Sector, and Other Essays on Philanthropy, Voluntarism, and Nonprofit Organizations* (Baltimore: Johns Hopkins University Press, 1992), x–xi.

30. This slogan can be found on the organization's fundraising website, https://www.givemn .org/organization/Eternal-Word-Television-Network.

Mother Angelica aligned with Pope John Paul II's priorities and criticized some Vatican II reforms, as well as abortion, the ERA, and any initiatives associated with feminism. When the 1993 World Youth Day celebration featured a dramatic performance with a woman in the role of Jesus, she rebuked liberal Catholics on-air, saying, "I'm tired of your witchcraft, I'm tired. . . . I'm tired of being pushed in corners. I'm tired of your inclusive language that refuses to admit the Son of God is a *man*! I'm tired of your tricks. I'm tired of your deceits. . . . I'm so tired of you, liberal church in America." This speech has been widely quoted and shared online.[31]

Although media scholars rate EWTN as a more effective conduit for messaging than any official organ of the church, Mother Angelica by no means spoke for, or even to, all American Catholics. Many American Catholics were enthusiastic about Vatican II, opposed Reagan's domestic and foreign policies, and defied church teachings on sexuality, using birth control and getting abortions at the same rate as the American population overall. Catholic voting patterns also roughly matched the country as a whole. From 1980 to 2020, the majority of Catholic voters (sometimes a very slight majority) opted for the eventual winner, Republican or Democrat. An exception was 2004, when Catholic voters split evenly, 48 percent for fellow Catholic John Kerry (Democrat) and 48 percent for the winner, incumbent George W. Bush (Republican). American Catholics' 48 percent support for Kerry was way down from the 80 percent support for Kennedy in 1960, a stark example of the degree to which party affiliation had supplanted denominational identification as a driver of behavior.

Evaluations and Reevaluations

At the turn of the twenty-first century, the mainstream view of the religious movement highlighted by *Newsweek* back in 1976 could be summed up by the title of a 1998 book by sociologist Christian Smith, *American Evangelicalism: Embattled and Thriving*. By "embattled," Smith meant that these religious Americans (he focused just on the Protestants, treating Roman Catholics as a separate category) saw themselves as being out of step with modern culture, more committed to absolute truths and sexual purity, less comfortable with pluralism or a "live and let live" response to other people's choices. They felt mocked and misunderstood. "We're almost a persecuted group," one woman told him.[32] By

31. Mother Angelica, "I'm Tired of Your Witchcraft," YouTube video, 22:54, https://www.you tube.com/watch?v=mGZocJZsMbk.

32. Christian Smith, *American Evangelicalism: Embattled and Thriving* (Chicago: University of Chicago Press, 1998), 131.

"thriving," Smith meant that evangelicals were succeeding on pretty much every criterion that social scientists knew how to measure: church attendance and membership, group cohesion, retention over years and generations, intensity of commitment, willingness to mobilize for mission. Smith deemed evangelicalism "more than alive and well," indeed "the strongest of the major Christian traditions in the United States today."[33] Journalists and other scholars generally concurred.

There were, however, other perspectives, both at the time and, increasingly, later. Book titles summarized these perspectives as well. On the topic of embattlement, no one argued that evangelicals (here including Protestants and Catholics, as Gallup did in the 1976 survey) did not *feel* persecuted, but the basis of that sentiment was countered with evidence that evangelicals played offense at least as often as they played defense, and that they frequently won. Sociologist D. Michael Lindsay looked for *Faith in the Halls of Power* (2007) and found numerous examples of evangelical influence in politics, academics, entertainment, and business. A shadowy group of political insiders who called themselves *The Family* (Jeff Sharlet, 2009) might more aptly be seen as an arm of the *American Fascists* (Chris Hedges, 2008) who would employ all available tactics to remake American society. These people were *The Power Worshipers* (Katherine Stewart, 2019) intent on *Taking America Back for God* (Andrew L. Whitehead and Samuel L. Perry, 2020). Even some erstwhile insiders lamented that evangelical culture warriors had been *Blinded by Might* (Cal Thomas and Ed Dobson, 1999). Evangelicals' dual allegiance to the Prince of Peace and the archetypal frontier gunslinger, *Jesus and John Wayne* (Kristin Kobes Du Mez, 2020), "corrupted a faith and fractured a nation," as the book's subtitle put it. To the extent that evangelicals were embattled, according to these interpretations, the primary cause was their own belligerence.

The notion of evangelical thriving also came in for scrutiny from a variety of angles. Some alarm bells rang within the evangelical world. Evangelical historian Mark Noll, then teaching at Wheaton College, bemoaned *The Scandal of the Evangelical Mind* (1994). "Despite dynamic success at a popular level," he warned, "modern American evangelicals have failed notably in sustaining serious intellectual life."[34] Representing the small progressive wing of the tradition, Canadian theologian Ronald Sider raised equally grave concerns about *The Scandal of the Evangelical Conscience* (2005). Michael Emerson, writing with Christian Smith, found white evangelicals unable and unwilling to confront the racism that caused the United States to be *Divided by Faith* (2000).

33. Smith, *American Evangelicalism*, 20.
34. Mark A. Noll, *The Scandal of the Evangelical Mind* (Grand Rapids: Eerdmans, 1994), 3.

White evangelicals' 81 percent support for Republican president Donald Trump in 2016 sparked intense self-examination within the community, particularly as that voting support was accompanied by a precipitous rise—from 30 percent in 2011 to 68 percent in 2020—in white evangelicals' willingness to overlook immorality in politicians.[35] In the evangelical news magazine *Christianity Today*, Ed Stetzer undertook "Debunking the 81 Percent," arguing that Trump's evangelical voters "were not enthusiastic about him as a candidate" and had many strategic and demographic reasons, rather than religious motivations, for selecting him.[36] Lifeway Research, a division of the Southern Baptist Church, contended in 2017 that half of self-identified American evangelicals were not evangelicals at all, based on agreement with beliefs the researchers considered essential to the tradition.[37] These researchers attributed part of the mismatch to sloppy labeling but also expressed concern that churches were inadequately teaching the truths of the tradition.

The most disturbing evidence of evangelical failure to thrive, however, came in an area where conservative white Christians professed to be specially invested: sexual purity. Waves of sexual abuse scandals hit the American Catholic Church, the Southern Baptist Convention, and other ecclesial bodies and mission organizations in the evangelical orbit, ranging from Jesus People USA, to pioneering megachurch Willow Creek, to Kanakuk Kamps, to Ravi Zacharias International Ministries. Although most of the scandals broke later, much of the abuse happened during and in conjunction with the rise of the religious right. To be clear, sexual abuse in churches and missions has been a problem throughout church history, but the abuse scandals of the late twentieth and early twenty-first centuries were unique in their scope and impact. They were not fabrications (like the Maria Monk hoax of the 1830s) or salacious but isolated incidents (like the adultery trial of pastor Henry Ward Beecher in 1875). They were wildfires consuming lives and causing billions of dollars in damage.

For a while, American Protestants thought that sexual abuse was mostly a Catholic issue and largely attributable to the mandate that Catholic priests be celibate. In 1984, Rev. Gilbert Gauthe became the first American priest convicted in a high-profile criminal trial for sexual abuse. He admitted to abusing thirty-seven children. The following year, another American priest, Rev.

35. Suzanna Krivulskaya, "The Diminishing Importance of Personal Morality in Politics, 2011–2020," PRRI, November 21, 2022, https://www.prri.org/spotlight/the-diminishing-importance-of-personal-morality-in-politics-2011-2020/.

36. Ed Stetzer, "Debunking the 81%," *Christianity Today*, October 2018, 21.

37. Bob Smietana, "Many Who Call Themselves Evangelical Don't Actually Hold Evangelical Beliefs," Lifeway Research, December 6, 2017, https://research.lifeway.com/2017/12/06/many-evangelicals-dont-hold-evangelical-beliefs/.

Thomas Doyle, coauthored a report, "The Problem of Sexual Molestation by Roman Catholic Clergy: Meeting the Problem in a Comprehensive and Responsible Manner," warning that abuse was widespread and that the church lacked adequate mechanisms for dealing with it. Church leaders ignored the report, disbelieved survivors' stories of abuse, and treated people pressing for reforms as gossips and troublemakers. Although abusive priests were by no means all conservatives, the church's overall approach of stonewalling abuse investigations was set (as later Vatican reports acknowledged) by the conservative Pope John Paul II, his conservative successor Pope Benedict XVI, and other church officials appointed by them to positions of leadership. By 2020, thousands of American clergy abusers had been identified, along with many more thousands of victims, and dozens of dioceses across the country—and the world—had been assessed multimillion-dollar penalties.

The American Catholic abuse crisis became major national news via reporting by the *Boston Globe* in 2002. Soon afterward, abuse victims in the Southern Baptist Convention, led by activists such as Christa Brown, started calling for investigations. The abuse problems in the two churches were different, notably in the profiles of victims. Whereas most of the Catholic victims were boys and young men, most of the Southern Baptist victims were women and girls, who charged that SBC teachings on female subservience and the church's lack of women in leadership roles created conditions that were ripe for exploitation. The SBC, like the Catholic Church before it, ignored reported abuses and attacked people seeking reforms; unlike the hierarchical Catholic Church, the SBC also claimed that its decentralized structure gave it no authority to investigate or punish abusive pastors.

The election of Donald Trump—a man who was facing multiple allegations of sexual assault and who bragged, in a recording, about forcibly groping women—convinced many American women to speak out about their own victimization. The resulting flood of disclosures, many of them shared on social media, became known as the #MeToo movement, with a #ChurchToo subsection focusing on abuse in churches. It was in this environment that SBC victims of abuse were finally able to press their cases. In 2017, former SBC vice president Paul Pressler, an architect of the conservative resurgence, was sued by a former assistant who claimed that Pressler raped him in 1980, when he was fourteen years old, and continued to abuse him for the next two decades. In 2018, another architect of the conservative resurgence, Paige Patterson, was fired from his position as head of Southwestern Baptist Seminary for a pattern of mishandling sexual assault allegations brought by students. The following year, the *Houston Chronicle* published an investigative series documenting roughly 380 SBC church leaders and volunteers who faced sexual misconduct charges from more than seven hundred

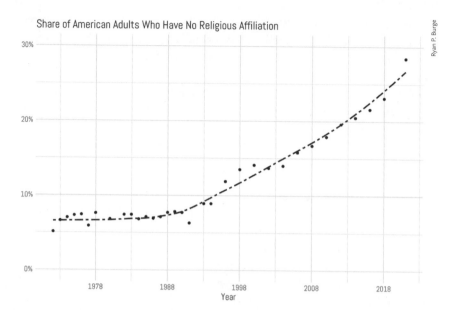

The rise of the "nones," or people who claim no religious affiliation when surveyed, is among the biggest trends in American religion in the twenty-first century. Data from General Social Survey.

victims. In spring 2022, despite years of claiming that its polity prevented the collection of such information, the SBC released its secret list of hundreds of church leaders who had been accused of abuse.

Cases like these, and dozens more at conservative Christian churches and institutions, provoked widespread disillusion. A 2021 survey found that 39 percent of Americans agreed with the statement "High profile misconduct by clergy has turned me off of religion." That sentiment was shared by nearly 45 percent of religious "nones" but also 42.7 percent of Catholics, 27.1 percent of nondenominational Christians, and 26.8 percent of evangelicals.[38] Searching for language to describe the magnitude of the crisis, some evangelicals were thrown back to Reagan-era themes: existential threat, fearful urgency, time running out. Longtime SBC insider Russell Moore described the events that convinced him to leave his church leadership position in an article titled "This Is the Southern Baptist Apocalypse."[39] Megachurch pastor Andy Stanley declared a "state of emergency" for evangelicalism and wrote that the movement's quest to save

38. Paul A. Djupe and Ryan P. Burge, "Are Evangelicals Exceptional in Their Sexual Abuse Beliefs?," *Religion in Public* (blog), May 24, 2022, https://religioninpublic.blog/2022/05/24/are -evangelicals-exceptional-in-their-sexual-abuse-beliefs/.

39. Russell Moore, "This Is the Southern Baptist Apocalypse," *Christianity Today*, May 22, 2022, https://www.christianitytoday.com/ct/2022/may-web-only/southern-baptist-abuse-apocalypse -russell-moore.html.

the nation had reduced members to "political tools. A manipulated voting demographic. A photo op."[40] Another megachurch pastor, Timothy Keller, asked, "Can Evangelicalism Survive Donald Trump?"[41]

The hopeful "Year of the Evangelicals," not even fifty years past, felt very far away. The movement's arc had shot up, then tumbled down, and its forward trajectory was impossible to predict.

◆

In 1993, a group of American evangelicals and Catholics, including clergy, scholars, and leaders of parachurch organizations, signed an ecumenical document, "Evangelicals and Catholics Together," in an effort to provide common witness for a new millennium. Portions of the document took the tone of a prayer.

> There is a necessary connection between the visible unity of Christians and the mission of the one Christ. We together pray for the fulfillment of the prayer of Our Lord: "May they all be one; as you, Father, are in me, and I in you, so also may they be in us, that the world may believe that you sent me" (John 17). We together, Evangelicals and Catholics, confess our sins against the unity that Christ intends for all his disciples. . . .
>
> By preaching, teaching, and life example, Christians witness to Christians and non-Christians alike. We seek and pray for the conversion of others, even as we recognize our own continuing need to be fully converted. . . .
>
> In considering the many corruptions of Christian witness, we, Evangelicals and Catholics, confess that we have sinned against one another and against God. We most earnestly ask the forgiveness of God and one another, and pray for the grace to amend our own lives and that of our communities.[42]

FURTHER READING

D'Antonio, William V., Michele Dillon, and Mary L. Gautier. *American Catholics in Transition.* Lanham, MD: Rowman & Littlefield, 2013.

Dowland, Seth. *Family Values and the Rise of the Christian Right.* Philadelphia: University of Pennsylvania Press, 2015.

40. Andy Stanley, *Not in It to Win It: Why Choosing Sides Sidelines the Church* (Grand Rapids: Zondervan, 2022), 15.

41. Timothy Keller, "Can Evangelicalism Survive Donald Trump?," in *Evangelicals: Who They Have Been, Are Now, and Could Be,* ed. Mark A. Noll, David W. Bebbington, and George M. Marsden (Grand Rapids: Eerdmans, 2019), 251–55.

42. "Evangelicals and Catholics Together: The Christian Mission in the Third Millennium," *First Things,* May 1994, https://www.firstthings.com/article/1994/05/evangelicals-catholics-together-the-christian-mission-in-the-third-millennium.

Hankins, Barry. *Uneasy in Babylon: Southern Baptist Conservatives and American Culture*. Tuscaloosa: University of Alabama Press, 2003.

Harding, Susan Friend. *The Book of Jerry Falwell: Fundamentalist Language and Politics*. Princeton: Princeton University Press, 2000.

Johnson, Emily Suzanne. *This Is Our Message: Women's Leadership in the New Christian Right*. New York: Oxford University Press, 2019.

Margolis, Michele F. *From Politics to the Pews: How Partisanship and the Political Environment Shape Religious Identity*. Chicago: University of Chicago Press, 2018.

Noll, Mark A., David W. Bebbington, and George M. Marsden, eds. *Evangelicals: Who They Have Been, Are Now, and Could Be*. Grand Rapids: Eerdmans, 2019.

Shea, William M. *The Lion and the Lamb: Evangelicals and Catholics in America*. New York: Oxford University Press, 2004.

Steinfels, Peter. *A People Adrift: The Crisis of the Roman Catholic Church in America*. New York: Simon & Schuster, 2004.

Williams, Daniel K. *Defenders of the Unborn: The Pro-Life Movement before Roe v. Wade*. New York: Oxford University Press, 2019.

Conclusion

The study of church history was added late, and only tenuously, to Christian higher education in the United States. Some educators believed that the subject was simply too boring to hold student interest, although the long-prevalent pedagogical method of asking students to memorize and recite textbooks was probably more to blame than the subject matter. Some educators found church history mildly appealing but refused to divert curricular hours devoted to ostensibly more important subjects. Still other educators believed that church history was too dangerous to teach. For example, at Andover Seminary in the early nineteenth century, students were required to take full years of Bible, theology, and sacred rhetoric, but the professors of those subjects let their colleague in church history give just a few lectures in the weeks before graduation—both because the other professors hated him (academic politics can be brutal) and because they feared that his lectures would threaten students' vocations. Skeptical professors asked, How could students who were exposed to "the multifarious forms of religious beliefs in past ages" and "the various and clashing opinions of different sects" stand firm in their faith? Surely the "opinions of fallible men," which church history fairly brims with, should be relegated to the margin of ministry preparation, lest the whole edifice crumble.[1]

Mixed as their motives were, the hostile professors were not entirely wrong in their assessment of church history. The subject could be dangerous, precisely because it highlighted human diversity and fallibility. Christians in the past—like all humans in all eras—made a lot of errors. They chose power instead of love. Or they meant well but caused harm. They were sure that the Bible said things that other Christians were equally sure it did not. Some of the most faithful Christians in the past faced the harshest treatment, from the world at large or

---

1. J. Earl Thompson Jr., "Church History Comes to Andover: The Persecution of James Murdock," *Andover Newton Quarterly* 15 (1975): 213–27.

from their own coreligionists. The gospel is good news; church history is often bad news. What good is bad news?

To be fair, the Bible contains a lot of bad news too. The Old Testament books of history, prophecy, and wisdom are full of trials and failures, warnings and bitter truths, hard-won lessons that later generations forgot. American Christians rarely plumb these depths, however. Studies of twenty-first-century American Christian sermons find a very strong preference for New Testament texts, and analysis of the most popular worship songs finds a dearth of lyrics about grief or pain. The lectionaries—schedules of weekly Bible passages—used in Roman Catholic and many mainline Protestant churches omit a lot of the heavier Old Testament texts. "The necessity of lamentation is nearly absent from church liturgy," noted seminary professor and musician George Robinson.[2]

Yet these texts and this mode of reflection are vitally important for helping people of faith understand where they came from, why their world looks the way it does, and how they ought to live out their religious principles. The now-popular sermon and song texts of the New Testament had not yet been collected when the apostle Paul wrote, "All scripture is inspired by God and is useful for teaching, for reproof, for correction, and for training in righteousness" (2 Tim. 3:16 NRSV). The scripture to which Paul referred was the Hebrew Bible, replete with history and heaviness. While postbiblical historians cannot claim that their work is divinely inspired, that work can serve similar purposes. History teaches. It rebukes. It shows crooked places that need to be set straight and wounds that need to be healed.

Unfortunately, instead of facing the hard truths of history, American Christians, and Americans in general, increasingly shy away from them. Books get pulled from shelves, and laws are passed to shield students from "divisive concepts" that might cause discomfort. This book itself could fall afoul of such laws, depending on how they are applied. Civil War–era preaching was pretty divisive. So, in various ways, were the First Great Awakening, the Scopes Trial, and the rise of the religious right. Reading about violence toward Indigenous people, Black Americans, and religious minorities could very well cause discomfort. Feeling left out of these chapters could cause discomfort too. A reader might wonder, Why aren't there more women? Where are the people who look like me or go to a church like mine? What about influences from other religions and other countries of the world?

A book like this one is necessarily incomplete and unsettling. There's a lot it cannot do. Best case, this book has communicated accurate information and

2. Quoted in Marty Duren, "Where Have All the Sad Songs Gone?," Religion News Service, October 10, 2018, https://religionnews.com/2018/10/10/where-have-all-the-sad-songs-gone/.

connected some dots that seemed scattershot before. It has attended to foundational categories of historical analysis: context, complexity, contingency, and change over time. It has helped to map the American Christian landscape while hinting at vistas that might have been or could yet be. This book might not always be inspiring, in the typical sense of raising shining examples to emulate, but any discomfort it causes might inspire something else: change. King Xerxes, the monarch in Esther 6 who called for a reading of history to help him fall asleep, ended up discovering a buried injustice and setting it to rights instead. Thanks to the records and annals, the king silenced a malicious adviser and disrupted a murder plot, restoring an unsung hero to a place of honor. Old news, even old bad news, has surprising power to reframe the present and alter the future—but only when people are brave enough to face it.

▼

One final example of the vagaries of history: In the late 1920s, the Church of England planned to revise its Book of Common Prayer, which had not been updated since 1662. Proposed revisions included a blessing that began "Go forth into the world in peace." English composer Martin Shaw penned a choral anthem using the same text. But in 1928, the British Parliament rejected the revisions, so the blessing was not officially approved for use in the Church of England. Some clergy used it anyway, in England and in other churches across the Anglican Communion, while Shaw's anthem was sung in an even wider variety of churches. The rejected liturgical fragment eventually became part of the Presbyterian Book of Common Worship (1946), gained popularity through the liturgical renewal movement of the 1960s, and was set to music again by English composer John Rutter in the 1980s. As human institutions intervened or interfered, these words of blessing persevered.

> Go forth into the world in peace; be of good courage; hold fast that which is good; render to no man evil for evil; strengthen the fainthearted; support the weak; help the afflicted; honour all men; love and serve the Lord, rejoicing in the power of the Holy Spirit. And the Blessing of God Almighty, the Father, the Son, and the Holy Ghost, be upon you, and remain with you for ever.

Index